An Ohio Portrait

An Ohio Portrait

GEORGE W. KNEPPER

Published for the Ohio American Revolution Bicentennial Advisory Commission by the Ohio Historical Society, Columbus, Ohio 43211

Since its formation in 1971 the Ohio American Revolution Bicentennial Advisory Commission has endeavored to develop programs and projects which would instill in all Ohioans a greater appreciation for the events of the American Revolution and a wider knowledge of Ohio's role in national life. This volume represents one of the commission's major efforts.

The bicentennial should be a time for reexamining our historical record, as we, as a people, enter our third century of national life. Hopefully, this volume will provide all Ohioans with a resource for gaining new perspectives on the state's social, economic, and political development. The following pages contain text and pictures that present a panoramic view of the growth of the first state to be carved from the old Northwest Territory.

The experiences of Ohioans were common to all Americans, and while national developments had a decisive impact on the buckeye state, what happened in Ohio affected the national scene. To an extent, Ohio can be viewed as a microcosm of the nation, and in understanding the history of this state in its broader context one achieves a greater comprehension of the national experience since the Revolutionary Era.

The commission is grateful for the dedicated assistance of the staff of the Ohio Historical Society in the preparation of this book. The commission is also appreciative of the financial support of the 111th Ohio General Assembly, whose members realized the importance of a meaningful bicentennial observance.

THE OHIO AMERICAN REVOLUTION
BICENTENNIAL ADVISORY COMMISSION

Alan E. Norris, Chairman
Ward Miller, Vice-Chairman
Michael J. Devine, Administrator

George Carmer	Thomas Moyer
Maxine Charlton	Henry Pierce
Marian R. Heiser	Robert T. Secrest
Grace G. Izant	David Skaggs
Dale Locker	Thomas Smith
Donald E. Lukens	Byron Walker

Library of Congress Catalog Number 76-14536
International Standard Book Number 0-87758-006-5
Printed in the United States of America.

Designed by Mlicki Advertising Design Associates, Inc.
Printed by The Watkins Printing Company, Columbus, Ohio

Table of Contents

Preface

Ohio can claim only a small corner of attention for its place in the American Revolution. Nevertheless, it was formed initially by people of the Revolutionary generation who transplanted to its soil their concept of republicanism. They built well. Just twenty years after the Peace of Paris recognized the independence of the United States, Ohio emerged as the seventeenth state, and the first to be carved from the national domain. In less than fifty years, it was already the third most populous state, drawing people from every section of America, from black, Indian, and white, and from every new wave of immigration. Indeed, Ohio was such a mixture of America's people, who found a land so well endowed with the resources necessary for both an agricultural and an industrial society, that they created in Ohio perhaps the most representative state in the nation.

An Ohio Portrait attempts to tell their story in a general yet comprehensive manner. The numerous illustrations serve to complement and expand the narrative. The nature of this publication sometimes precludes extensive analysis of a historic topic or period. However, it is hoped that this book will reach a public whose appreciation for, and knowledge of Ohio will be enhanced for having read it.

Many people contributed to this work. I would like to express appreciation to Michael Devine, administrator of the Ohio American Revolution Bicentennial Advisory Commission, for his support, his management of production details, and for his reading of the manuscript drafts. Representative Alan Norris, chairman of the commission, has been most supportive of the effort as has Thomas Smith, director of the Ohio Historical Society, who made the fine resources of the society available to me. The manuscript was read in its entirety by Professor Charles Alexander of Ohio University, and William Keener of the Ohio Historical Society, and in part by various subject specialists of the Ohio Historical Society. I am in their debt for correcting errors and for helpful suggestions. Since the final decision on content was mine, I am responsible for any mistakes of omission or commission which may remain.

A very special thanks must go to Mrs. Arlene J. Peterson, specialist in graphic materials for the Ohio Historical Society, whose knowledge of Ohio's pictorial resources and whose unfailing energy and interest in the project were central to the completion of the book. Special thanks go also to Ron Mlicki whose involvement and interest went far beyond what was required in his official role as designer of the publication. I owe my education in visual journalism to them both.

Mrs. Debbie Lynch, administrative assistant to the administrator of OARBAC, typed the manuscript and coordinated much of the work with gracious efficiency. Nancy Essex performed editorial services with skill and imagination. To Harold Stevens, James Richards, and Michael Harden, a special thanks for unselfish work done well. Our debt to various picture repositories is reflected in the picture credits.

This book is dedicated to those who love Ohio, *Imperium in Imperio* (an empire within an empire). May their affection and regard be broad enough to encompass occasional failures as well as striking accomplishments.

May 10, 1976   George W. Knepper

An Ohio Portrait

NATURAL VEGETATION OF OHIO

At the Time of the Earliest Land Surveys

prepared by

Robert B. Gordon

1966

The Setting

In the bicentennial year of American independence, Ohioans should remember the impact of the American Revolution on their state's development. We usually do not think of the Ohio Country as a colonial area. Yet in the aftermath of the War of Independence, a great national domain was formed "North and West of the River Ohio" from lands formerly claimed by Virginia, Massachusetts, and Connecticut. For the first time the Confederation Congress had an opportunity to impose a pattern upon the land, to determine the course of its development, and to establish policies that would result in a particular type of social creation.

The state of Ohio — the first state carved out of the public domain, the first fruits of the Northwest Territory — served as the model for all ensuing development of public lands. Since Ohio was admitted into the Union in 1803, only twenty years after the Peace of Paris had formalized American independence, the state was a creation of Revolutionary generation men. Therefore, Ohio presumably embraced a settlement pattern, social structure, and political organization endorsed by those who had made and sustained the American Revolution. Those elements persist today, although the overlay of two centuries of productive activity has nearly concealed them.

The Ohio Country was prime land, "a country beautiful and fertile, and affording . . . all that nature has decreed for the comfort of man," as the English traveler Morris Birkbeck found it in 1817. The land was named for the great river called "Oyo" in the Iroquoian tongue, known to early French explorers as *La Belle Riviere*, or beautiful river. By this avenue men and women approached a distant region, hidden long behind the Appalachian barrier and the equally effective barrier posed by powerful and often hostile Indian nations. The river brought the

Glaciers scoured grooves in the rocks on Kelleys Island. (1)

Cedar Bog is a glacial remnant in Champaign County. (2)

people in, took their goods out, and provided the waters that ultimately supported an impressive industrial concentration.

Ohio's topography was determined primarily by the last great glacier, an ice sheet that covered all but the southeastern third of the future state. Strangely enough, despite the leveling action of the glacier, Ohio's highest and lowest points, Campbell Hill (elevation 1,550 feet) near Bellefontaine and part of Hamilton County (elevation 440 feet) near Cincinnati, both lie in the glaciated area. The unglaciated southeast remained a knobby, broken country where hills were interlaced with numerous streams, many of them navigable for small boats and canoes. Only along the river bottoms was the soil good enough to support an intensive agriculture. In time, much of the great virgin forest that covered the land would be timbered off, or would be indiscriminately cleared to make room for crops and pasturage. Underlying the grudging soil along the ridges and hillsides were rich mineral deposits that would be exploited soon after the earliest settlements began to mature.

South of Lake Erie, the glacier smoothed off the northern and western portions of the Allegheny Plateau whose highlands cover nearly all of eastern Ohio. The glacier also left a fertile lake plain which extends inward from Lake Erie, forming a narrow band in the eastern part of the state and widening to the west into a broad, poorly drained area once known as the Black Swamp. The lake plains to the east supported settlement from an early time, but the supersaturated lands of the Black Swamp were a formidable barrier that helped make the northwestern part of Ohio the last to be settled. Significant deposits of limestone, sandstone, and salt located in the lake plains contributed to Ohio's development.

Putnam Hill limestone mine, Muskingum County. (3)

Big Muskie dwarfs conventional equipment in a strip mine near Cumberland (Guernsey County). (4)

Vinton County clay mine. Clay was also mined in surface pits. (5)

Large areas in eastern Ohio still show the effects of strip mining. (6)

The glacier's work is perhaps most evident in the central plains, sometimes called the till plains, an area that embraces most of central and western Ohio. Gently rolling land, watered by numerous springs and streams and amenable to machine farming, characterizes this region. Its rich soils make it Ohio's premier farming region. Like the rest of Ohio, this land was once heavily forested except for occasional natural prairies.

Ohio is further divided, both geologically and geographically, by a great continental divide that bisects the state in a generally east-west direction, separating the waters that flow north into Lake Erie from those that flow south into the Ohio River. Swamps and small natural lakes lay on the poorly drained portions of the divide. Game trails and Indian portages crossed it at key points, and the fall of waters away from its heights provided mill sites.

Much that a pioneering people needed was available in the Ohio Country. The area was accessible from the Ohio River and its many navigable tributaries—the Muskingum, Hocking, Scioto, Little Miami, and Great Miami — and from Lake Erie where streams like the Grand, Chagrin, Cuyahoga, Black, Huron, Sandusky, and Maumee provided routes to the interior. Timber resources were incredibly varied: buckeye, oak, tulip, pine, hickory, beech, maple, elm, sycamore, chestnut, cherry, ash, gum, and walnut were each favored for particular uses. Woodsmen, sophisticated in their understanding of timber qualities, made axe handles of shock-absorbing ash, furniture of sturdy and beautiful walnut and cherry, and used the versatile buckeye for so many different purposes that it became closely tied to the identity of the emerging state. Stone of good building quality was abundant, and most early

Buckeye Furnace (restored) in Jackson County produced iron from local ores and charcoal in the nineteenth century. (7)

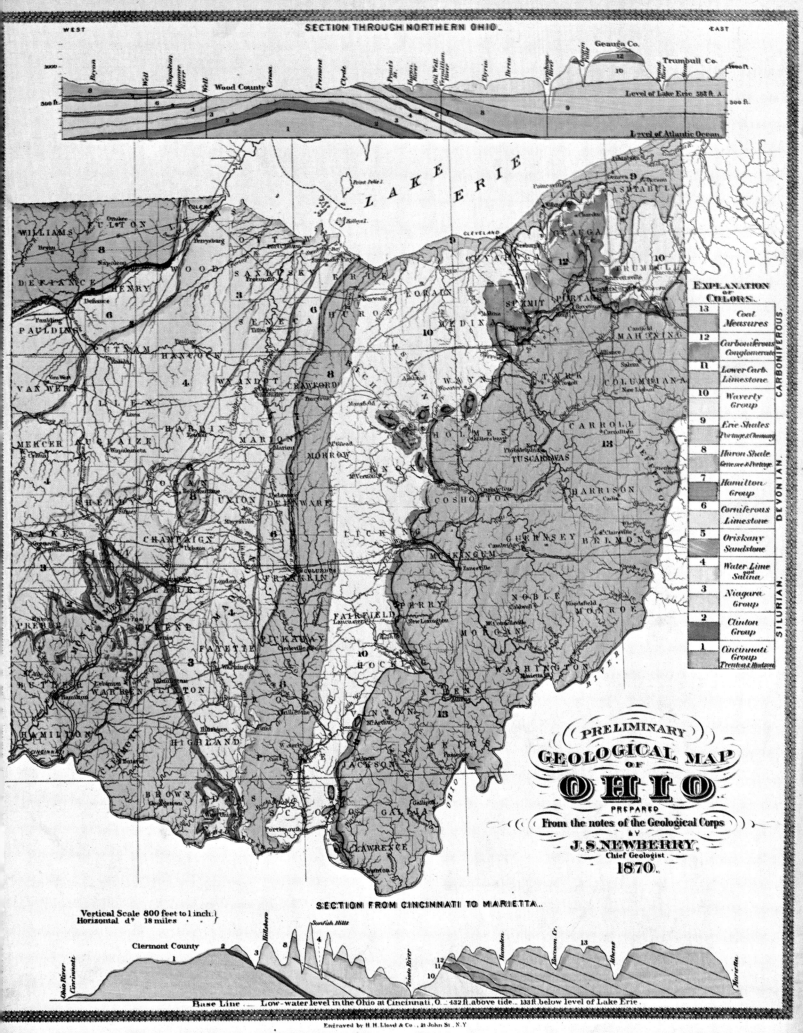

SECTION THROUGH NORTHERN OHIO.

WEST   EAST

Geauga Co.

Trumbull Co.

Level of Lake Erie 565 ft. A.

Level of Atlantic Ocean

LAKE ERIE

EXPLANATION OF COLORS.

13	Coal Measures
12	Carboniferous Conglomerate
11	Lower Carb. Limestone
10	Waverly Group
9	Erie Shales Portage & Chemung
8	Huron Shale Genesee & Portage
7	Hamilton Group
6	Corniferous Limestone
5	Oriskany Sandstone
4	Water Lime and Salina
3	Niagara Group
2	Clinton Group
1	Cincinnati Group Trenton & Hudson

CARBONIFEROUS

DEVONIAN

SILURIAN

PRELIMINARY
GEOLOGICAL MAP
OF
OHIO
PREPARED
From the notes of the Geological Corps
BY
J. S. NEWBERRY,
Chief Geologist.
1870.

SECTION FROM CINCINNATI TO MARIETTA.

Vertical Scale 800 feet to 1 inch.
Horizontal d⁰ 18 miles

Clermont County

Hillsboro

Sunfish Hills

Base Line.   Low-water level in the Ohio at Cincinnati, O. 432 ft. above tide. 133 ft. below level of Lake Erie.

Engraved by H. H. Lloyd & Co., 21 John St., N.Y

The Corning limestone quarry near Covington (Miami County). (9)

Mining salt on a grand scale at Cleveland. (10)

Ohio buildings that used stone were built from materials quarried locally. Salt springs, while not abundant, helped meet the needs of the first settlers. Later generations found enormous sources of salt lying deep under the earth, especially near the Ohio and within a band stretching south about fifty miles from Lake Erie. Clay was found in a region from the Ohio River westward to the valley of the Tuscarawas. Rough crockery and tableware eventually gave way to the production of chinaware, brick, tile, and vitrified pipe.

All of this natural wealth was particularly useful since Ohio's climate was excellent for agriculture. Ohio's temperate climate allows a growing season which varies from 125 days in Mahoning and Knox counties to 206 days in Hamilton County. Precipitation is adequate throughout the state, averaging about 38 inches a year, but there is considerable variation in rainfall between the 44 inch per year average of Clinton County in the Southwest and the 29 inches received in an average year along portions of the south shore of Lake Erie.

In addition to timber, salt, clay, limestone, and sandstone, Ohio had coal and iron ore, minerals which enabled Ohioans to establish a diversified manufacturing base. Coal in abundance was found in eastern and southern Ohio. Iron ore, first smelted with hardwood charcoal and later with coking coal, was abundant in southern and eastern Ohio. Today names like Ironton, Buckeye Furnace and Vesuvius serve as reminders of this indigenous industry. Oil, found as early as 1859 in southeastern Ohio, was first exploited in commercial quantities in western Ohio in the 1890s, and fields at widely scattered sites across the state were discovered and developed later. Power from natural gas gave rise to several important industries, including the glass industry ultimately centered in the Toledo area

"Don't Tread on Me!" An Ohio copperhead. (11)

Artist's conception of the "Great Hinckley Hunt,"
December 24, 1818. More than 500 hunters in
Medina County killed seventeen wolves, twenty-one
bears, 300 deer, and turkeys, foxes, and raccoons. (12)

Flint Ridge, Licking County, since prehistoric times a source of flint. (13)

where natural gas and silicates of proper quality were brought together. Sand and gravel deposits, shale, and even a small gypsum mining operation provided additional materials of commercial significance. The march of industrialization passed by Ohio's oldest exploited mineral, the many-colored flint of Flint Ridge. Prized and widely traded by prehistoric Indians, flint is now valued as a source of jewelry and as the official state stone.

Newcomers to the wilderness sustained themselves for long periods on the game animals, fowl, and fish that abounded in the Ohio Coun-

Flint in its natural state (above), and polished (below). (14)

try, and as these settlers became more established, they continued to supplement their diets with this natural bounty. Deer, elk, beaver, buffalo, bear, and squirrel were the primary game animals. About 300 kinds of birds could be found in Ohio, with the wild turkey and the passenger pigeon being the principal quarry of hunters. Stories of "big hunts" in the early nineteenth century almost defy belief. An 1817 hunting party operating near Ohio's new capital city, Columbus, killed three bears, thirty-three deer, and 117 turkeys. The accommodating passenger pigeons fairly begged to be slaughtered by roosting in overwhelming density upon low tree limbs from which they were knocked with clubs. Rather than taking flight at the sound of a gun, roosting pigeons seemed to cluster even closer. An English traveler wrote that "a fowling piece well charged with dust shot might bring down a bushel of these willing game dead at your feet." Indiscriminate slaughter quickly thinned even these seemingly inexhaustible flocks, and by 1914 the last known passenger pigeon had died in the Cincinnati Zoo. Some game animals were considered a nuisance: in 1822, 200 hunters operating near Columbus for three days killed 19,660 squirrels. These animals had been so destructive of crops that the Ohio General Assembly at one time required every taxpayer to kill between ten and 100 squirrels annually.

Fish stories are synonymous with exaggeration, and some stories from early Ohio are difficult to believe, but there were too many reliable witnesses to fabulous catches to dismiss these tales routinely. In 1796, John Heckewelder reported that the Cuyahoga River beneath the big falls teemed with fish of many kinds. Ohio's rivers produced enormous catfish and sturgeon. Lake Erie was until recent times one of America's richest fishing grounds. Stocking from hatcheries to-gether with cleaning Ohio's waterways may one day reestablish the state's position as a primary source of this valuable commercial and recreational asset.

Not all game was beneficent to the settler. In addition to the considerable crop damage by beast and bird, that master builder, the beaver, caused flooding problems for farmers, canalers, and road and railroad builders. Still other species of wildlife posed a direct threat to human safety. Wolves, bears, and wildcats caused injury to man and his domestic animals. Perhaps a more omnipresent threat was posed by poisonous snakes which proliferated in the rocky crevices of eastern and southern Ohio and in the swamps of central and western Ohio. Timber and swamp rattlesnakes and copperheads were the most dangerous species. The rocky banks of deep-cut river courses in northeastern Ohio provided a congenial environment for rattlesnakes. Along Wetmore Creek in Stow the village blacksmith lowered himself into a rocky den filled with rattlers still torpid from their long winter hibernation. Laying about with a club, he killed over sixty-five of the creatures, a feat of enough interest and significance that worshippers poured from a nearby log church to witness the deed.

Both the agricultural and industrial pioneers of Ohio had at their fingertips a splendid diversity of the resources and conditions necessary for growth. While all of these productive elements could have been used with care and to best advantage, such is not "civilized" man's record either in Ohio or elsewhere. Sometimes the settlers were the victims of natural forces. By planting their fields and building structures on the natural flood plains of rivers and streams, they made themselves vulnerable to periodic floods of disastrous proportions. The more the land was cleared and the natural reservoirs drained, the

Severe sheet erosion in a Muskingum County wheat field. Most Ohio farmers now use techniques to conserve their soil. (15)

Wave action threatens property along portions of Lake Erie's southern shore. (16)

worse the effects of these floods. At other times, the dependable rains on which Ohio farmers usually could count during the spring and summer disappeared for prolonged periods. Drought was especially severe in the mid-1930s. Late frosts in the spring and early frosts in the fall frequently damaged crops, especially the vulnerable fruit crop, much of which is now planted along Lake Erie, whose waters minimize the effects of these unseasonable frosts. From spring to

fall the heavens above Ohio are apt to be a battleground for cold air masses from the North clashing with warm, moist air masses from the Gulf of Mexico. The fury of the winds thus generated can rip apart the dirigible *Shenandoah*, can smash through a Lorain or devastate a Xenia. Tornadic winds are probably the most feared natural phenomenon to which the state is now subject. Extensive and wise flood-control measures have greatly reduced the threat to towns

Mid-section of *Shenandoah*, broken apart by a line squall, near Ava (Noble County) in 1925. Fourteen crew members died in the wreckage. (17)

The 1883 Ohio River flood at Portsmouth. (18)

An Ohio Portrait

The Lorain tornado, June 28, 1924, destroyed this
fire station and church. (19)

The disastrous 1913 flood devastated Dayton. (20)

Xenia, shattered by a tornado in 1974. (21)

like Dayton, devastated by flood waters in 1913, and the Ohio River towns which suffered repeated inundations such as the record flood of 1937.

The eternal optimism of the pioneers convinced them that the resources they enjoyed were limitless. If profligate farming methods wore out the soil in one spot, they could always move on to another virgin location where wasteful farming methods produced the same result all too often. Far-sighted reformers like John Locke of Cincinnati urged soil conservation methods well before the Civil War, and in the mid-nineteenth century concerned farmers began to learn ways of conserving their lands while making them more productive. State and county agricultural associations, fairs, farmer's organizations like the Farm Bureau and the Grange, 4-H Clubs which originated in Ohio, agricultural colleges, farm magazines, and ultimately university extension programs, radio programs, and the work of county agents, all combined to change old attitudes and gain acceptance for new and superior agricultural management. These efforts were just in time; in the decade following World War I, more than one million acres of farm land were taken out of production as Ohioans moved in record numbers to the cities. Although acreage in production continues to decline in the vicinity of major urban concentrations, Ohio's agricultural output has stabilized at a respectable and profitable level, with the state now ranking twelfth among the fifty states in value of its agricultural products.

Some of the farm land taken out of production serves residential, business, transportation, and recreational uses, but some has been ravaged by strip mining operations. Heated controversy has raged in recent decades over the economic advantages of the coal produced by strip mining,

Acid drainage pollutes streams miles beyond the mines. (22)

as opposed to the physical and social devastation attributable to untrammeled stripping. The world's mightiest shovels devour the land and leave a sterile moonscape in great portions of Belmont, Harrison, Carroll, and adjoining counties. Recent legislation requires reclamation efforts that may restore the ravaged land.

Lumber production peaked in Ohio about 1900, but by that time a great part of the state's forests were gone. To a pioneer farmer, trees were the enemy to be cut down and rooted up to make room for crops and grazing land. The voracious appetite for agricultural land resulted in the denuding of vast portions of the state. Photographs taken in the late nineteenth century often reveal a nearly treeless landscape, something that seems incongruous in Ohio. Although Caleb Atwater early urged forest conservation, only belatedly did reforestation efforts and forest management programs help Ohio recover from her wasteful course. Today, the highway engineer who recommends sacrificing trees for the sake of

In 1886, Findlay boasted of its "inexhaustible" supplies of natural gas for illumination, heating, and power. (23)

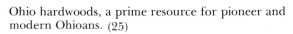
The Cow Run oil field near Marietta, ca. 1885. (24)

Ohio hardwoods, a prime resource for pioneer and modern Ohioans. (25)

widening or improving highways must fight off the resistance of a concerned citizenry. Probably trees never had so many friends as they now have in an increasingly urban society that retains a nostalgia for and an appreciation of unspoiled nature.

Other evidences of the wasteful use of resources in Ohio exist. One example is the inefficiency of early mining methods which failed to get maximum returns from coal mines and clay beds. A most spectacular example of negligent waste occurred in the 1880s and 1890s in and around Findlay, when millions of cubic feet of natural gas were allowed to escape. Not until a supposedly inexhaustible resource had vanished forever did its exploiters realize the extent of their error. They had been warned! The able state geologist, Edward Orton, said, "these stocks of buried light and heat and power are small at the best and demand the most careful husbandry."

Orton also called attention to the serious decline in water quality in Ohio's rivers. In 1880 he warned, "the rivers cannot possibly be replaced as sources of water-supply, while on the other hand, it is not only possible, but abundantly practicable to filter and disinfect the sewage, and, as a result of such correction to return only pure water to the rivers." During Ohio's first century, said Orton, not a single town had attempted to meet "this urgent demand of sanitary science," but he predicted that purification efforts would be well begun before the turn of the next century. Were he alive today, he would know that the battle has just begun, but he would see the extensive public and private efforts now underway to restore good water quality to Ohio's lakes and streams. Some of Ohio's resources — land, water, forest — are being restored, too slowly some might say, but the problem is monumental. Fish hatcheries, game preserves, bird sanctuaries, the preservation of scenic lands, and new controls on loggers and miners are abetted by legislative programs aimed at environmental controls and land use planning. These create promise that Ohio might continue to be one of nature's favored places.

(26)

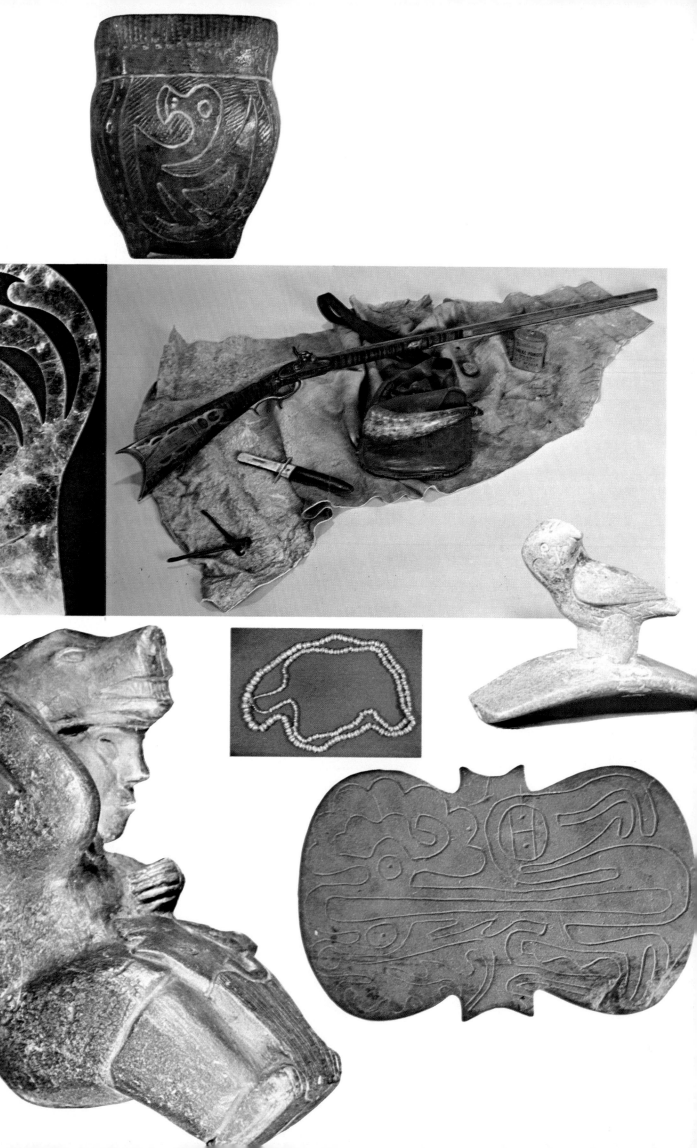

First Arrivals in the Ohio Country

The first Ohioans were prehistoric Indians known only by the relics they left behind. About 20,000 years ago, a Mongoloid people from Asia made their way eastward across a land or ice bridge then connecting Siberia with Alaska. They apparently were pushed out by powerful adversaries or perhaps by climatic shifts that made their homelands a desert. Over thousands of years, they migrated southward along the western and central reaches of North America to the Central Plateau of Mexico and adjoining lands. From this southward thrust, the fringes of migration pushed eastward periodically, and successive waves of these Indians washed across the Mississippi and Ohio valleys.

Traces of the earliest arrivals in the Ohio Country date possibly from 11,000-12,000 B.C. These people and their successors for some 9,000 years were stone age hunters and gatherers — the ancient ones, the archaic people. Later arrivals possessed a more advanced culture. First appearing in Ohio about 1,000 B.C. were the Adena people who were so named because an early excavation of one of their mounds took place at Adena, the country estate of Thomas Worthington just outside Chillicothe. Possessing interesting cultural traits, they were hunters and gatherers who experimented with agriculture, growing beans, pumpkins, squash, gourds, and sunflowers. Their dwellings appear to excel in size and structure the wigwams of later forest Indians. They were craftsmen of a high order, creating beautiful shell ornaments and working also in copper and mica. Some of their carvings reveal sophisticated skills and artistic sensitivity.

The Adenas were true "mound builders," most often using their mounds as burial sites. Today their Ohio remnants, including the sixty-eight foot cone called the Miamisburg Mound, are concentrated in the valleys of the Great and

An Ohio Portrait

Marietta earthworks along the Muskingum as depicted in a 1795 painting. (1)

Little Miami, and the Scioto and its tributaries. Among their mounds, none is more impressive or intriguing than the great Serpent Mound, one of several effigy mounds discovered in Ohio. Its dramatic location on a bluff overlooking a small river valley in Adams County heightens the visitor's sense of awe. With imagination one can visualize arcane rites carried out by priestly functionaries.

On the property of a Ross County farmer named Hopewell, mounds of another impressive culture were first studied. These Hopewell people appear at one time or another to have occupied areas from Kansas to New York. They arrived somewhat later than the Adenas and are well represented in southern Ohio with major mound groupings found in Ross, Licking, and Hamilton counties. A sedentary people who lived in rectangular dwellings, they supplemented hunting and fishing with agriculture, raising some maize, beans, and squash. An extensive trading activity accounts for objects made from obsidian — obtainable only in the distant West, copper — most likely from Michigan's northern peninsula, mica, and sea shells. Artifacts from these and other materials are found in their mounds, many of which are laid out in geometric patterns. A funerary cult was associated with burial practices and is indicative of the elaborate organization of community life.

The people who bridge the time span from the Adenas and Hopewells to those historic Indians who later greeted the Europeans are not very clearly defined. Considerable debate surrounds the people of this late woodland period. Who were the Fort Ancient people? They were incorrectly credited with construction of the impressive Fort Ancient complex in Warren County, a Hopewell site which they occupied at one time. They may have been ancestors of the wandering Shawnees, who appeared in the Ohio Country in the early eighteenth century. And what of the Cat Nation — the Eries? Some contemporary scholars doubt that these Iroquoian-speaking people who built palisaded towns and earthwork defenses on nearly inaccessible sites throughout northeastern Ohio were a distinct people at all. The *Jesuit Relations* describe the final defeat of the so-called Eries by their Iroquoian brethren near modern Erie, Pennsylvania, in 1656. Other Erie sites, such as Fort Island in the old Copley Swamp near Akron, have been wrongly identified as the locale of the Eries' last stand.

Fascination with these early people continues to grip modern visitors to Ohio's extensive, well-preserved remnants of past cultures. Imagine the wonder attending those who first came across the great mound groupings or who first saw, through a covering of brush, a great earthen serpent stretching over a thousand feet across a deserted landscape. Some of these grave sites have been desecrated because of ignorance, greed, or well-intentioned curiosity. Others have been preserved. The classically educated New Englanders of Marietta preserved the mounds and attached to one construction of the forest builders the name "Via Sacra," to commemorate the ancient people who left monuments upon the land.

For more than a half-century after the disappearance of the late woodland people, Ohio was largely unpopulated, crossed occasionally by wanderers or by Iroquois war parties intent upon conquest far to the west. If "nature abhors a vacuum," it would appear the nomadic Indians did also. By the early 1700s, several different Indian peoples were moving into the Ohio Country, partly as the result of pressures forcing them from their previous homes, and partly because

John and Johanna Maria Heckewelder,
missionaries to the Delawares. (2) (3)

choice lands were there for the taking.

From the west came the Miamis. An attractive people who brought vestiges of a prairie culture to their new homes, they settled along western Ohio from the valley of the Miami of the North (Maumee) to the valleys of the Great Miami and Little Miami and their tributaries. Their principal village was Pickawillany, near modern Piqua. Here, by the 1740s, a chieftain called *La Demoiselle* by the French, and Old Britain by the English, presided over trading activity where pelts were exchanged for French trade goods.

Another people of Algonquian linguistic stock, the Delawares or *Leni-lenape*, which means true men, moved westward across Pennsylvania to escape the advancing frontier and the Iroquois enemy and settled in the Tuscarawas-Muskingum watershed. In the 1760s and 1770s the center of their power was at Goschochgung, modern Coshocton; but by the end of the American Revolution their principal towns were near those of the Wyandots in the Sandusky River area. Long association with American colonials resulted in the Delawares acquiring some non-Indian practices: much tea was sold to the Delawares by English traders, many of the men favored European dress when obtainable, and they were the only Ohio Indians of the eighteenth century who accepted Christianity in considerable numbers. Their conversion was the work of extraordinary Moravian missionaries such as Christian Frederick Post, David Zeisberger, and John Heckewelder. The efforts of these Moravians were supported by Chief White Eyes, who permitted them to establish mission villages along the Tuscarawas at Schoenbrunn, Gnadenhutten, Salem, New Schoenbrunn, and at Lichtenau on the Muskingum. Some Delawares, however, were hostile to the missionary activity; among them

Adena house as reconstructed from archaeological evidence. (4)

Mound city in Ross County is a Hopewell site. (5)

Most famous of the effigy mounds is Serpent Mound in Adams County. (6)

Seip mound, near Bainbridge, built by the Hopewell culture. (7)

The Reverend David Zeisberger, Moravian missionary to the Delawares, from an old print. (8)

Gentle and honest, Tishcohan of the Delawares scouted the Ohio Country in 1758 for the Moravian Christian Frederick Post. Chin whiskers were rare among Indian men. (9)

"The Power of the Gospel" by Christian Schuessle depicts David Zeisberger preaching to the Indians. (10)

was Hopocan, or Captain Pipe, an implacable foe of the white men.

The Shawnees were an Algonquian people who first appeared in Ohio around the middle of the eighteenth century. They wandered from the Carolinas and Tennessee to settle in south-central Ohio, initially along the Scioto but soon spreading to the west toward the two Miamis. Perhaps the most warlike of the Ohio Indians, they resisted encroachment on their newfound lands with fierce dedication. However, their effectiveness was sometimes lessened by the inability of their main tribal divisions to agree on policy. At their principal villages in the Scioto Valley from Circleville to Chillicothe (a Shawnee word for "town"), Cornstalk, his formidable sister the Grenadier Squaw, and a number of able war chiefs concocted strategies to preserve their lands.

Two of Ohio's important Indian peoples were Iroquoian speaking — the Mingoes and the Wyandots, a splinter group of Hurons. Pushed out of Huronia on the Ontario Peninsula by the fierce Iroquois Confederacy, a group of Hurons moved to the French post at Detroit and from there a group called Wyandots then migrated into northcentral Ohio. Settling principally along the Sandusky and its feeder streams, their chief towns were near Upper Sandusky. Determined foes of the Americans through the Revolutionary period and during the Indian wars of the 1790s, many Wyandots later fought alongside William Henry Harrison in the War of 1812.

The fifth major Indian group in Ohio included various Iroquois — Cayugas, Mohawks, Tuscarawas, but mostly Senecas — who were known collectively as Mingoes. Their settlements were scattered, but northeastern Ohio, the upper Ohio River Valley, and an area extending southeastward from the vicinity of Columbus were

their main homesites. The Mingoes' long relationship with encroaching white society gave them considerable insight in their dealings with pioneers. The best known Mingo associated with the Ohio Country was John Logan, who was reputedly part Cayuga and part French. His friendship for whites was turned to hatred by the indiscriminate slaughter of his family by white border ruffians. Not until Logan had taken revenge by lifting some thirty scalps was he placated. His famous lament, couched in Biblical imagery, became an American classic.

Sporadically, other tribes located in the Ohio Country. Ottawa villages were spread widely around Ohio and were especially numerous in the northwestern part of the future state. Chippewas had a village on the lake named for them in Medina County. From time to time an occasional Mohican, Pottawatomie, Munsey (Delaware), Wea (Miami), or Piankeshaw (Miami) appeared, but only in limited numbers.

All Ohio Indians combined sedentary agriculture with hunting and fishing. Corn was the main crop. Early travelers reported fields stretching two or three miles along rich river bottom lands. Beans, squash, gourds, pumpkins, berries, nuts, and maple sugar were other food products favored by Ohio Indians. By the time American frontiersmen pushed up against these Indians in the Ohio Country, they had already learned the Indians' skills — woodcraft, animal lore, cultivation methods, housing, and clothing. They reaped the benefits of Indian experience. Sometimes Americans gave the Indians things of value — some persons on the frontier were well-intentioned toward the Indians. But all too often what the Indians received from the frontiersmen — whiskey and rum, disease, a desire for trinkets, baubles, and useless objects — proved to be their undoing. Dependent on European guns and supplies, they became pawns in power struggles. The French used Indians against the English, and the English used them against the Americans. Indian resistance to American encroachment played a most important part in the saga of Ohio's settlement.

The fundamental differences which separated Indian and white were nowhere more evident than in their concepts of land use and ownership. To the white settler, land was real property to be owned outright (in fee simple); the owner had full right to exclude trespassers. The Indian did not own land. As a tribal member he shared with his people a use-right of all the lands habitually regarded as theirs. The difference was expressed graphically to Moravian John Heckewelder by a Delaware who explained:

My friend, it seems you lay claim to the grass my horses have eaten because you had enclosed it with a fence:

now tell me, who caused the grass to grow? Can *you* make the grass grow? . . . the grass which grows out of the earth is common to all; the game in the woods is common to all . . . then be not disturbed at my horse having eaten only once of what you call *your grass*, though the grass my horses did eat, in like manner as the meat you eat, was given to the Indians by the Great Spirit. Besides, if you will but consider, you will find that my horse did not eat all your grass.

In modern Ohio one cannot escape an awareness of the Indian who forms an important part of historical displays throughout the state. His story is dramatized in outdoor amphitheaters near New Philadelphia and Chillicothe. At Schoenbrunn, Gnadenhutten, Piqua, Maumee, and elsewhere, one is reminded of his presence. But nowhere is this memory more evident than in Ohio counties named Huron, Erie, Seneca, Wyandot, Tuscarawas, and Delaware; rivers

Cabins used by Ohio pioneers featured many handmade items. Some metal and chinaware was brought from the East. (11)

An Ohio Portrait

The Shawnee chief, Black Hoof. (12)

named Ohio, Muskingum, Cuyahoga, Miami, and Scioto; towns named Wapakoneta, Chillicothe, Ottawa, Mingo Junction, and Shawneetown; indeed, in the very name of the state itself.

The earliest known penetration of the Ohio Country by Europeans occurred relatively late when one considers that Robert René Cavelier Sieur de La Salle did not reach the Ohio River until 1669. By that date the French had long-established posts along Lake Huron and had penetrated the western lakes and the interior of the Illinois Country far to the west. This western penetration was late only in terms of French activity, for in 1669 there was not yet a Pennsylvania, New York had been won from Dutch settlers just five years earlier, and English settlements were confined to a narrow coastal littoral.

La Salle explored the shores washed by *la belle riviere*. His exact route is unknown, and generations of local enthusiasts throughout the midwest have made extravagant claims about his

presence in their area. The powerful Iroquois Confederacy held hegemony over the Ohio Country and posed an effective barrier to the exploitation of that region by the French. No permanent French post was established in Ohio. By the 1740s, however, French trading relationships with the Miamis and Ottawas were threatened by George Croghan, Conrad Weiser, and other aggressive Pennsylvania traders who had moved into the Ohio Country with their rum, blankets, steel axes, guns, and trade goods.

The threat was pronounced because Croghan was a persuasive forest diplomat and because British traders were giving the Indians more and better trade goods in exchange for pelts than were the French. Moreover, the frontier of British settlement was expanding westward at a rate that alarmed the French and their Indian allies. Already, ambitious land schemes were being organized. Speculators in Virginia and Pennsylvania and their allies in London cast covetous eyes on the Ohio Country. The most direct threat was the Ohio Company, largely a Virginia enterprise, whose scout Christopher Gist traveled as far west as Pickawillany (in modern Shelby County) in 1750 and 1751. Virginia claimed all of the Ohio Country under her charter of 1609. In 1752 her agents negotiated the Treaty of Logstown with the Iroquois and Delawares, who ceded to Virginia lands south of the Ohio, near the Kanawha River, and authorized the Ohio Company to build a fort and settle this region.

Earlier French efforts, including the bizarre journey made by Céleron de Bienville along the Allegheny and Ohio, where he planted lead plates claiming the lands for the French king, had failed to stop the aggressive British. A more direct warning was required. In the summer of 1752, French settlers under Charles Langlade and their Indian allies led by the Ottawa war chief, Pontiac, smashed the trading post at Pickawillany and killed many Miamis who had dealt there with British traders. The pro-British Miami chief, *La Demoiselle*, was killed and his heart was eaten by the victors, but the gruesome object lesson was ineffective in stifling competition. In 1753 Lieutenant Governor Robert Dinwiddie of Virginia sent the veteran Christopher Gist to accompany his young agent, George Washington, on a mission to warn the French away from their fort-building activities on the Upper Ohio. This mission and a follow-up military expedition in 1754, also under Washington's leadership, were failures. The stage was now set for the greatest of the colonial struggles — the French and Indian War.

In this war, the initial advantage enjoyed by the French and their Indian allies evaporated by 1758 or 1759 as Britain developed new energies under able war minister, William Pitt. None of the major actions occurred in the Ohio Country. French influence was curtailed by the loss of Fort Duquesne (1758), which was promptly renamed Fort Pitt, and by the fall of Fort Niagara, which interrupted supply lines to the western posts. The posts to the north and west of Ohio were surrendered in 1760 as a consequence of the fall of Montreal and Quebec. Major Robert Rogers, an energetic colonial and leader of a band of skilled woodsmen and fighters named Rogers's Rangers, moved into the Ohio Country on his way west to take the surrender of Detroit and Fort Michilimackinac. He apparently met Pontiac near the mouth of the Cuyahoga, a site just twenty miles from an Ottawa village called Ponty's Town near modern Boston in the Cuyahoga Valley. Only years later, however, could the British reach the distant Illinois posts and replace French authority with their own. The

Peace of Paris of 1763 ended hostilities, and France relinquished her claim to all of New France and Louisiana, one of the richest colonial prizes ever lost.

British authority now lay unchallenged over the Ohio Country, or so the government of George III believed, but in fact the Indians controlled it. The western Indians were extremely displeased by the defeat of their French allies and by increasingly shoddy British trade goods and restricted distribution of the customary "presents." Every British post in the West except Fort Pitt and Detroit was lost to Indian raiders, who acted in enough concert to cause British officials and some later historians to speak of "Pontiac's conspiracy" because this pro-French Ottawa was its leading figure. In Ohio proper only one small trading post, Sandoski (near modern Sandusky) was destroyed by Indian raiders, but the raids made by Ohio Indians against the exposed settlements of western Pennsylvania and Virginia resulted in hundreds of white prisoners being carried into the Ohio Country, where some were adopted into Indian families and others were killed.

Initial British countermeasures were unsuccessful. The Royal Proclamation of 1763 described a line along the Appalachian crest beyond which settlement was prohibited; the Ohio Indians would thus be sheltered from many of the irritations that had caused them to take up the hatchet.

The Proclamation was aimed at preserving the fur trade while reducing the expense to Great Britain of maintaining garrisons throughout the West. The plan was doomed from the beginning. No one could stop the colonials' relentless search for land, as the acquisitive habits of Americans were too well developed. They interpreted this proclamation as an infringement on their colo-

An Ohio Portrait

Simon Kenton

Simon Kenton, the border runner, as an old man. Kenton (1755–1836) is buried at Urbana. (13)

A council between Colonel Henry Bouquet and the Ohio Indians along the Muskingum, 1764. (14)

An artist's representation of Pontiac, an Ottawa war chief whose "conspiracy" nearly drove the British from the West in 1763 and 1764. (15)

nial charters and as evidence that selfish interests in Great Britain were to be served at the expense of colonial rights.

A second response to Indian initiative in the West was better received by the colonials. A Swiss mercenary, Colonel Henry Bouquet, led about 1,500 men, including units of the colorful Black Watch regiment, into the heart of the Delaware nation. There along the Muskingum in 1764, Bouquet dictated peace terms, the most dramatic of which required the northwestern Indians to return all white captives regardless of age, length of captivity, and status within Indian society. The Indians generally complied. For recent captives, return to their own people was usually a welcome release. For many of those who had become fully

Colonel Bouquet's treaty with the Ohio Indians (1764) required them to deliver up their white captives. Here, along the Muskingum, the delivery takes place. (16)

An Ohio Portrait

Logan, the famous Mingo leader, was possibly part French. His lament was memorized by generations of Ohio school children. (17)

During the Revolutionary War, Samuel Brady escaped pursuing Indians by leaping this Cuyahoga River chasm. This spot lies near the heart of modern Kent. (18)

Cornstalk, a chief of the Shawnees, was murdered by border soldiers at Point Pleasant (West Virginia) in 1777. (19)

integrated into Indian society, it was often a trauma, a feeling one can best appreciate by reading Conrad Richter's realistic and moving *A Light in the Forest*. A second punitive expedition, led by Colonel John Bradstreet, met with little success as it progressed westward on Lake Erie close to the Ohio shore. Failure to carry out its mission caused anxiety to the British command in America for years to come.

Perhaps more important ultimately than military might in restraining the Ohio Indians was the work of the Moravian missionary Christian Frederick Post, who is credited with persuading the Delawares to abandon their old allegiance to the French. Soon after this, George Croghan persuaded Pontiac himself to cooperate with the British. These efforts were undoubtedly aided by the new British policy of restricting the westward movement of its colonials. Also helpful was the Board of Trade Plan of 1764, which restricted trade with the Indians to licensed traders operating out of established posts. By this method control could be maintained and steps taken to minimize unfair practices that had earlier goaded

the Indians to war. Thus, by the mid-1760s, it appeared that peace had returned to the Ohio Country.

Peaceful conditions did not last long. A gulf of misunderstanding was widening between Great Britain and her American colonies as a whole series of actions and counteractions in the political and economic spheres created new tensions. Colonial radicals like Sam Adams of Massachusetts thought that those "rights of Englishmen" coveted by colonials were being sacrificed to the selfish interests of British politicians and merchants. Royal ambition and authority was evident in the eastern seaboard communities, but in the frontier West the only visible manifestations of imperial power were the tiny British garrisons in the isolated posts reestablished after Pontiac's War.

In 1774, however, Parliament passed the Quebec Act, designed in part to redefine administrative control over the West. The act provided that lands north of the Ohio extending westward from Pennsylvania to the Mississippi should be part of the Old Province of Quebec, administered from a distant capital, Quebec City, a thousand miles away from the Ohio Country. At the time of its passage, the only colonials living in the Ohio Country were a few itinerant Indian traders and a handful of Moravian missionaries maintaining peaceful villages among their Delaware converts on the Tuscarawas. Nevertheless, the Quebec Act effectively stripped some provinces of the benefits of their western land claims and placed a crimp in the land speculation schemes of influential colonials and Englishmen.

The Quebec Act never received a fair trial in the West, because its promulgation coincided with a crisis which soon had the British government and American colonials in arms against one another. Some called the Quebec Act a "coercive" act, and colonials clearly did not intend to observe its provisions. Strangely it was John Murray Lord Dunmore, the Royal Governor of Virginia, who most effectively ignored the Quebec Act.

Virginia was competing with Pennsylvania for control of Fort Pitt and its surrounding area, the key to the Ohio Country. Among the American settlers in this region were many rough, aggressive people, some of whom were involved in atrocities against the Ohio Indians. The most infamous of these atrocities was perpetrated by Daniel Greathouse and fellow ruffians, who lured a number of Indians, including members of Logan's family, to Baker's cabin on the Virginia side of the Ohio where they murdered them in barbaric fashion. Enraged by this deed, Logan conducted his personal vendetta along the frontier. To quell renewed Indian raids on Virginia settlements, Dunmore organized an expedition designed to force the Shawnees and Mingoes to accept peace terms.

In the summer of 1774, Dunmore moved down the Ohio from Fort Pitt to the Hocking River, where he expected to be joined by Colonel Andrew Lewis and nearly 1,000 men from the Virginia settlements. Lewis was delayed. In early autumn his encampment at Point Pleasant, where the Kanawha flows into the Ohio, was attacked by about 1,000 Shawnees, with a representation of other Ohio Indians, under the command of Cornstalk. This battle of Point Pleasant, one of the bloodiest in the Ohio Valley, was a draw, although the Indians left the field to Lewis's men. Dunmore, meanwhile, moved up the Hocking River to the Scioto, where he approached the Shawnee towns in the Pickaway Plains. By the time Lewis joined him, he had concluded with the Shawnees terms that permitted unmolested navigation of the Ohio as well as assurance that Virginians south of the Ohio would be safe from In-

dian attack. The nearby towns of some intransigent Mingoes were burned, and Dunmore's party then withdrew. While returning to Virginia they paused at Fort Gower, a hastily erected fortification at the confluence of the Hocking and the Ohio. Here, in the Fort Gower Resolutions, Dunmore's officers pledged support of the work lately performed by the First Continental Congress, but also expressed confidence in Dunmore and his leadership. For the next year and a half a tenuous peace prevailed along the Ohio.

The Ohio Country was of great importance throughout the War of Independence. It was located between Detroit, the principal British outpost in the West, and Fort Pitt, the colonials' most advanced post and the supply center for all American activity in the West. It was also positioned between Detroit and the nascent Kentucky settlements, prime targets for Indian raids. Following Dunmore's War and the final split between Great Britain and her colonies, both British and Americans sought to make allies of the Ohio Indians. Despite the sincere and well-motivated efforts of men like Colonel George Morgan to win Indian friendship and support, the land hungry Virginia "long knives" were held in fear and distrust. Only the Christian Delawares remained friendly or neutral. The rest — Shawnee, Miami, Wyandot, Mingo, Ottawa, the Wolf Clan of the Delaware — were allies of the British, whose commander at Detroit, Lieutenant Governor Henry Hamilton, earned the grim sobriquet "Hairbuyer" for his practice of paying bounties for American scalps, although he did not invent this practice.

Organized warfare with the western Indians broke out in 1777. Cornstalk and his son were treacherously murdered at Fort Randolph by Americans whom he had come to warn that his

First Arrivals in the Ohio Country

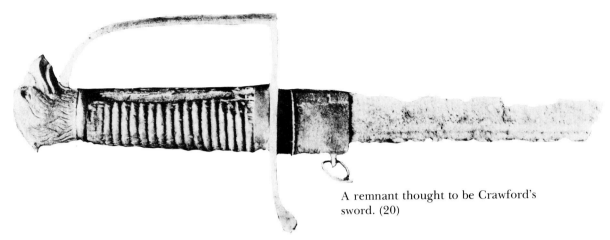

A remnant thought to be Crawford's sword. (20)

The Delawares take revenge. Colonel William Crawford at the stake in 1782 near Upper Sandusky. (21)

An Ohio Portrait

Simon Girty, infamous on the Ohio frontier as a
turncoat, as he was pictured in an 1891 children's
history of Ohio. (22)

"Here triumphed in death ninety Christian Indians,
March 9, 1782." This marker in the Gnadenhutten
cemetery commemorates the tragic massacre which
demonstrates frontier violence at its worst. (23)

Shawnees were about to violate the peace settlement imposed by Dunmore. The Ohio Indians
rose to avenge him and, for the next six years,
attacked Kentucky and Virginia settlements. The
Ohio Indians were supported by British officers,
supplies, and sometimes troops. In almost every
case, retaliatory raids were mounted against Indian villages, especially those of the Delawares,
Shawnees, and Miamis, which were most vulnerable to attack from Fort Pitt and from the Ken-

tucky settlements. The most spectacular American raid, George Rogers Clark's capture of Kaskaskia, Cahokia, and Vincennes in 1778 and
1779, occurred outside Ohio. Hamilton was captured at Vincennes, but his replacement at Detroit, Major Arent De Peyster, continued un-
abated the British support of border warfare. In
1780, however, Clark led about 1,000 Kentucky
backwoodsmen into Ohio and defeated a small
number of Shawnees in the inconclusive Battle of
Piqua. After burning Indian towns and crops,
Clark's men retired.

A somewhat more ambitious scheme had
been mounted at Fort Pitt late in 1778. General
Lachlan McIntosh, hoping to neutralize the Ohio
tribes and also to establish a post on the way to
Detroit, marched to the Tuscarawas where he
erected Fort Laurens on the site of modern
Bolivar and garrisoned it with Virginia and Pennsylvania troops. Inadequate supplies and manpower combined with poor timing frustrated
McIntosh's hopes. After enduring a prolonged
siege by Indians from the Sandusky, led by Captain Bird and the famous renegade Simon Girty,
the garrison received reinforcements. Fort
Laurens was abandoned, however, in the summer of 1779.

Amid the bloodshed and brutality characteristic of border warfare, one act stands out for
sheer savagery. In 1781 the Christian Delawares
and their Moravian leaders were forced by Indians of the Sandusky area, principally Wyandots
and Delawares, to leave the Tuscarawas and go to
the Sandusky so they would be isolated from
American influence. These "captives" nearly
starved in their new homes before some were
permitted to return to their villages and gather
corn still on the stalk. While engaged in this pursuit, they were approached by an informal band
of border men who were incensed over recent

murders along the Ohio. Led by Colonel David Williamson, the invaders collected arms from the unsuspecting Delawares and herded most into buildings at Gnadenhutten. All but eighteen of the nearly one hundred attackers voted to kill the prisoners who, when informed of their fate, spent the night singing Psalms and praying. In the morning they were led out, two by two, to the slaughter houses where some sixty-two of these peaceful Indian men and women, plus thirty-four children, perished. Congress was so mortified that in the great Land Ordinance of 1785 lands were provided for the descendants along the Tuscarawas, but the Moravian Indians never stayed again for any length of time in that shadowed valley.

Ohio's final act in the Revolutionary drama was played out by Colonel William Crawford, former land agent for George Washington and leader of over 400 mounted men, who pressed west in 1782 toward the hostile Indians in the Sandusky towns. Surprised by superior numbers and defeated at Battle Island on the Olentangy, Crawford's force broke for safety, but the Colonel was captured and cruelly tortured to death by Delawares and Wyandots.

The Peace of Paris in 1783 brought formal recognition of independence to the United States of America, and with it an immensely valuable bonus — the rich lands stretching westward from the Appalachians to the Mississippi. That part of this wilderness empire lying north of the Ohio River was inhabited only by Indians except for the small French remnant in the Illinois Country, some squatters along the Ohio, and those British traders who stayed on in the posts at Niagara, Detroit, and Michilimackinac, all on United States soil.

Congress intended to open the Ohio Country to settlement, but first Indian title had to be removed. Commissioners from Congress met in 1785 with representatives from the Wyandots, Delawares, Ottawas, and Chippewas at Fort McIntosh, just downriver from Fort Pitt. The commissioners told the Indians that, as allies of the defeated British, they too had been defeated — a sophistry that was not persuasive for long. Plied with food and strong drink, the Indians signed away their rights to what is now the eastern and southern two-thirds of Ohio. This Treaty of Fort McIntosh confined the Ohio Indians beyond a line drawn from the mouth of the Cuyahoga, upstream across the portage to the Tuscarawas, to Fort Laurens, to Loramie's Store (near Piqua), and finally to the Ohio River. The treaty was rejected by most Ohio Indians. The Shawnees agreed in 1786 to move west of the Great Miami, but for some years to come the Ohio Country was still a perilous place to settle. Only the brave and the fortunate would successfully dare the Indians' wrath.

(24)

Connecticut Land Company, ss.

Nᵒ 63

HARTFORD, Sept. 5th, 1795.

THIS CERTIFIES, That _____

is entitled to the Trust and Benefit of _____

_____

Twelve Hundred Thousandths of the Connecticut Western Reserve, *so called, as held by* John Caldwell, Jonathan Brace, *and* John Morgan, *Trustees in a Deed of Trust, dated the Fifth Day of September One Thousand Seven Hundred and Ninety Five, to hold said Proportion or Share to* _____ *the said*

_____

Heirs and Assigns, according to the Terms, Conditions, Covenants and Exceptions contained in the said Deed of Trust, and in certain Articles of Agreement entered into by the Persons composing the Connecticut Land Company; *which said Share is transferable by Assignment, under Hand and Seal, witnessed by two Witnesses, and acknowledged before any Justice of the Peace in the State of* Connecticut, *or before a Notary Public, or a Judge of the Common Pleas in any of the United States, and to be recorded by the Clerk of the Board of Directors.*

John Caldwell
Jonathan Brace — Trustees.

A State Carved From the Wilderness

Ohio was the testing ground for the procedures by which the government of the United States converted the public domain into states—Indian removal by treaty and by war, land surveys, the sale or other disposition of lands, establishment of territorial government, and the statehood process. Several of these procedures might be underway simultaneously. In Ohio's experience the situation was further complicated by the presence of the Virginia and Connecticut reserves which, although lying within the emerging state, were separately controlled for a short period.

Responsibility for creating the public lands and for initiating the territorial system rested with Congress. In 1780, while the War of Independence was still raging, Congress resolved that states with western land claims should surrender them for the purpose of creating a public domain. These lands would then belong to the United States and would be used for the benefit of the new nation. New York was first to respond; it surrendered its vague claims to the Ohio Country. Within the next six years Virginia, Massachusetts, and Connecticut relinquished their rather more substantial claims.

In surrendering its western lands, Virginia retained a huge area lying between the Scioto and Little Miami rivers. Virginia used these military bounty lands to indemnify its Revolutionary War veterans. Land certificates or warrants were issued to each veteran, the amount of land varying from 200 acres for a private to 15,000 acres for a general. If the veteran did not wish to take up the Ohio land to which he was entitled, he could sell his warrant at a steep discount to a speculator who hoped to grow rich by resale of the land at inflated prices. Connecticut also reserved Ohio land, more than three million acres lying between the forty-first parallel of north latitude and Lake Erie, extending westward 120

An Ohio Portrait

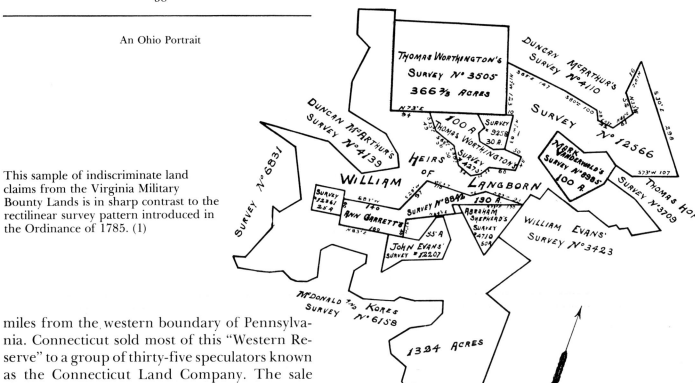

This sample of indiscriminate land claims from the Virginia Military Bounty Lands is in sharp contrast to the rectilinear survey pattern introduced in the Ordinance of 1785. (1)

miles from the western boundary of Pennsylvania. Connecticut sold most of this "Western Reserve" to a group of thirty-five speculators known as the Connecticut Land Company. The sale price of $1.2 million was placed in a fund for the support of public education in the Nutmeg State. The westernmost part of the reserve, modern Huron and Erie counties, was granted to the "sufferers" burned out of their coastal properties during the late war by British raiders. This area, called the Firelands, retained a distinctive character until recent times.

As noted earlier, Congress first attempted to reduce Indian title to the Ohio Country by treaty. While that process was underway, Congress passed the Land Ordinance of 1785, surely one of the most influential and far-reaching acts in American history. This act for the survey and sale of the "lands Northwest of the River Ohio" established a rectilinear survey system which lay a gridiron of north-south, east-west lines across the land. The basic units of the survey were townships, six miles square, with each township divided into thirty-six sections, each one mile square (640 acres). Townships were arranged in north-south rows called ranges. Every range, township, and section was numbered according to a standard code, thus obviating any chance for overlapping or mistaken claims except where surveyors' errors caused difficulty. Section sixteen of each township was set aside for the support of public education, and four sections were reserved by Congress for later sale. The same rectilinear pattern was used in the Connecticut Western Reserve except that the grid was based on five-mile-square townships, as was true also of a limited part of the Congress Lands.

Actual survey started with a forty-two mile "base line" running west from the point at which the Pennsylvania border met the north shore of the Ohio River. The running of this line, as well as the larger survey, was the responsibility of the geographer of the United States, at that time Thomas Hutchins. In 1787, before the survey of these first "Seven Ranges" was complete, Congress authorized sales to begin at the Pittsburgh land office. The smallest unit of land sold was a section, sold at auction at a minimum price of one dollar an acre. Payment was in cash or in federal land certificates, with no provision for credit.

Poor subsistence farmers had little chance of accumulating the minimum $640 needed to purchase land in the Seven Ranges. Even if they had the money, farmers purchasing land sight unseen would be taking a great risk. Sales limped along with speculators providing most of the limited action. Since Congress had been counting on land sales to secure general revenue funds, finding ways to speed up the process was important. The ultimate solution—a liberalization of sale terms—lay in the not-too-distant future but, in the meantime, Congress approved several sales of huge tracts of Ohio land to speculators and private land companies. The sales were made at bargain prices far more generous than the terms available to the individual purchaser. Once in the hands of private owners, the land was surveyed and then disposed of by whatever terms pleased the land company. Thus the small farmer was able to secure a reasonable plot at prices and terms he could manage.

Josiah Harmar's troops remove squatters illegally occupying Ohio land. (2)

Thousands of Americans did not wait for the survey or concern themselves about sale terms; they simply moved into the Ohio Country and settled where they pleased. These "squatters" saw no reason why unoccupied lands should not be used. They were part of an American tradition which went back to the first settlements. It was impossible to keep a restless people from straying out into the open country beyond the control of settled societies. Some contemporaries regarded the squatter as the best representative of the free man seeking to better himself through his own labors and risks; others regarded him as a loafer, shiftless and improvident, siring "brats" who would have to be supported eventually by more responsible people. Congress wanted these people cleared out and gave the job to Colonel Josiah Harmar, who established Fort Harmar at

Josiah Harmar (1753–1813). (3)

Fort Harmar, an early artist's view. (4)

Map of the State of Ohio Taken from the returns in the OFFICE of the SURVEYOR GENERAL By John F. Mansfield

Manasseh Cutler, whose effective lobbying helped
secure the Ohio Company of Associates grant. (6)

the mouth of the Muskingum to aid in the project. A sense of the difficulties he encountered can
be gained from one of his subordinates who reported his experience with squatters near modern Steubenville:

> At Yellow Creek I dispossessed two families and de-
> stroyed their building . . . I read my instructions to the
> prisoner [Joseph] Ross who declared they never came
> from Congress, for he had late accounts from that
> honorable body, who, he was convinced, gave no such
> instructions to the Commissioners . . . if I destroyed
> his house he [said he] would build six more within a
> week. He also cast many reflections on the honorable
> Congress, the Commissioners, and the commanding
> officer.

As one would surmise, efforts to clear the squatters failed in Ohio as they had failed and were to
fail elsewhere in a developing America.

While Congress was experiencing certain
frustrations with its land survey and sale policies,
it was taking steps to provide an orderly administration for the Northwest. Thomas Jefferson's
Ordinance of 1784, though never put into effect,
paved the way for a territorial system operated on
the assumption that the wilderness should be
transformed into settled, republican states, and
that this process should take place in several steps
which were consistent with the state of development of the area. The provisions finally applied
to the Ohio Country were contained in the famous Northwest Ordinance of 1787. In the first
stage, a governor, secretary, and three judges
chosen by Congress were to administer the
Northwest Territory using laws drawn from
existing state codes. When a census revealed that
there were at least 5,000 free adult males in the
Northwest, qualified electors could choose a legislature, but the governor would retain an absolute
veto over their bills. The legislature could choose
a delegate to Congress. This delegate could in-
troduce legislation and debate, but he could not

vote. When the territory boasted 60,000 inhabitants it could apply to Congress for admission as a
state, and Congress would then take the necessary steps. At least three and no more than five
states were to be created out of the Northwest.

The Northwest Ordinance also protected the
civil liberties of the people in its "articles of com-
pact." This is interesting because the new federal
Constitution then being drafted was severely
criticized for not having such safeguards, until
the first ten amendments, the famous Bill of
Rights, were added in 1791. Slavery was forbidden north of the Ohio; education and religion
were to be encouraged; the Indians were to be
dealt with fairly and honorably. The Northwest
Ordinance was first applied in the evolution of
Ohio to statehood. Every state coming into the
Union after Ohio, except Texas, would go
through a modified form of this statemaking
process.

Certainly one reason that Congress established
administrative control over the Northwest Territory at this early time was to hasten the sale of
public lands. A civil population must have government. The effective lobbying of agents for the
Ohio Company of Associates, especially the Reverend Manasseh Cutler, speeded the process.
Sale of land to the Ohio Company would bring
income to the Treasury and people to the wilderness. The blandishments of the versatile Mr. Cutler were persuasive, especially since the president of the Congress, Arthur St. Clair, was the

most likely prospect to become governor of the Northwest Territory.

Passage of the Northwest Ordinance was followed soon by the first authorized settlement in the Ohio Country. A group of Revolutionary War veterans led by Rufus Putnam and Benjamin Tupper had organized the Ohio Company of Associates in Boston in March, 1786. The company won from Congress 1.5 million acres along the Ohio and west of the Seven Ranges, for a price of $1 million, half of which was to be paid immediately and half when the survey was complete. Ultimately the company was granted 1,782,000 acres, for which it paid in depreciated government securities some twelve and a half cents an acre in true value, certainly one of the great land bargains of all times.

On April 7, 1788, boats constructed at Sumrill's Ferry, Pennsylvania, brought Rufus Putnam and his party to the mouth of the Muskingum.

Rufus Putnam, leader of the Marietta settlement. (7)

The settlement at "the point," Marietta, ca. 1790. (8)

There on the east bank, across from Fort Har-mar, they established a village named Marietta in honor of Queen Marie Antoinette and the French Alliance. These New Englanders were colonists of a high order. Many were well edu-cated, skilled, and sensitive to their new environ-ment and its opportunities. They built a fortified center, the Campus Martius, laid out town lots and out lots, preserved the mounds and focused their town around them, and quickly established familiar institutions. Some moved on up the Muskingum, even to remote and exposed loca-tions like Big Bottom and the Donation Tract, where lands were granted to settlers brave enough to form a shield on the far reaches of company land.

At one point, the Ohio Company venture was tangled in the more ambitious schemes of the so-called Scioto Company which planned to se-cure about five million acres east of the Scioto. This ill-fated venture resulted in the disillusion-ment of hundreds of gullible French émigrés who were lured to Gallipolis (city of the French, or Frenchtown) under the most blatant misrepre-sentations. These tragic victims found a raw wil-derness instead of the gentle, pastoral Eden they were promised and for which their genteel skills were suited. Only a small number stayed on along the Ohio even after an embarrassed Congress in 1795 ceded lands called the French Grants for their succor.

More successful by far was the sale in 1788 of a large tract between the Miamis to Judge John Cleve Symmes of New Jersey. He sent energetic settlers from various eastern states. Their first settlements were Columbia and Losantiville, communities which later combined to form Cin-cinnati. Early settlers in the Symmes Grant were more varied in background than the New Eng-landers of Marietta.

Arrival of the French settlers at Gallipolis. (9)

Cartoon of French settlers cutting trees near Gallipolis. (10)

An Ohio Portrait

Nathaniel Massie, founder of Chillicothe. (11)

As one would suspect, the Virginia Military District attracted settlers primarily from the Old Dominion and Kentucky. In this region the rectilinear survey was not used. Instead the Virginians relied on a random system of claims and indiscriminate surveys, and to this day this part of Ohio reflects the irregularities of that system. Manchester on the Ohio was the district's first settlement, but leaders like Nathaniel Massie and Thomas Worthington soon made Chillicothe on the Scioto its center of influence. Like the New Englanders in Marietta, the southerners who settled the Virginia Military District gave a pronounced regional flavor to this part of Ohio, and their influence was to have a profound effect on the state's development politically, economically, and socially.

A distinctly different cast was given to the Western Reserve where New Englanders dominated early settlement. General Moses Cleaveland of the Connecticut Land Company led a party of surveyors to the mouth of the Cuyahoga in 1796 where they platted a town. The proposed town languished, however, and showed no signs

Territorial government is inaugurated, 1788. (12)

Arthur St. Clair, first governor of the Northwest Territory. (13)

that it would one day be the metropolis of a great state. These early surveyors triumphed over difficult terrain, sickness, short supplies, lost equipment, and various other hazards.

Other towns were established in the reserve before the end of the eighteenth century, including Youngstown, settled by the New Yorker John Young in 1796, Warren (1799) and Ravenna (1799).

Many other Ohio land grants were made for specific purposes—the Donation Tract abutting the Ohio Company lands; the Refugee lands; the Moravian tracts; Zane's grants; and several others. When lands granted by Congress for special purposes were not used, they usually reverted to the public domain or were disposed of under a revised set of conditions. Nearly all Ohio land not previously identified was designated Congress Lands. Most of these lands were surveyed on a six-mile grid. Portions of the Congress Lands, especially in the northwestern part of Ohio, were later donated to the state for support of its road and canal building efforts.

Thus the great variety of patterns imposed on Ohio made it a field laboratory for testing government land policies. The six-mile township became the standard for all later surveys, special grants to land companies were abandoned, special grants to individuals for services rendered (for example the Zane grants or the Dohrman grant) virtually ceased, and no further "reserves" of lands retained by established states were to be found further west.

In July, 1788, just three months after the establishment of Marietta, the new territorial governor, Arthur St. Clair, former Revolutionary War general, and president of the Confederation Congress, arrived at the new settlement to establish temporary civil government in the Northwest. He was joined by Winthrop Sargent, secre-

tary of the territory, and by the three judges—James M. Varnum, Samuel H. Parsons, and John C. Symmes. Temporary government was established immediately and, by 1795, in concert with the judges, St. Clair had selected laws from the codes of existing states, mainly Pennsylvania. The first stage of territorial government as outlined in the Northwest Ordinance was underway.

Newcomers did not flock to Ohio in great numbers during these earliest years of settlement. The difficult journey and the slow pace of the survey were not what deterred them; rather it was the hostility of the Ohio Indians which kept the would-be stream of migration to a trickle. Primitive defenses had been erected upon first landings, and most communities soon had fortified retreats ready to meet the expected emergencies. Those who went into the interior to settle often paid dearly. In 1791 twelve persons were killed at Big Bottom, upstream from Marietta on the Muskingum. Clearly the Indians did not intend to abide by the treaties of Fort McIntosh and Fort Finney, but then these inept treaties were scarcely to be taken seriously by those who had no hand in them or who had cooperated with the congressional commissioners out of fear. Why should the Indian sit by and observe the final alienation of his lands while getting in return little more than the disease, drink, and debauch that always followed upon the white man's heels?

By 1790 the Indian situation had become acute. Some 600 United States troops stretched out along the Ohio were too few to send against a formidable foe supplied as of old from the British post at Detroit. Congress authorized President George Washington to call out the militia, and men from Virginia, Pennsylvania, and Kentucky assembled at Fort Washington (Cincinnati) where they joined the regulars under the command of

An Ohio Portrait

Fort Washington, erected 1790 in Cincinnati. (14)

The care with which Anthony Wayne prepared his troops resulted in complete victory over the Indians at Fallen Timbers. (15)

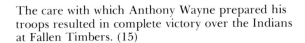

General Josiah Harmar. Harmar pushed north into Indian country before he had his fractious, ill-trained militia under control. He met disaster. After destroying Indian villages and crops near modern Fort Wayne, Indiana, his forces were routed by the northwestern Indians under the Miami war chief, Little Turtle, and driven back to Fort Washington in disgrace.

Another attempt to reduce Indian power was made in 1791. Governor St. Clair himself took charge of an army of some 3,000 men who were as unruly and as inept as Harmar's. He constructed a number of fortified posts north of Fort Washington in the Indian country. Counting on them as advanced bases and as potential refuges, St. Clair advanced with about half of his original force and camped on the eastern branch of the Wabash near the present Ohio-Indiana line. There Little Turtle's braves surprised and routed the inept and confused army. Despite St. Clair's personal bravery, his forces suffered about 900 casualties, one of the worst defeats in American military history.

President Washington was determined to prevail and sought the best military leadership he could find to take on the task of reducing Indian power in the Northwest. His choice, Anthony Wayne, called "Mad Anthony" because of his sometimes impetuous nature, did the job well. He arrived at Cincinnati in 1793, bringing some 2,500 men with him. He then drilled and trained his force for the task ahead. St. Clair's line of forts was strengthened and extended, a final post being erected at the confluence of the Maumee and the Auglaize. This post was named Fort Defiance and from it Wayne sortied through the surrounding region. Meanwhile, the British had erected a post called Fort Miamis at the site of modern Maumee, thus clearly revealing their intent to supply and aid the Indians. Finally, on

Little Turtle, Chief of the Miamis, and victor over Harmar and St. Clair. (16)

August 20, 1794, Wayne attacked the Indian forces led by the Shawnee war chief Blue Jacket (an adopted white whose real name was Marmaduke Van Sweringen) at Fallen Timbers along the Maumee just above the rapids. Wayne's disciplined troops drove the defenders from their natural barricade of trees felled by tornadic winds. He then pressed on to the very gates of Fort Miamis, where he held his famous temper in check, fortunately perhaps, for the United States was in no condition for a showdown with Great Britain. After burning Indian villages and crops Wayne and his men returned south to Fort Greeneville. Here in June, 1795, more than 1,100 Indian warriors gathered including Blue Jacket, Little Turtle, Tarhe, a Wyandot, and the Delaware Buckongahelas. By August a treaty was signed. The most significant provision of the Treaty of Greene Ville was to set a boundary line, similar to the line of the Fort McIntosh Treaty, separating Indian lands from those of eastern and southern Ohio now open to American settlement.

Although some young warriors like the redoubtable Shawnee Tecumseh were displeased with this arrangement, the new effort to isolate Indian and frontiersman from one another was largely successful. With a new degree of safety present in the Ohio Country, the tide of settlement swelled.

So many newcomers arrived in so short a time that, by 1797, St. Clair agreed to a census. It revealed that there were now more than the 5,000 free adult males needed for entry into the second stage of territorial development. In December, 1798, elections were held to choose the twenty-two members of the lower house of the territorial legislature. These representatives met in Cincinnati early in 1799 and promptly nominated ten men, from whom President John Adams selected

five to form the council, or upper house, of the legislature.

The Northwest Territory now had representative government. The new legislators were concerned primarily with questions of organizing militia, regularizing judicial procedures, controlling the sale of liquor to the Indians, and establishing taxes. Their effectiveness was curtailed by the governor's tendency to veto much of their legislative program, a practice which built resentment against St. Clair and which would ultimately lead to his undoing. Perhaps the most interesting action of the legislature was to deny a petition from Virginians who wished to bring their slaves into the Northwest Territory. Fellow Virginians sitting in the legislature took the lead in denying the petition because they knew the limitations and evils of a slave society and were not about to see their new homeland take on that psychic and social burden. As their delegate to the Congress of the United States, the legislature chose William Henry Harrison, a young Virginian who had served effectively as an officer in the recent Indian wars.

The friction between Governor St. Clair and the lower house of the legislature focused on more than the governor's autocratic ways and his liberal use of the veto. St. Clair was a Federalist, and since the legislature was dominated by Jeffersonians (Democratic-Republicans) from the

Wayne's men clear the defenses at Fallen Timbers, 1794. (17)

The Treaty of Greene Ville, 1795, as depicted by Howard Chandler Christie. Anthony Wayne dictates terms to the northwestern Indians. (18)

Line Drawing of the Principal Figures in the Painting.
1. Anthony Wayne; 2. Little Turtle; 3. William Wells; 4. William Henry Harrison; 5. William Clark; 6. Meriwether Lewis; 7. Isaac Zane; 8. Tarhe, The Crane; 9. Blue Jacket; 10. Black Hoof; 11. Buckongehelas; 12. Leatherlips; 13. Bad Bird; 14. White Pigeon; 15. The Sun; 16. David Jones; 17. Henry De Butts; 18. John Mills; 19. The Treaty of Greene Ville; 20. Greene Ville Treaty Calumet. (19)

Noted Wyandot chief Tarhe the Crane fought against the American troops in 1790–1794 and with them in 1813. (20)

RT GREENE VILLE
(GREENVILLE, OHIO)
ADQUARTERS, GENERAL
THONY WAYNE, 1793–1796
HIS CAMPAIGN AGAINST THE
IFEDERATED INDIAN TRIBES
OLD NORTHWEST TERRITORY.
Site of
TREATY OF GREENE VILLE

Named for Nathaniel Greene of Revolutionary War fame, Fort Greeneville was located in the town of Greenville, Darke County. (21)

An Ohio Portrait

Thomas Worthington of Chillicothe, "Father of Ohio Statehood," played a central role in Ohio's emergence from territorial status. (22)

Virginia Military District and elsewhere in the territory, strain was inevitable. The contest between governor and legislature centered more and more on the statehood issue.

St. Clair had long been interested in the possibility of dividing the Northwest Territory in such a way that the Jeffersonian influence in the Scioto Valley would be minimized. Should the territory be divided, a line running north from the mouth of the Scioto would not only split the seat of Jeffersonian power, it would also fragment the most settled portion of the territory and thus delay ultimate statehood for any part. Legislative leaders, however, urged Harrison to present Congress with a different plan, which Congress adopted on May 7, 1800. There were to be two separate governments in the Northwest Territory: a line from the mouth of the Kentucky River to Fort Recovery would extend northward to the international boundary. West of that line would be the new Indiana Territory with its capital at Vincennes. East of it would be Ohio (called the "Eastern State") with Chillicothe named as the seat of government. St. Clair's position deteriorated rapidly as his political enemies gained the ear of Congress and played skillfully on his autocratic actions and attitudes. Thomas Worthington, a young Virginian who had settled along the Scioto, and Edward Tiffin, an English-born physician, were leaders of the anti-St. Clair faction, and they and their associates persuaded Congress to overrule the governor's efforts.

The ultimate triumph of the statehood-seeking Republicans was assured when Congress passed the Enabling Act in April, 1802. The western and northern boundaries of the new state were set by establishing a meridian north from the point at which the Great Miami intersected the Ohio to the point where it joined an east-west line drawn eastward through the southernmost tip of Lake Michigan. That east-west line was to extend to Lake Erie. The act also established the terms for electing a constitutional convention, and when the delegates, chosen by male residents of one year who paid taxes, assembled in Chillicothe on November 1, 1802, they represented the Republican strength of the Ohio Country and they proceeded to draft a constitution that reflected their political biases. Governor St. Clair, in one last effort, spoke to the convention in terms that President Thomas Jefferson regarded as intemperate, and he promptly removed St. Clair from office. The governor then retired to his Pennsylvania properties where he died a disappointed man.

Under the leadership of Edward Tiffin, the presiding officer, the convention formed a constitution that served Ohio for fifty years. It established a bicameral general assembly which was all-powerful. The assembly appointed most executive officers and judges; the governor, elected for a two-year term, had no veto and was

This Chillicothe building served as Ohio's first capitol (1803–1810). (23)

The English-born physician Edward Tiffin, president of the Constitutional Convention (1802), first governor of Ohio, and brother-in-law of Thomas Worthington. (24)

largely a figurehead. The franchise was granted to adult males who paid taxes, but work on the roads would also qualify a non-propertied man to vote. Blacks were disenfranchised by the constitution when a seventeen-to-seventeen vote in the convention was broken by Tiffin who cast the ballot against black suffrage. A bill of rights and an amendment procedure were included in the document as was a specific prohibition of slavery. Thomas Worthington rode off to Congress with the convention's handiwork in his saddlebags, and when Congress approved it in February, 1803, the constitution was official even though never submitted to Ohioans for ratification.

Early in 1803, Edward Tiffin was elected Ohio's first governor. The office represented little but honor, as Tiffin and like-minded associates in the constitutional convention had made certain. The real power rested with the general assembly which, duly elected, met on March 1, 1803, to inaugurate state government in Ohio. Through an oversight, Congress failed to pass a resolution admitting Ohio, an error that was rectified 150 years later during Ohio's sesquicentennial year when both houses of Congress resolved to admit the state retroactive to 1803! Thus Ohio emerged as the seventeenth state of the Union and became the model for future state-building. Although many features of its development were unique, its pattern of progress from underdeveloped public land to constitutionally established republican state was the pattern for the future of America.

The members of the new state government were not without political experience since many holding elective or appointive office had served in the territorial government. Chillicothe was selected as the state capital, but from the start it had competitors. Zanesville captured the prize from 1810 to 1812 after which it reverted to Chil-

licothe. But then, in 1816, the capital was moved permanently to the new, more centrally located Columbus, on the east bank of the Scioto across from Franklinton.

The general assembly's early legislative record was relatively undramatic as it dealt mostly with the formation of new counties, taxation, and the incorporation of institutions of various sorts. The governor, lacking a veto, was only as influential as his personality and his political connections allowed. The judiciary was subject to political maneuverings since judges were appointed officials, but in the case of *Rutherford* vs. *McFadden*, the Ohio Supreme Court won the right to review the constitutionality of acts of the general assembly.

One area of legislative activity which stands out with special force was the enactment of "black laws" imposing severe restrictions on Ohio's black citizens. Although Ohio was shielded from the "peculiar institution" of slavery, it was in no way free from the common attitudes of the day held by the white majority toward the black minority in the North. Today these attitudes would be labeled "racist" based as they were on assumptions of black inferiority. As early as 1804 the assembly enacted laws prohibiting blacks from serving on juries or from testifying against a white man in court.

The most egregious act, an 1807 provision that required a Negro coming into Ohio to post bond of $500, was obviously directed at restricting black immigration. These acts were rationalized in non-racist terms—economic contingencies and the need for Ohio businessmen to placate slaveholding neighbors with whom the state did so much business—but there was no mistaking the real intent; Ohio was to be white man's territory. Few serious attempts were made to enforce the $500 bond requirement. When

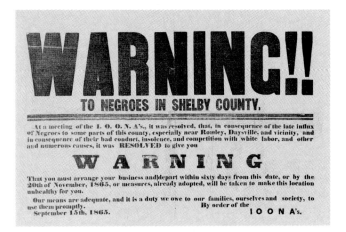

Broadside. (25)

Adventurer Aaron Burr precipitated
excitement on the Ohio frontier (1805–07). (26)

some Cincinnatians made such an effort in 1829,
a delegation from the black community scouted
out possible homesites in Ontario. The threat of
losing its supply of cheap labor was enough to
cause Cincinnati to reconsider. Some blacks did
move to Canada, however, where they formed
villages and established farms in the backcountry
and where they continued to seek that elusive
equality that evaded them in Ohio and its sister
states of the North. Not until 1849 would Ohio
repeal the last of its black laws, and then as much
because of political expediency as for any enlightened regard for the rights of its black citizens. (The extension of the franchise to blacks
was delayed until after ratification of the Fifteenth Amendment to the Constitution of the
United States.)

The two most dramatic events of Ohio's first
decade were the Burr Conspiracy and the onset
of the War of 1812. The former had romance,
intrigue, suspense, and involved a number of colorful personalities. The latter offered the threat
of renewed frontier terror, the mobilization of
the new state's resources, and assorted acts of
heroism and misplaced valor. The Burr story can
be quickly told.

The conventional picture of Aaron Burr
portrays him as a man of charm, family, and
achievement who lost all as a result of killing
Alexander Hamilton in the nation's most famous
duel, and also as a result of his nefarious, perhaps
treasonous, maneuverings in the West. In his
western adventures (1805–07), his story touches
Ohio. To this day no one knows what Burr hoped
to achieve, whether an independent nation beyond the Appalachians, a consolidation of certain
United States territory with Spanish territories,
or whatever, but he was in touch with some influential Ohioans. These and others whose only
accounts of Burr's activities came second hand

Harmon and Margaret Blennerhassett entertained
many travelers of note at their island home near
Belpre. (27) (28)

The Shawnee Prophet, younger brother of
Tecumseh. (29)

Portrait presumed to be Tecumseh, the Shooting
Star of the Shawnees. He would have been a great
man in any society. (30)

William Henry Harrison (1773–1841). Portrait by
Rembrandt Peale, 1814, in a general's uniform. (31)

managed to find some credence in the notion that
Burr was engaged in treasonous activities.

His base in the West was Blennerhassett's
Island, a romantic Ohio River retreat below Belpre where the Irish émigrés, Harmon and Margaret Blennerhassett, lived in style in their handsome home. Blennerhassett assisted Burr by paying for building of boats and gathering of
supplies. This activity, coupled with Burr's mys-
terious comings and goings, plus concern expressed by President Jefferson, ultimately caused
Governor Tiffin, whom Burr had visited, to in-
form the general assembly in December, 1806,
that Burr might be engaged in treasonous activities. The legislature approved taking pre-
cautionary measures. Tiffin called out the militia
which seized Blennerhassett's boats and supplies
while the Virginia militia, apparently fortified
with libations from Blennerhassett's wine cellar,
looted the great mansion. The Blennerhassetts
became wanderers on the land. Burr, meanwhile,
was caught far to the south, and was taken to
Richmond, Virginia, where he was acquitted of
treason in a trial conducted by Chief Justice John
Marshall.

The significance of this adventure lies not so
much in Burr's purportedly treasonable activities

An Ohio Portrait

Return Jonathan Meigs, Jr., governor of Ohio (1810–1814) for whom a fort and a county were named. (32)

as it does in its revelation of how easily rumor and innuendo could spread into genuine fears in the backcountry. More important, however, is the lesson as old as the nation: let any portion of the people feel that government is not sufficiently responsive to their needs and they start talking about alternatives. The West at this time, and for some years to come, saw itself as subordinate to the developed East, and if a government dominated by eastern interests proved unresponsive to western goals—internal improvements, an adequate supply of currency, low tariffs on manufactures—then thoughts of other arrangements became alluring.

A much more real problem for Ohio came from the renewal of warfare which threatened to send Indians against the growing western settlements from the Western Reserve to central and western Ohio. The Treaty of Greene Ville had seemed a final solution to Indian-white problems. It was augmented in 1805 by the Treaty of Fort Industry, (modern Toledo) which removed Indian claims to more of northwestern Ohio. Indians remaining within the state were to be confined to the northwestern sector. The British had relinquished their posts on American soil in 1796 as required by Jay's Treaty, but they had erected new posts across the Canadian border. From these refuges they continued to supply the Indians of the northwest. These Indians increasingly looked to the great Tecumseh, the Shawnee Shooting Star, for leadership. Despite their defeat in 1811 at Tippecanoe, Indiana Territory, Tecumseh's people presented a formidable threat to the Ohio frontier.

Western farmers represented in Congress by "War Hawks" were said to favor war with Great Britain if it meant ending the renewed Indian threat and if it might result in opening a new agricultural frontier in Canada. Yet there is no

evidence that Ohio was overwhelmingly for war. Only a vocal minority seems to have pressed the issue. Senator Thomas Worthington cast his vote in Congress against war, while Ohio's other senator, Alexander Campbell, was absent and did not vote. The governor, Return Jonathan Meigs, Jr., was apparently ready for the conflict if it came. He placed Ohio's militia on call even before Congress finally declared war against Great Britain in June, 1812.

Most Ohioans who saw duty in the War of 1812 served within the state boundaries. Some, however, were with the inept General William Hull at Detroit in 1812 when he surrendered that bastion of American strength in the West to General Isaac Brock without a struggle. In the first months of war, other Ohio militia, including those from the Western Reserve under the command of General Elijah Wadsworth, garrisoned the little fortifications that shielded central Ohio and the Reserve from expected British and Indian attack.

Overall command of American forces in the northwest was given to William Henry Harrison, who was admired in the western country for his aggressiveness in dealing with the Indians. This veteran of frontier warfare was not always well served by his subordinates. General James Winchester of Tennessee, for example, prematurely pushed an advance party toward Detroit only to be surrounded and forced to surrender at the River Raisin, near Monroe, Michigan. His disarmed troops were then massacred by General Henry Proctor's Indian allies.

By 1813, Harrison had established his main post at Fort Meigs near modern Perrysburg at the rapids of the Maumee where his army successfully withstood a siege by a British and Canadian army supported by Indians under Tecumseh. In August, Proctor led about 1,200 soldiers and In-

Major George Croghan.

Major George Croghan led the spirited defense of Fort Stephenson (Fremont) in 1813. (33)

dians up the Sandusky, but his thrust was turned back by the heroic defense of Fort Stephenson (modern Fremont) by Major George Croghan and his small garrison who made effective use of their lone field piece, "Old Betsy."

The turning point of the war in the West came late in the summer of 1813 when a hastily constructed fleet under the command of Commodore Oliver Hazard Perry defeated a British fleet of roughly equal size at the Battle of Lake Erie, fought near Put-in-Bay on South Bass Island. By gaining control of the lake, Perry cut the British supply line thus forcing the abandonment of Detroit. The Indian army under Tecumseh was now vulnerable and withdrew into the Ontario peninsula. Harrison's troops, many of whom were ferried across the lake on Perry's ships, took up the chase and met and defeated the retreating army at the Battle of the Thames, dur-

ing which Tecumseh was killed. This effectively ended the war for Ohio. The young state had carried its share of the burden, contributing manpower and substantial supplies to the armies. Civilians served as well as soldiers. Young John Brown, for example, who left his Hudson home at age fifteen to drive cattle westward for Harrison's army, was just one of hundreds who served behind the lines. Three times Ohioans were taxed additionally to pay the costs of war. Approximately 24,500 enlisted men and 1,750 officers served their state in military service, while a number of Ohio blacks sailed and fought with Perry. In addition to Harrison, Ohio leaders like Duncan McArthur and Lewis Cass achieved visibility that was later useful in furthering political ambitions. With external threat removed, Ohio finally could turn its undivided attention to internal development.

(34)

An Ohio Portrait

Oliver Hazard Perry moves his command from the shattered *Lawrence* to the *Niagara* (35)

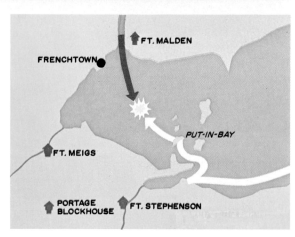

(36)

A State Carved from the Wilderness

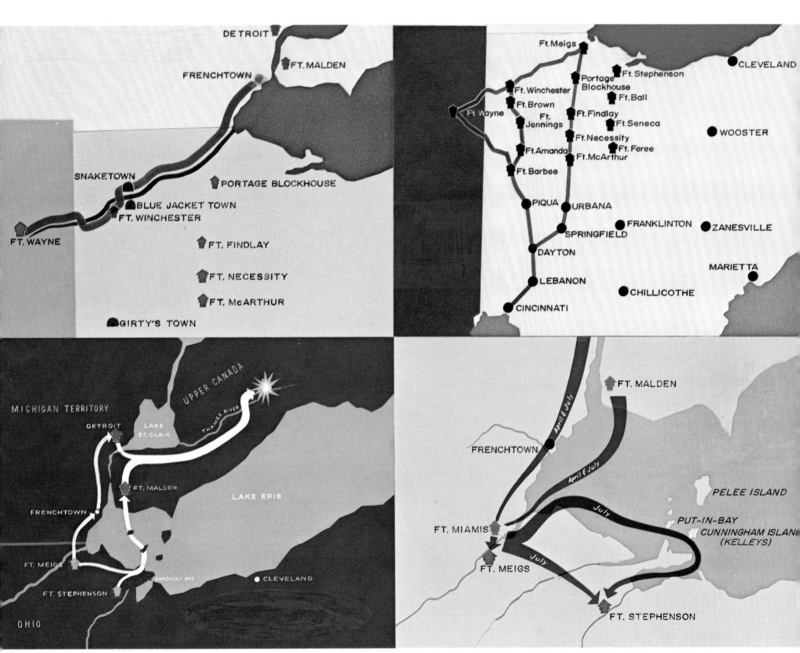

The map (upper left) shows General Winchester's
1812–1813 campaign. Proceeding clockwise are
maps of General Clay Green's 1813 campaign;
Indian activities in the vicinity of Fort Meigs; and
the Battle of the Thames, 1813. (37)

Building a Society: The Material Side

The surge of people moving into Ohio as part of the great migration to the West following the War of 1812 could not conceal the fact that Ohio was still in its early pioneer stage. Although some 7,360,857 acres of the surveyed lands registered in Ohio land offices had been sold by 1821, millions of acres were still available. Much of this land was in the relatively isolated and poorly drained northwestern part of the state. Here lived the approximately 2,400 Shawnee, Seneca, Wyandot, Ottawa, and Delaware Indians on a number of "reservations." By 1842 the last of these Indians had departed for lands offered by the federal government west of the Mississippi, and their abandoned tribal lands soon supported an alien people.

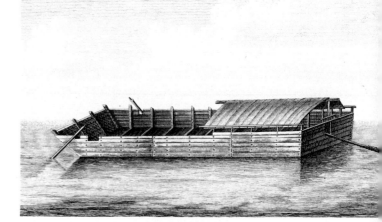

By 1820 Ohio had sixty-six organized counties and a population of 581,000. Many newcomers came by steamboat, but some still arrived by keelboat, flatboat, or raft, drifting down the Ohio. In the post-war period, increasing numbers came overland across forest traces. Some started their trip across the National Road, which was completed to Wheeling by 1817, and from there took boats for the last leg of the journey. Northerners crossed the Genessee road in New York and then transferred their goods to lake boats risking all on Lake Erie's often tempestuous waters. Once ashore they had great difficulty moving through the forest. Zane's Trace (1797) from Wheeling to Maysville, Kentucky, was the first road in Ohio but was in such poor condition that it was virtually impassable in places.

Once situated on land bought either from the United States Land Office, a previous owner, or a private land company (or on which he had simply squatted), the settler often erected a crude half-faced shelter until he and his neighbors, if he had any, could erect a cabin. As life became more settled and the farmer had the time and means, he

An Ohio Portrait

"A road accident. A glimpse through an opening of the primitive forest, Thornville, Ohio." Engraved by W. J. Bennett, N.A. from the original painting by G. Harvey, ANA. (1)

Map showing Indian reservations prior to removal of the Ohio Indians. (2)

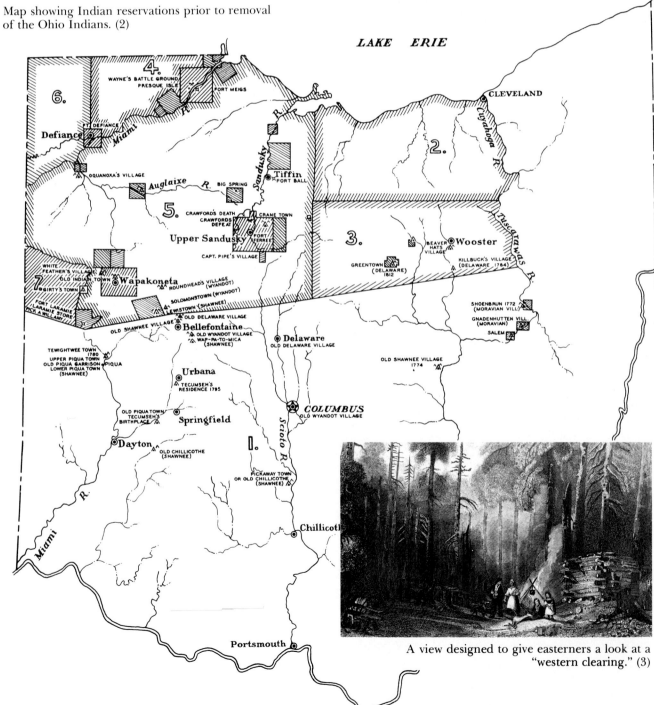

A view designed to give easterners a look at a "western clearing." (3)

Cabin raisings were often community efforts. (4)

added refinements. A loft, real shingles fixed with nails, glass for windows, board siding and other improvements could convert a plain cabin into a more adequate farm home.

Cabin building often had to wait until land was cleared and a crop was in. Woe to the newcomer who arrived too late to "make a crop": he and his family had to hoard their flour and meal while depending on the land to supply game, fowl, and fish to supplement their diets.

Work more exhausting than clearing the land is difficult to imagine, but many of these pioneers were experts with the axe and inured to hardship. New settlers arriving in the spring commonly had several acres planted in time to reap a respectable crop. Ephraim Cutler described how he prepared ground for planting in 1799: "The timber was large, principally beech and sugar trees, all of which we cut down and piled, and burned the most of it. Four acres were cleared ready to plant by the fifteenth of June. . . ." He raised 150 bushels of corn, much of which he fed to his livestock except for the hogs which foraged in the forest where "the supply of nuts and acorns was inexhaustible." Sometimes the great trees were "girdled" by cutting through the bark layers completely around the trunk. Crops could then be planted among them since sunlight could now reach the forest floor through the leafless branches. When time permitted the dead trees would be cut and burned.

Great palls of woodsmoke hung over Ohio for years while this clearing process was at its height. Not only the felled trees but the stumps too were fired, creating Ohio's first air pollution problem. Prudent farmers used the hardwood ashes to make potash, which was a valuable commercial product that brought much needed income. Because burning out stumps was too slow and imperfect a process, manpower, ox-teams,

and sometime later a mechanical gadget called a "stump-puller" were more commonly used.

Farmers in pioneer Ohio had to be men of many skills. Living in the wilderness, far from storekeepers and tradesmen, farm families looked to themselves for their basic needs. When the long winters came, a variety of home industries kept families occupied. A pioneer of Lima recalled: "Our house was a cabin containing a parlor, kitchen and dining room. Connected was a shoe shop, also a broom and repair shop. . . . After supper each knew his place. In our house there were four mechanics. I was a shoemaker and corngrater. My father could make a sledge, and the other two boys could strip corn. My sisters spun yarn and mother knit and made garments. . . . Thus our evenings are spent in our wild home."

Household furnishing were few, consisting of possessions brought on the long trek west but often supplemented by homemade furniture, kitchenware, and utensils. An iron pot, a kettle, a few plates, and cups often constituted the entire range of kitchen implements. Women and girls had unending chores to occupy their energies.

Candlemaking was a common activity of pioneer women. (5)

An Ohio Portrait

To accommodate a growing family, an addition was often added to a log cabin. This sketch of an Ohio cabin is by Lefevre J. Cranston. (7)

A view in the backwoods of Ohio. Drawn from nature by E. Whitefield. (6)

The kitchen range eased women's work. It was an early "labor saving device." (8)

Household Receipts Given for What they are Worth.

GINGER SNAPS.—One pint of molasses; boil fifteen minutes; stir in while boiling one cup of butter, one teaspoonful soda, and one tablespoonful ginger. Let it cool; then add a sufficient quantity of flour to roll very thin; then bake in a quick oven.

ONE-EGG CAKE.—This makes a very good cake, and not expensive: One egg, one cup of sugar, one and a half cups of flour, six tablespoonful of melted butter. If you use baking powder, take a heaping teaspoonful; if not, take one half teaspoonful of soda, and one of cream tartar. Add flavoring.

PUFFS FOR TEA.—One quart of sweet milk; one quart of sifted wheat flour; four eggs well beaten; two tablespoonsful of melted butter; two tablespoonsful of sifted sugar; half a teaspoon of salt. Bake in brown ware cups, from twenty-five minutes to half an hour, in a brisk oven.

DELICATE CAKE.—Take the whites of four eggs, beaten to a stiff froth; one cup of sugar, one cup of flour, half a cup of sweet milk, three teaspoonsful of butter, one teaspoonful of soda, and three of cream tartar.

GINGER COOKIES.—One cup of molasses, one of sugar, one of warm water; two tablespoonsful of pulverized alum; one cup of butter or fried meat fat; flour to make a dough; roll, but not too thin; cut out, and bake in a quick oven. Dissolve the alum in water, and add to the other ingredients the last thing.

RAISED WAFFLES. — One pint sweet milk; a heaping teacupful of butter; three eggs (yolks and whites beaten separately;) a tablespoonful of thick brewer's yeast, or half a penny's worth of baker's yeast; one quart of flour; one fourth table-

(9)

Once cleared and fenced, eastern Ohio farmland took on a settled, pastoral appearance. (10)

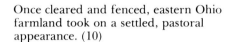

The farm woman's unending chores often took her outside the house. (12)

Clermont County farmers using grain cradles. The cradle was the most efficient cutting tool prior to machinery. (11) & (13)

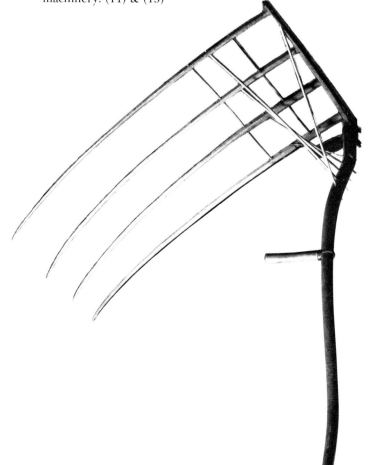

Not only did they manage the household, cook, sew, preserve and raise vegetables, but many of them also worked alongside the men and boys in the fields and took on arduous chores like soap making. They did all this while raising large families which often boasted ten to fifteen or more children.

Generalizing about the pioneer farmer is tempting, but the experiences of hundreds show that they represented a surprisingly wide range of competence, energy and achievement. They were as much a mix as any other group of human beings. Some labored, some loafed; some prospered, some failed; some responded enthusiastically to the challenge, some faltered. Few fit the later stereotype of the vigorous, assertive, handsome, rugged individualist; for deprivation, hardship, accident, and disease took a toll as well as the uncompromising loneliness of the great woods. Despite all, however, they persevered and prevailed by the hundreds of thousands and formed the population core of a vigorous people in a rapidly developing state.

Ohio's population experienced a great burgeoning from 1820 to 1850, and by the latter year

An Ohio Portrait

The rich wool yield of Merino sheep made them a favored breed in Ohio. (14)

Milling was early Ohio's chief industry. Forsyth's Mill on the Olentangy River. (15)

A primitive corn pounding technique used by early settlers. (16)

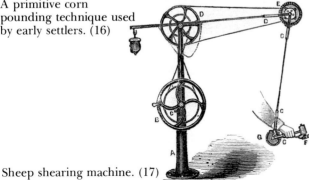

Sheep shearing machine. (17)

Ohio became the third most populous state in the nation, with 1,980,329 residents. A substantial percentage of these Ohioans were born elsewhere in the United States, with the largest numbers coming from Pennsylvania, New York, and Virginia. Over eleven percent were foreign born, with Germans, Irish, English, French, Welsh, Scots, and Canadians prevailing, in that order. More than 25,000 blacks lived in Ohio with the largest concentrations in Hamilton, Ross, Franklin and Gallia counties.

Most Ohioans continued to live on farms, and their agricultural productivity brought Ohio close to the top among the states. The average Ohio farm in 1850 consisted of 125 acres valued at about $2,500, both figures being close to the average for farms in the northern states. Corn, wheat, oats, and rye were the principal field crops raised, but other crops like tobacco and fruits of various sorts, also received much attention. Nicholas Longworth of Cincinnati stood out as one of the most resourceful early experimenters with new agricultural products. He not only brought grape cultivation and wine making to Ohio, but also introduced the strawberry and an improved black raspberry.

Livestock was abundant and varied on Ohio farms. Sheep raising, concentrated in the northeastern counties, made the state first in this important activity. Ohioans were among the first Americans to import Merino sheep, coveted for their fine wool. By the 1830s, the progenitor of the Poland-China hog was developed in the Miami Valley. Improved breeds of cattle also were introduced in the first half of the nineteenth century to upgrade Ohio's herds. Gone were the days when livestock had to be driven to market long distances over hazardous roads. By mid-century, canals and railroads put the cattle and hog raiser in easy range of his market, and made it

Building a Society: The Material Side

Workmen scraping hides at the George E. Roth tannery, Circleville. (18)

Haymarket in Akron, located along present day Market Street. (19)

Wine makers at Engel & Krudwig Winery (1895), Sandusky. (20)

An Ohio Portrait

Nicholas Longworth by Robert S. Duncanson. (21)

worth his while to abandon the tough lean animals that foraged in the woods for the more productive domesticated livestock, carefully bred and fed to produce optimum market value.

Farming methods changed radically in the decades just prior to the Civil War. Foremost among the changes was the introduction of all kinds of farm machinery, from improved iron plows to Obed Hussey's reaper, although only a few farmers used machines at this time. Scores of inventive minds worked on the development of farm implements, and by the 1850s Ohio was a prime producer of farm machinery of all types. Of equal importance was the spread of knowledge about good agricultural techniques. Some principles of good soil management had long been known, but virgin Ohio land was initially so fertile that most early farmers ignored sound practices even when they were aware of them. As the land was reworked over many years it could retain its fertility only with careful management—draining, fertilizing, allowing fields to lie fallow, planting legumes, strip or contour plowing, and similar methods. John R. Buchtel used some of these techniques in Summit County in the 1840s and early 1850s to farm profitably lands that his neighbors claimed could not be made productive. The general assembly created the State Board of Agriculture in 1846 to assist farmers in acquiring this knowledge. With the cooperation of county societies, district fairs displayed prize livestock and produce and demonstrated improved farming techniques. Farm journals such as the *Farmers Reporter and United States Agriculturalist* (1830) and the *Ohio Farmer and Western Agriculturist* (1844) publicized innovations in farming. But a writer complained to the *Ohio Farmer:* "Unfortunately I find a large portion of our farmers prejudiced against every variety of improvement, particularly where the knowledge of that improvement is to be acquired from books." Nevertheless by mid-century some Ohio farmers had moved into the modern, mechanized era to a limited extent.

Focusing initially on the farmer is natural in describing a pioneer society, for he was the dominant personage in the early years of state development. But as Richard Wade reminds us, an urban frontier existed almost from the earliest days of the westward movement, and some towns developed urban characteristics at an early time.

Marietta, Cincinnati, and Chillicothe soon were challenged for hegemony by a host of new towns that emerged in the first decades of the nineteenth century. However, none could keep pace with Cincinnati, which was a bustling town of 6,500 by 1815 and a city of over 16,000 just ten years later. By then Cincinnati had a municipal government, a hospital, college, museum, theater, fine churches, and newspapers. Already it was touted as the Queen City; "an astonishing place," as the western traveler Basil Hall termed it. Proximity to its amenities caused nearby land to soar in value, up to $150 an acre for good unimproved land. Columbus at this time could boast close to a thousand inhabitants. Chillicothe, Zanesville, Dayton, Canton, Hamilton, Springfield, and Steubenville each were convinced of a prosperous future. In the Western Reserve, where the great population increase would follow completion of the canals, Warren, Ravenna, and Youngstown continued to be the principal towns with smaller settlements at Painesville, Hudson, Canfield, Jefferson, and other places. Cleveland had little but promise and a good location for future growth; in 1815 it had only 150 inhabitants. Sandusky to the west and Mansfield to the southwest had been recently founded. Toledo, later the metropolis of northwestern Ohio, had not yet appeared on the map.

Building a Society: The Material Side

The Buckeye Mower, developed in large part by the inventive genius of Lewis Miller. (22)

The Buckeye Mower and Reaper plant in Canton, ca. 1860. (23)

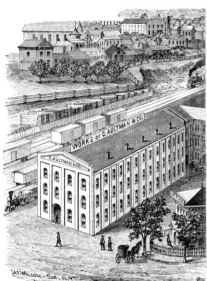

Danver's seed sower. (25)

Wheeler's thresher. (24)

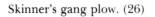

Skinner's gang plow. (26)

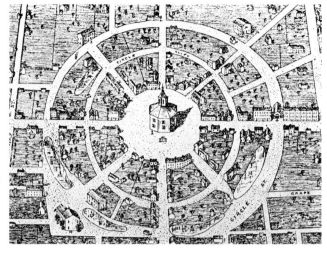

Early town plat of Circleville. Later development eliminated the circular pattern. (27)

Among the interesting aspects of Ohio town growth were the planned communities, whose founders believed the layout of the town would create a prosperous and salubrious environment. The Reverend David Bacon tried to make the new community of Tallmadge in the Western Reserve fit his religious ideals. From the town circle in the heart of the township, roads radiated out to the eight points of the compass. The Congregational church was the literal as well as the spiritual focus of his community. In Pickaway County, Circleville was laid out in concentric circles relating to prehistoric Indian earthworks and reflecting its founder's sense of order and beauty. The New England-style towns which graced the

Western Reserve—Hudson, Canfield, and Elyria, for example—were laid out around a green, sometimes rectangular, sometimes oval or circular. Churches and public buildings around the green enhanced the image of community and of orderly development.

By 1850, many Ohio towns had become small cities with municipal governments, a few handsome edifices, churches, residences, commercial and manufacturing activities. Brick and stone had replaced wood as a building material for many of these structures. Cincinnati, with 115,435 inhabitants in 1850, had far outdistanced other Ohio cities; indeed, it had become one of the preeminent cities of the nation. An

Plan of the Quaker town of Mount Pleasant in Jefferson County. The town is now on the National Register of Historical Sites. (28)

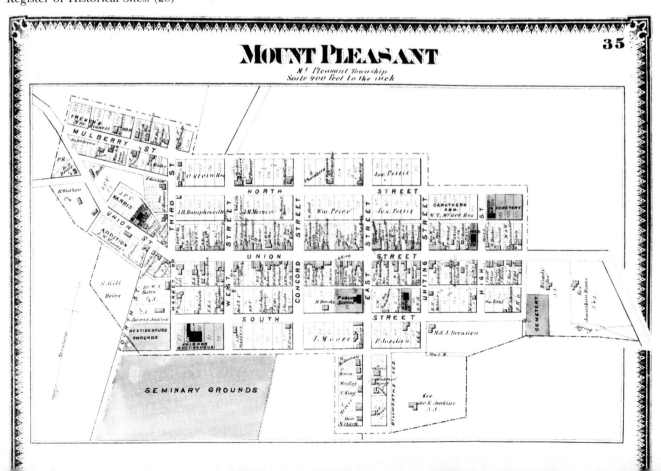

Cincinnati's elegant Burnet House opened in 1851. (29)

By midcentury, many Ohio towns had the solid look of Lancaster, seat of Fairfield County. (30)

English traveler asserted that within half a century Cincinnati had achieved more architectural distinction in its buildings than "any city of the same age on the surface of the globe," and when Burnet House was completed in 1851 it could boast a hotel "undoubtedly the most spacious and probably the best . . . in its interior and domestic arrangements of any in the world." Cincinnati's substantial and diverse industrial base assured the economic undergirding required to remain a prosperous and cosmopolitan city.

The growth of modern cities is a function of economic development, which in turn is related to the availability of transportation. Ohio found it imperative to build a network of roads and canals to supplement the Ohio River system and Lake Erie, which had served to move goods and people in the earliest years. The Enabling Act of 1802 required that 3 percent of the money from the sale of public lands in Ohio go toward building and repairing roads, but this sum was inadequate to the task.

By 1812 roads connected towns like Marietta, Zanesville, Chillicothe, Franklinton (Columbus), and Cincinnati with their hinterlands. Several military roads ran north through the Miami Valley and on toward the frontier. In the Western Reserve, Cleveland and Warren were on primitive roadways. Most early roads had been hacked out of the forest by those coming to claim their lands, like Turhand Kirtland of Wallingford, Connecticut, who cut a road into Chardon in Geauga County, or Benjamin Tappan, Jr., who in 1799 moved his goods up the Cuyahoga to modern Boston and cleared a road to Ravenna using oxen.

An Ohio Portrait

The Conestoga Wagon, an important freight hauler on the National Road. (31)

This covered bridge in Athens County is one of many such structures remaining in Ohio. (32)

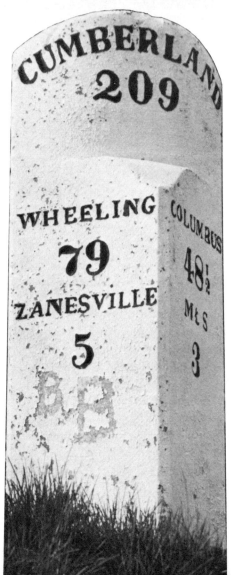

These early roads almost defy description, "devilish" and "wretched" being favorite adjectives applied to them. Perhaps this folktale tells it all:

A man riding along the Black Swamp road spied a beaver hat floating on a puddle of water. He picked up the hat and found a man under it and called for help. The man said "leave me alone stranger, I have a good horse under me, and have just found bottom."

As late as 1828 freight shipments by road from Cleveland to Columbus took six to eight days. Many roads were built as private ventures by turnpike companies and later taken over by county or state governments. In 1843 the general assembly authorized county commissioners to collect taxes for road building. The introduction of plank roads, macadam pavement, bridges, draining by ditching and similar improvements greatly enhanced Ohio's main roads by the time of the Civil War. However secondary roads and back lanes remained in poor condition until many years after the advent of the automobile.

The National Pike, most famous of all Ohio roads, ultimately connected Cumberland, Maryland to the east with Vandalia, Illinois to the west. Although Congress donated some lands to the state for road building purposes, the National Pike was one internal improvement built almost totally at the expense of the national government. Completed to Columbus by 1833, it did not reach the Indiana border until five years later. A considerable traffic moved across this road, and memories of its coaching taverns, S-bridges, and milestones lived until the present day of this great highway now paralleled across Ohio by Interstate 70.

Important as roads were, the movement of large quantities of heavy freight required canals. Talk of a canal system developed almost from the beginning of statehood, but a poor state was in an

Milestone along the National Road. (33)

Alfred Kelley; artist unknown. (34)

Cincinnati Public Landing, 1835, watercolor by John Casper Wilde. (35)

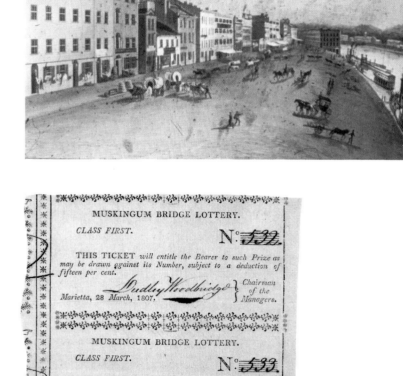

unfavorable position to assume the necessary large debt. After the War of 1812, a burgeoning population gave some promise that the tax base of Ohio would grow and provide the state with the potential to create a canal system by selling construction bonds secured by a pledge to use the state taxing power if necessary. Governor Ethan Allen Brown favored the undertaking and urged the legislature to take appropriate steps. On February 4, 1825, the general assembly passed an act creating a Board of Canal Commissioners to oversee construction and another commission to manage funding of the project. The basic political compromises about routes had already been made and, with skilled engineering and labor available from the newly completed Erie Canal in New York, construction could proceed immediately.

The first bond issue was sold, construction money was available, and work started on the great project. The Ohio and Erie Canal was to be built first stretching a total of 308 miles from Cleveland up the Cuyahoga Valley to the Portage Summit (Akron), down the Tuscarawas to Coshocton, southwestward across Licking Summit to the vicinity of Buckeye Lake, west to Lockbourne just south of Columbus on the Scioto, and down the Scioto to Portsmouth. Over 3,000 contracts were let for the channel, locks, aqueducts, reservoirs, and other features. An extraordinary public servant, Alfred Kelley, a canal commissioner from Cleveland, personally oversaw construction, riding hundreds of miles in all kinds of weather to see that contracts were fulfilled and that the state received full value. After a ceremonial ground breaking at Licking Summit on July 4, 1825, actual construction began at Portage Summit.

In just two years the thirty-seven miles to Cleveland, including the two turning basins and

Money for internal improvements was sometimes raised by lottery as with this Muskingum Bridge Lottery. (36)

An Ohio Portrait

At a lock on the Ohio-Erie Canal. (37)

Plan of a combined lock. (38)

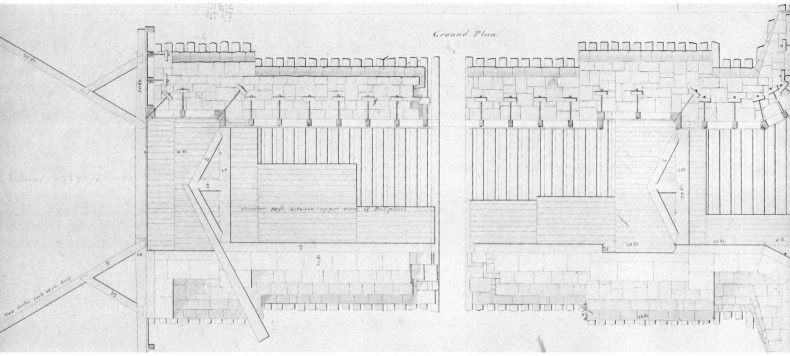

seventeen locks at what is now Akron and the twenty-five additional locks to Cleveland, were completed. The first boat, the *State of Ohio* built at Akron, carried dignitaries to Cleveland and opened a new era for the state. By 1832 the great ditch, twenty-six feet wide at the bottom, forty at water level, and four to four and a half feet deep with a ten foot towpath on one side, was completed all the way to Portsmouth. At a fare of two cents a mile, a packet boat could carry passengers from Lake Erie to the Ohio River in eighty hours.

Construction was initiated on the Miami and Erie Canal during this time to assure residents of other sections of Ohio that their needs would be met, and work proceeded from Cincinnati to Dayton. However, the canal was not completed to Toledo until 1845. Construction was aided by liberal federal land grants, by state land grants, and by donations. Many "feeder" canals were constructed with state funds. Politics also dictated connections from the Ohio-Erie Canal to Columbus and to the Muskingum Valley, as well as giving state aid to certain private ventures like the important Penn-Ohio or "Cross-cut" Canal that linked the Ohio-Erie at Akron with the Mahoning Valley and Pittsburgh to the east. Although short lived the Penn-Ohio brought an economic boom to portions of northeastern Ohio which had lagged behind the more prosperous river towns to the south. Many grand schemes failed. The Big Sandy Canal connecting Bolivar on the Ohio-Erie with the Ohio River to the east, literally did not hold water. This canal was but one of many whose promoters had buoyed their hopes only to see them crash with the venture's collapse.

Claims that the canals were ineffective are partially legitimate. The state did not receive enough in tolls to cover the cost of construction

Ohio's Canal system (right) was travelled by packets like those advertised in a Cleveland newspaper.(39)

and maintenance; the canals were frozen over for several months of the year; floods, vandalism, and accidents put stretches out of operation for extended periods; and they were confined by geography to largely north-south routes. But these arguments present only one side of the story. The economic and psychological impact on Ohio and its people was positive indeed. Consider population: Cleveland began its rise to eminence after becoming the northern terminus and trans-shipment point for canal traffic. Akron was a child of the canal. Founded in 1825 by Simon Perkins, a farsighted land speculator and banker from Warren, Akron became a diversified man-ufacturing town of 1,500 within a decade and five years later was the seat of government for newly formed Summit County (so named because of Portage Summit). Massillon and Canal Fulton in Stark County, Canal Dover (now Dover) in Tus-carawas, Coshocton in Coshocton, Lockbourne in Franklin, and Waverly in Pike, all grew because of the Ohio-Erie Canal. In the west, Troy and Piqua in Miami County, St. Mary's in Auglaize, De-fiance in Defiance, and Toledo in Lucas owed much to the Miami-Erie Canal. Some towns not on the state system prospered from local canals. For instance, Milan in Erie County, now land-locked, became briefly the country's premier wheat shipper because of a short canal connect-ing it to Lake Erie.

As a result of the canals, construction money was spent in Ohio and wages were paid to Ohioans, some of whom were local farmers while others were transient Irish and German laborers. Many of the Irish and Germans stayed and settled often in canal towns. The canals had a pro-nounced effect on prices. Ohioans could now buy imported hardware, clothing, furniture, and hundreds of other items for a fraction of their former cost. With freight rates now dramatically

Boat on the Ohio-Erie Canal near Piketon, ca. 1850. (40)

The ferryboat *Welcome* on the Ohio from Boude's Ferry (Brown County) to Augusta, Kentucky. (41)

An Ohio Portrait

Walk-in-the-Water (ca. 1820), the first steamship on Lake Erie. (42)

reduced and new markets available, Ohio producers received better prices for the products they had to sell. The canals indeed did much to benefit the state and its people.

Travelers on Ohio's canals could board steamboats at either Lake Erie or the Ohio River. These romantic vessels, fighting lake gales or river hazards, were important links in the transportation chain. The *Orleans* had amazed spectators along the Ohio in 1811. Only seven years later, the *Walk-in-the-Water*, the first steamboat on Lake Erie, churned from Buffalo to Detroit in three days with stops at Cleveland and Sandusky. By mid-century the colorful steamboat era produced great boats which competed with one another for supremacy even if high-pressure boilers exploded in the process. This free-wheeling spirit coupled with abundant natural hazards made steamboating a risky business. But who could resist the allure of the lighted ships with their grand salons, crystal chandeliers, and gay music as they navigated the Ohio or the lakes with their engines throbbing with a powerful beat? No less romantic were the stern or side wheelers, manned by roustabouts and deck hands, many of whom were free Negroes, which churned from port to port carrying passengers and cargo short distances though on occasion they went all the way to Buffalo on the lakes or to Cairo or even New Orleans on the rivers. Shipbuilding became an important industry for Cincinnati, Marietta, and several other Ohio River ports, while along Lake Erie nearly every town or sizeable river mouth was the scene of construction activity.

Both canals and steamboats were ultimately victimized by the versatile railroads whose ubiquitous tentacles soon reached into formerly obscure Ohio areas. In 1832 the state legislature granted the first effective railroad charters in Ohio, but some time elapsed before the first lines were operating. From Sandusky, whose citizens were still angry over being left out of the canal system, the Mad River and Lake Erie Railroad extended to Xenia. The Mansfield and Sandusky City went to Mansfield, where it joined the Columbus and Lake Erie to Newark. A line connecting Cincinnati to Columbus joined another that carried on to Cleveland, and from Cleveland a short line ran southeast to Ravenna. These early routes were built by private companies, but after 1837 nearly all profited from state aid. Few towns were so small that some local boosters did not seek funds through stock subscriptions to run track into them to connect them with the larger world. Many such schemes existed in the larger towns. For example, the great booster Alfred Kelley had much to do with making Cleveland a railroad center. Scores of railroad building ventures failed, bringing ruin and disgrace in their wake, but the spirit of the age was to build, and business would not be denied. Little uniformity of equipment or practice developed in the first years of railroading. However, during the 1850s completed mileage increased to 2,946 and by 1870 had reached 3,376 miles of track. The Erie, Pennsylvania, New York Central, and Baltimore and Ohio emerged as through systems. They gave a great boost to Ohio commerce, took business from the canals, and reoriented trade routes in an east-west direction, a move that had momentous political consequences in the decade before the Civil War.

The growth of a transportation network was vital to increasingly sophisticated and specialized industry at a time when technological innovation began to make expansion from local to regional and national markets possible, although that level of development is more clearly associated with the post Civil War period than with the early

A sketch of *Houses Along the Upper Ohio* by Lefevre J. Cranston. (43)

Cleveland Lakefront Railroad Terminal, ca. 1850. (44)

Meat processing that helped Cincinnati become "Porkopolis." (45)

decades of the nineteenth century.

From 1815 to 1850 shops and mills became both more numerous and more widely distributed about the state. Some depended on waterpower but a growing number used steam. Flour and grist mills were Ohio's leading industrial activities and these plus distilleries and lumber mills were widespread. Many industrial establishments in Ohio were still relatively small, although leaders of a few firms had begun directing their companies toward employing more workers at specialized tasks. Ohio's clothing industry, second in value in the pioneer state, employed an average of 11.3 men in each establishment, even though each factory averaged only $3,615 in machinery. Owners of pork and beef packing houses, whose products led the nation in that industry and ranked third in value among Ohio's manufactures, invested an average of $36,803 in their businesses and supervised an average of 10.3 workers. A visitor to Cincinnati, the nation's leader in meatpacking and Ohio's greatest industrial city, witnessed the daily routine of one establishment and marveled at the efficiency and specialization of labor:

> In this establishment, hogs weighing five or six hundred pounds are killed, scraped, dressed, cut up, salted, and packed in a barrel, in twenty seconds, on an average. . . . The great secret of such rapidity is, that one does one thing only, and thus, learns to do that one thing with perfect dexterity. We saw a man there who, all day and every day, knocks pigs down with a hammer; another who does nothing but "stick" them; another who, with one clean easy stroke of a broad, long-handled cleaver, decapitates the hugest hog of Ohio.

Technological innovations, accelerated demands for iron from steam engine and machinery manufacturers, and improved means of transportation made Ohio's iron industry the most heavily capitalized and largest employer in the state's manufacturing sector. Using steam for harder and more continuous blowing, manufac-

An Ohio Portrait

(49)

(50)

turers expanded furnace capacity from about three to nearly ten tons daily. The replacement of charcoal by coal (coke) in the smelting process increased furnace output to twenty-five tons per day and led to the building of fifteen furnaces in the coal-rich Hocking Valley alone. Between 1820 and 1850 the Hanging Rock and Mahoning Valley regions had their greatest expansion in furnace building. By 1850 Ohio ranked second to Pennsylvania in the value of its iron furnaces. On the average, these furnaces had $52,394 invested

Nineteenth century Ohio banknotes. (46–51)

(46)

(47)

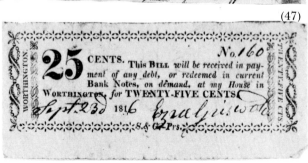

(48)

in machinery and facilities, and they were manned by 77.8 employees.

The diversity of Ohio's manufacturing activities was extraordinary even in that relatively unspecialized age. Other Ohio manufactures included all sorts of clay products—crude crockery, fine chinaware, bricks, and tile—matches, glassware of all kinds from fine tableware to bottles, hardware, clothing, furniture, farm machinery, paper, soap, carriages and wagons, tools and the machines that were used in the manufacture of other items. The list could be extended substantially.

As elsewhere, all business in Ohio relied upon an adequate supply of dependable currency, but it was seldom available in the early years. Barter could suffice for a primitive economy, but only a money system could sustain more sophisticated requirements.

Bank notes from the Bank of the United States circulated in Ohio, but they were not adequate to meet the state's needs. The first general assembly chartered the Miami Exporting Company in 1803 with certain bank features, including the right to issue notes. In 1808 and 1809 charters were granted to banks in Marietta, Chillicothe, and Steubenville, each of which could issue notes without limit except that each bank's total indebtedness was limited to three times its capital. New banks were chartered for Warren, Zanesville, Cincinnati, and Dayton between 1812 and 1814; by 1818 Ohio banks numbered twenty-five.

The sound practices of Ohio banks was undermined in the panic of 1837 when specie redemption of bank notes ceased. Also, a number of uncharted banks were operating and issuing notes, sometimes with no secure backing. "Keg money," the sprinkling of thin layers of coin over kegs of scrap metal to inflate reserves, and other

(51)

such ruses were common. The proliferation of bank notes was a powerful temptation to counterfeiters, some of whom operated on a grand scale. The Brown brothers, whose "money shop" was located in the Cuyahoga Valley, were wholesalers of "queer," a term for counterfeit money. They ran relatively little risk since they did not personally circulate the counterfeit. "Retailers"—tavern keepers, livery stable operators, and boatmen—bought the counterfeit from them and circulated it.

Everyone was victimized by the instability of the money supply. Accepting a note from an insecure or fraudulent bank could mean ending up with severely discounted or worthless paper. Newspapers ran charts from time to time showing the rate at which certain bank notes were discounted. Among the most famous of the bank frauds was that run by Mormon leaders at Kirtland. The loss of money in the Mormon bank fraud was as much responsible as religious prejudice for the hostility their neighbors expressed toward the Mormons. In 1845 the legislature passed the Kelley Act, authored and promoted by Alfred Kelley, which created a state bank with branches and independent banks arranged so that all twelve districts in the state had banking service. This law served Ohio until the National Banking Act of 1863 brought a new degree of regularity to America's banking practices.

In addition to shortages of currency and loan money, Ohio had a banking problem that merited national attention. The Second Bank of the United States was chartered by Congress in 1816. In 1817 it opened a branch in Cincinnati and in 1818 another in Chillicothe. When the state auditor seized $100,000 from the branches in compliance with an act of the general assembly, the bank sued for return of the money and interest. In 1824 in the case of *Osborne* vs. *Bank of the United States,* the United States Supreme Court upheld a lower court order to Ohio to pay back the money. The principle of the McCulloch decision of 1819 which ruled state taxation of federal government agencies illegal, was upheld.

Part of the hostility toward the Bank of the United States sprang from western suspicion of eastern money men, part from the bank's draining specie from Ohio, and part from its lending policies. By calling due loans in somewhat summary fashion, the bank helped bring on the Panic of 1819 in Ohio. The state and its people suffered considerable economic loss in the collapse of an inflationary economy characterized by an overextension of credit. Another severe national panic, that of 1837, also caused much hardship in Ohio, as did the next great economic collapse twenty years later. These were but temporary setbacks, however, for the state continued to grow in numbers and material well-being.

(52)

New Years Greetings

A Happy New Year

A·Buckeye·Greeting
From Columbus

Ho! fill a cup of the heartiest cheer,
A toast to the state we all hold dear.
The grandest state the Nation knows.
For there the Buckeye blossom blows;
Go travel north, south, east or west,
You'll find Ohio is the best;
To all she says: Behold my Pearls;
And shows a bevy of Buckeye Girls.

True Love

Early Ohio Social Concerns

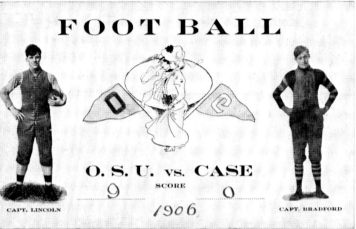

Having arrived in Ohio, the newcomer found that staying alive was often a tricky business. For every settler killed by Indians or accident, thousands died of pestilential diseases, some of which were endemic to the region. Illness, poor diet, exposure, overwork, and lack of suitable medical and dental care made people old before their time, and many forty-year-olds with toothless gums and haggard faces appeared twice that age. "Respecting the healthfulness of this country," said James Kilbourne, journalist and legislator, "I have to repeat that it is in fact sickly in a considerable degree."

Marshes and river bottoms which gave off "effluvial airs" from dank, rotting vegetation were especially lethal areas. Canal builders who frequently worked to their waists in such oozing masses sickened and died in great numbers, many going to unmarked graves along the ditch. High, well-drained land was regarded as healthy land; frequently towns or institutions would boast of their healthy locations on hills or ridges. As late as the 1870s Buchtel College in Akron advertised in its bulletin its healthy location on "one of the highest points in the state."

In September, 1823, more than half of the people living within a fifty mile radius of Columbus were reported to be sick. Ague, a term for intermittent fever, was a common frontier illness that helped account for such staggering statistics; malaria was another. Cholera morbus, bilious fevers, diarrhea, typhoid, and milk sickness ("puking fever") were common. In addition the usual contagious diseases — mumps, measles, scarlet fever, chicken pox, diphtheria, whooping cough, and smallpox—struck the West as severely as the communities in the settled East.

In his magnificent study of the Old Northwest during the pioneer period, R. Carlyle Buley devoted a fascinating chapter to pioneer "ills,

An Ohio Portrait

A cartoon of the doctor on horseback. Frontier physicians were sometimes called "death on a pale horse." It was said they "killed quick but cured slow." (1)

(2)

cures, and doctors." His material, gleaned largely from newspapers and travelers' accounts, gives rich detail about these subjects. With medical knowledge so limited and ignorance of proper medication and treatment so universal, frontier settlers relied on charm cures and on certain botanic specifics learned from the Indians or brought with them from their former homes. The latter often had merit, but the former were nothing but superstition: whopping cough could be cured by a bag of ground bugs hung around the neck, and diphtheria could be warded off by a poultice of cow dung held in place by a stocking turned wrong side out. Calomel, ipecac, lobelia, and quinine (Peruvian bark) were widely used. Many believed strongly in purging the system. When Seth Pease "felt unwell" while surveying the Western Reserve, he "took a puke . . . after I had done pukeing my pain gradually subsided." Bleeding was widely used, and patients often felt cheated when not enough blood was taken by cup or leeches. When leeches failed to take hold, they were encouraged by putting cream, sugar, or blood on the patients' skin or by putting them in a saucer of beer which made them lively. "It will be seen with astonishment how quickly they bite."

Some western doctors, especially the untrained practitioners out in the forests, were little help to their patients. Their rigorous practices "killed quick but cured slow." However, many of the better trained provided Ohioans with as much skill and competence as was then available anywhere. From an early time they had some of the latest equipment and techniques, such as stethoscope, microscope, vaccination, and anesthesia. In a few spectacular cases they performed experiments or radical operations not yet attempted in the East.

Slowly medical education got the attention and support it was due. Dr. Daniel Drake's school

Dr. Daniel Drake, Cincinnati's distinguished physician, author, and man of all talents. (3)

in Cincinnati was chartered in 1819 as the Medical College of Ohio. By 1850 Ohio had four medical schools with an enrollment of 518 students. Dr. John Harris opened the nation's first dental school in 1828 at Bainbridge, in Ross County. Further specialties developed quickly, and by the time of the Civil War Ohio was as well supplied with professional medical services as most states and better supplied than many.

Pioneer Americans were reputedly contentious people, but perhaps Ohioans had less cause to seek legal help than those who settled in areas where indiscriminate land surveys prevailed. Ohio lawyers were no more advanced than doctors in their professional development in the earliest days. In 1833 a private law school was organized in Cincinnati by John C. Wright and Timothy Walker and by mid-century was incorporated in the law department of Cincinnati College. Ohio was apparently somewhat more demanding than some other states in admitting men to practice before the bar. In 1823 Lucius V. Bierce, a young graduate of Ohio University, read law for two months with a lawyer in Alabama and thus successfully passed the bar examination of that state. On returning to Ohio later that year, however, he found that further reading in the office of an Ohio lawyer would be necessary before he sought admission to the Ohio bar. Some lawyers such as the able Elisha Whittlesey of Canfield had great success in training young lawyers of distinction. As in the present time, many Ohio lawyers then sought political careers. By mid-century they replaced farmers as the occupational group best represented in Ohio's political offices.

Preparation for the ministry, as for medicine and law, was not well defined in early practice. Some denominations, such as Congregationalists and Presbyterians, required an educated clergy

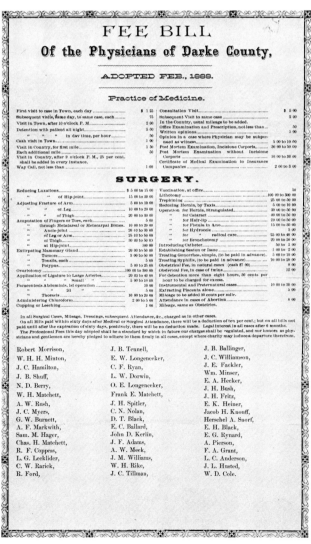

Fee bill of a Darke County physician, 1888. (4)

An Ohio Portrait

The Starling Medical College, Columbus. (5)

STARLING MEDICAL COLLEGE.
ORDER OF LECTURES (until January, 1880.)*

	Monday.	Tuesday.	Wednesday.	Thursday.	Friday.	Saturday.
9 A. M.	Dr. Drury's Clinic.	Prof. Loving.	Prof. Loving's Clinic.	Prof. Loving.	Prof. Loving.	C. C. Howard.
10 A. M.		Prof. Wheaton.		Prof. Wheaton.	Prof. Wheaton.	Prof. Pooley's Clinic.
11 A. M.	Prof. Pooley.	Prof. Pooley.	Prof. Pooley.	Prof. Pooley.	Prof. Pooley.	
2 P. M.	Prof. Gilliam.	Prof. Frankenberg.	Prof. Gilliam.	Prof. Frankenberg.	Prof. Gilliam.	
3 P. M.	Prof. Fullerton.	Prof. Fullerton.	Prof. Fullerton.	C. C. Howard.	C. C. Howard.	
4 P. M.	Prof. Landis.	Prof. Dunlap.	Prof. Landis.	Prof. Landis.	Prof. Landis.	

* After January 1st, other Lecturers will be added and the schedule re-arranged.

(6)

Cincinnati College of Law (1845–1869). (7)

Judges going to court. Riding circuit through the back country was often part of a judge's duty. (8)

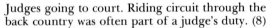

even on the frontier, while Methodists, Baptists, and others were slow to establish formal educational criteria for their ministers. Most early Ohio ministers with formal education were simply graduates or former students of liberal arts colleges and studied the curriculum common to such schools. By 1850 however, Ohio claimed seven theological seminaries with 105 students served by eighteen professors.

Training the clergy was essential to meet the needs of Ohio's church growth. From the beginning of settlement many religious establishments were founded in the state. The Moravian missions in the Tuscarawas Valley held regular services for the Indian converts. Even before 1800, Presbyterians, Congregationalists, Baptists, and Methodists had built churches, however rustic in appearance, in communities along the Miami and Ohio rivers. In the Western Reserve the Calvinist tradition of New England persisted, and virtually every village that emerged had its Congregational or Presbyterian church on the green or in a conspicuous location. Few Episcopalians migrated to Ohio in the early years.

Many early settlers of Ohio did not attend church services. Some were too distant from any congregation; some were unbelievers who could better escape in the West the constraints religion had placed upon the older established societies of the East. Two religious institutions that served the isolated frontier were the camp meeting and the circuit rider. The camp meeting was an intense, emotional revival service commonly held in a camp ground near some woodsy community. Preaching, singing, and praying would continue for days, and at night the scene was lit by torches as religious excitement burned high. Under intense religious hysteria, reputedly aided on occasion by frequent draughts of home-distilled "corn likker," converts would fall prostrate, testifying to

The Reverend Peter Cartwright and his wife. Cartwright was a great evangelistic preacher. (9)

their sins and redemption. Some were afflicted by jerks or trembling, some ran around on all fours barking in an effort to "tree the devil," and some spoke in tongues. These meetings provided a social as well as an emotional outlet. As with the militia muster, the social effects were perhaps as important as the stated purpose of the gathering.

The circuit rider was a clergyman, generally Methodist, who rode a regular circuit through the back country bringing religious solace to isolated individuals and congregations. He would preach, christen a child, say words over a grave, or solemnize a marriage. The Reverend Mr. Stauch, sent to Ohio by the German Lutherans of Pennsylvania, reported that during 120 days in 1806 he traveled 1,300 miles, preached sixty-seven times, and baptized 212 children. The devotion displayed by many of these men is impressive considering the awesome loneliness and the hazards and discomforts of life and travel in the forests in every season and all kinds of weather. Other itinerant preachers, many of them self-

Camp-Meeting, by A. Rider. (10)

An Ohio Portrait

The Reverend Lyman Beecher of Cincinnati, father of Harriett Beecher Stowe. (11)

"Two-horned" Congregational Church, Marietta, dedicated May 28, 1809. Oldest frame church northwest of the Ohio River. (12)

The Friends (Quaker) Meeting House at Mount Pleasant. The partition could be lowered to divide the room. (13)

proclaimed, did not follow any prescribed route but wandered the backcountry as they saw fit.

Early Ohioans were largely Protestant when they claimed religious affiliation. No old French Catholic nucleus existed in Ohio such as Detroit provided in Michigan, or Cahokia and Kaskaskia provided in Illinois. Roman Catholic growth in Ohio dates from the arrival of sufficient Irish and Germans to constitute parishes. The first Catholic church in Ohio, built in Perry County in 1818, was soon followed by a small church in Cincinnati. By 1826 a brick cathedral had been built in Cincinnati to meet the needs of a growing diocese. Anti-Catholic sentiment rose in the state. Certain Protestant leaders, especially Lyman Beecher, an influential Presbyterian minister of Cincinnati, worried lest the Ohio and Mississippi valleys lose their chance to be great centers of enlightened Protestantism.

The Germans brought not only Catholicism to Ohio but also Lutheranism and the German Reformed faith. Within one block of one another in the small canal town of Akron before the Civil War, the German Catholic, German Lutheran,

and German Reformed churches were established. A similar concentration could be found in other Ohio cities and towns. Many Germans settled in farming communities, especially in western Ohio, where their church buildings reflected the architecture of their homeland.

The Society of Friends, or Quakers, came into Ohio at an early time. They settled in the eastern counties, primarily Columbiana, Jefferson, and Belmont, but were found throughout the state. Mount Pleasant in Jefferson County was an important Quaker town and the site of the yearly meeting. Quakers played a conspicuous role in the antislavery movement. The Shakers, sometimes called Shaking Quakers, located in Ohio in 1812 at Union Village near Lebanon, and later at Watervliet, Whitewater, and North Union, now Shaker Heights. These plain people were industrious farmers who made clean-lined implements and furniture which is now much admired. Their tradition of absolute celibacy doomed them to ultimate extinction. Unitarians and their "poor country cousins," the Universalists, came to Ohio in small numbers with Cincinnati the focus of the

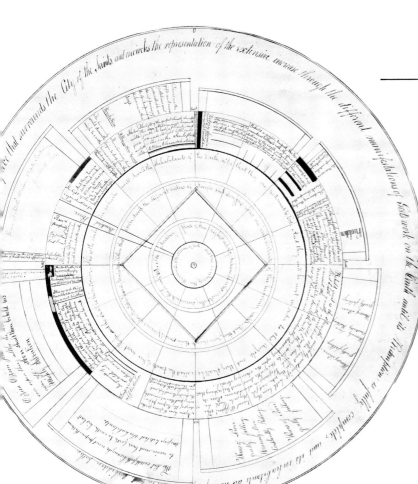

Early Ohio Social Concerns

The Shaker Tree of Heaven. (14)

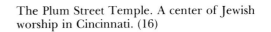

The Plum Street Temple. A center of Jewish worship in Cincinnati. (16)

at meeting. The religious dance, 1870. (15)

The Cathedral of St. Peter in Chains, Cincinnati, built 1839. (17)

An Ohio Portrait

Johnny Appleseed. Commemorative
postage stamp, 1966. (18)

Rabbi Isaac M. Wise (1819–1900), founder of
American Reformed Judaism. (19)

Farmers in Zoar, late nineteenth century. (20)

Unitarians and the small rural towns the focus of most Universalist activity. Jews, some of whom traveled Ohio roads as itinerant peddlers, formed a few congregations in Ohio before the Civil War. Under the leadership of Rabbi Isaac Wise, the Jews of Cincinnati with their Hebrew Union Seminary were the prime influence in the development of Reformed Judaism in America. German Pietists, called Mennonites and Amish, settled rich Ohio farm lands early in the nineteenth century, first in Holmes and Wayne counties but later in Madison, Union, Putnam, and Allen counties, where cheaper lands were available. Ultimately the Amish spread to Stark, Geauga, and several other counties. In 1817 a group of German Separatists under the astute leadership of Joseph Bimeler settled on 5,000 acres in the Tuscarawas Valley. Their community, given the Old Testament name Zoar, prospered from canal contracts, agriculture, and

manufacturing, and maintained its cohesive character until final dissolution in 1898. The Swedenborgian influence in Ohio rests largely with the unique and colorful John Chapman, who as "Johnny Appleseed" wandered the Ohio and Indiana countryside planting apple orchards, befriending Indians and isolated settlers, and talking about his mystical beliefs.

Most interesting in Ohio's religious scene is the prevalence of indigenous groups. Of these Alexander Campbell's followers, the "Campbellites" formally known as Disciples of Christ, were the most orthodox and most successful at establishing enduring congregations. Minimizing creed and hoping to unite all Christians on the great beliefs they shared in common, Campbell and his followers soon won numerous converts largely from the Baptists and Presbyterians. Ultimately this movement to reduce denominationalism resulted in the creation of yet

Older girls tending the younger children at Zoar, late nineteenth century. (21)

another denomination.

A former Campbellite, Sidney Rigdon, became a Mormon convert and persuaded the young New York farmer, Joseph Smith, to move his followers from central New York state to Kirtland in the Western Reserve. Here the Mormons briefly flourished, built a great temple through sacrifice and hard labor, and then fell on hard times as many of the 1,000 believers resisted an effort to make all property communal. Further disheartened by the exposure of Smith's fraudulent banking practices that affected non-Mormons as well as the faithful, many left for the West leaving only a remnant which called itself the Reorganized Church of Jesus Christ of the Latter Day Saints. Another New York farmer, William Miller, preached that the world would end in 1843. His numerous Ohio followers responded by selling their property, settling their affairs, and on the appointed day going to high places in their white "ascension robes." When nothing happened "Father" Miller recalculated, and the whole scenario was run through a second time in 1844. Miller then gave up the prediction business, but his movement had split many congregations beyond repair.

In addition to the Shakers, whose communal societies were organized around a religious ethic, Ohio was the site of a surprisingly large number of secular communal experiments. Fourier Phalanxes were established in Trumbull, Belmont, and Clermont counties. The little Ohio River town of Utopia reveals in its name its origins as a communitarian experiment. Kendal, in modern Massillon, and Robert Owen's Miami Valley communities are other examples of short-lived communitarian societies. The availability of inexpensive land, a reasonable degree of isolation from skeptical and hostile neighbors, and the relative looseness of social controls and constraints

The Mormon Temple at Kirtland (Lake County) as it appeared 1898. (22)

in a pioneer society all contributed to the choice of an Ohio location. In time, the filling up of the land, improved access to the outside, the loss of the young to broader fields of interest and opportunity, and the loss of the strong, often charismatic leader whose vision and talent held groups together, account for the rapid demise of most of these groups.

After the Civil War, Ohio was no longer the open, pioneer place it had been just a few decades before. Victorian influences had their effect on society. The so-called Protestant ethic, or work ethic, became entrenched. Family, church, and school tended to be mutually reinforcing in their efforts to train young people to be industrious, frugal, and prudent. A rise in wealth and capital accumulation allowed affluent congregations to raise great temples to their faiths. Great revival meetings spurred on the faithful and the newly converted to fresh exertions.

Increasing wealth and conformity in social

An Ohio Portrait

Samuel Lewis. (23)

expectations made Ohio less attractive than in former years to those whose vision of the good life was out of step with the dominant Protestantism. Spiritualists, "free love" advocates, and others who pursued unorthodox courses were barely tolerated. Somewhat better accepted were Christian Scientists whose beliefs seemed in tune with the developing scientism of the age.

As with religion, Ohio settlers brought their educational practices with them. Newly established villages characteristically set up a subscription school as one of their first projects, though only a small minority of eligible children attended. Settlers in the back country remained without schools for prolonged periods, often for several decades. When families were removed from schooling a noticeable decline in general learning and literacy took place. Thus the original settlers, particularly those with a New England background, often had a better formal education than did some second or third generation Ohioans.

An understandable dichotomy existed in the West about the matter of formal schooling. The Northwest Ordinance—with its famous assertion that "Religion, morality and knowledge being necessary to good government and the happiness of mankind, Schools and the means of education shall forever be encouraged"—was written by educated men from settled areas of the nation. While most newly arriving Ohioans probably concurred with the sentiment, they faced such immediate and enormous tasks simply to stay alive that not much energy, resource, or sympathy was left for "book larnin." Although the Land Ordinance of 1785 reserved section sixteen of every township for the support of education, this land often went unused, or when it was used, produced income inadequate to support a school. Initially, those who wished their children to re-

ceive schooling had to pay for it directly, and most commonly neighbors banded together to hire a teacher for their children.

Teachers were recruited from all walks of life. Teaching was one occupation open to women at this time, but qualified women were in short supply in certain areas. When Duncan McArthur instructed his wife in 1824 to secure a schoolmistress to tutor their daughters, he reflected that "a woman of education and correct habits" could not readily be secured in southern Ohio. Along with the "schoolmarm," another teaching stereotype was the old Irish teacher, who was coarse, mean, anti-intellectual, and equated education with corporal punishment. Some teachers were able young men who spent their late teens and early twenties teaching school to tide themselves over until they could enter their true life's work. Teacher training and state certification would ultimately improve the climate for teaching and, perhaps, the quality of teaching as well. However, that was well in the future.

An organized effort to create a public school system was under way in Ohio before 1820, when concerned citizens convinced newspapers to support the movement. In 1825 the general assembly passed a law that required county commissioners to assess one-half mill on all taxable property for school purposes. The law was imperfectly observed and frequently modified. In 1837 Samuel Lewis became the first Ohio State Superintendent of Common Schools and displayed great dedication and energy by riding to every county seat in Ohio to encourage support for public education. The general assembly enacted the Ohio School Law in 1848, modeled after the Akron School Law of 1847. This law provided all the elements of a modern school system, including school districts, support by public taxation, and

A cartoon depicting a schoolmaster who believed that to "spare the rod" was to "spoil the child." (24)

The Line Schoolhouse, East Palestine (Columbiana County). (25)

Schoolhouse at Madeira (Hamilton County), 1874. (26)

an elected school board which hired a superintendent to administer the system.

Education for black children was a special consideration in early Ohio. For a time black property owners in some counties were taxed for schools which would not admit their children, although that practice soon ceased. Schools for blacks were usually supported by blacks or by philanthropic whites. Only in parts of northern Ohio, where few black children lived, did they customarily attend schools with whites. At one time Cleveland had a few black teachers instructing classes with both black and white children.

Children who acquired a grammar school education, usually consisting of the old triumvirate, "readin', 'ritin', and 'rithmetic," could attend one of the numerous academies throughout the state. Many of these were minimal, short-lived affairs but represented the zenith of formal education for the great majority. In the 1840s Cincinnati opened a public high school, and other cities and large towns followed soon after, spelling doom for most of the private academies. The better high schools offered botany, music, mathematics, French, German, history, geography, physiology, Greek, and Latin in addition to English grammar and composition.

Several Ohioans contributed in a large way to

An Ohio Portrait

William Holmes McGuffey (1800–1873) pioneer educator, was a faculty member at Miami University and Cincinnati College, and was president of Ohio University. (27)

Chart used for reading instruction in the McGuffey system. (28)

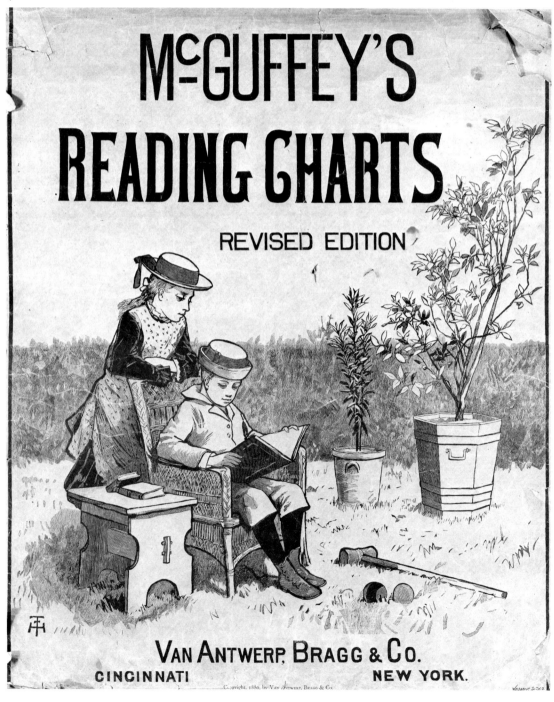

The arithmetics of Joseph Ray were used throughout the country. (29)

the instructional process by developing textbooks. Most famous of these perhaps was William Holmes McGuffey, whose popular *Readers* were produced by the millions over many decades. They taught moral homilies and good citizenship along with reading. Joseph Ray of Cincinnati wrote one of the nation's most widely used arithmetic books. Platt Spencer of Ashtabula County was the creator of Spencerian Script, a handwriting widely taught and used a hundred years ago. Most instruction was by "recitation," which emphasized rote memorization instead of thought processes. School libraries, laboratories, and gymnasiums were refinements which came after the 1850s.

The old-fashioned school bus. (30)

The penmanship taught by Platt Spencer to an age that fancied elegance in style. (31)

An Ohio Portrait

Miss Helmick's eight-grade class at Dueber School
(Stark County), 1906. (32)

(33)

(35)

(36)

(37)

1895 physics class, Ohio State University. (38)

Early citizens of Amesville (Athens County) sold pelts and bought these books of the "Coonskin Library" which now rest in the Ohio Historical Society's rare book room. (40)

View of the reading room, Cleveland Public Library. (41)

The first newspaper in Ohio, published in Cincinnati in 1793, by William Maxwell. (39)

An Ohio Portrait

Otterbein University, Westerville (Franklin County). (42)

Ohio has long been noted for its extraordinary number of colleges. Land was reserved in the Ohio Company Grant and in the Symmes Purchase for the support of colleges. Ohio University at Athens, which developed out of the former, was chartered in 1804 and began instruction in 1809. Miami University, after much difficulty in organizing, opened in 1824. Kenyon College at Gambier began in 1828 as a venture of the Episcopal Church and its Bishop, Philander Chase. Western Reserve opened in 1826 in Hudson with Presbyterian and Congregational support and moved to Cleveland in 1882. Other early Ohio colleges included Marietta, Oberlin, Denison at Granville, St. Francis Xavier at Cincinnati, Wittenberg at Springfield, Capital at Columbus (Bexley), Otterbein at Westerville, Baldwin (later Baldwin-Wallace) at Berea, Heidelberg at Tiffin, Ohio Wesleyan at Delaware, and many others. Nearly all had strong church connections, but some—Oberlin and Western Reserve, for example—soon had only minimal denominational ties.

The first Cincinnati College building. (43)

Several Ohio colleges had unique traits at this early time. Oberlin was the first college to adopt coeducation as a policy and was also the first college which actively sought out black students. Oberlin's first coeds paid dearly for their honor. They cleaned the rooms of men students, took care of their clothes, and for these tasks were paid two and three-quarters cents an hour. But despite these difficulties, three women graduated in 1841, the first women in the United States to be granted degrees on an equal basis with men. A new college, the first of its kind, was established in 1856 at Wilberforce in Greene County to provide collegiate education for black students. Antioch at Yellow Springs, under its distinguished president Horace Mann, sponsored academic innovations during a later period, including cooperative education which placed young men and women

Galloway Hall, Wilberforce University (Greene County). (44)

Female Seminary, Cleveland. (45)

in jobs during portions of their college careers. Ohio was also a leader in the development of municipal universities with Cincinnati, Toledo, and Akron each establishing city-supported schools.

From an early time Ohio also had libraries and what would now be called adult education programs. Ohio's first public library was organized in Belpre in 1796, with a second opening in Dayton in the first decade of the nineteenth century. The famous "coonskin library" of Amesville in Athens County provides a graphic example of the importance books had for some early settlers. Most Ohio cities and sizable towns had subscription libraries long before the Civil War. By 1814 Cincinnati had a circulating library, and the little town of Delaware opened one in 1825. Some 160 libraries had been incorporated in Ohio by the end of 1840.

Lyceums appeared in Akron and Cleveland in the 1830s. Many Ohio towns promoted these lecture programs and also organized philosophical societies that discussed everything from the causes·of milk-sickness to the military strategy of the Austro-Sardinian War. Book publishing appeared at an early time with Cincinnati emerging as the leading publishing center of the entire West. Many years later, Dayton, Springfield, Akron, and Cleveland would become major publishing centers.

Newspapers were important features of Ohio life from its earliest days. The *Centinel of the North Western Territory* was published at Cincinnati in 1793. By 1810 papers were also published at Chillicothe, Marietta, Lebanon, St. Clairsville, Steubenville, Zanesville, Dayton, and Lisbon. Among the most influential Ohio papers were the *Cincinnati Advertiser* later called the *Daily Cincinnati Enquirer, The Cleveland Herald,* the *Ohio State Journal and Columbus Gazette,* the *Ohio Statesman,*

Professor Silas Martin's Ohio State University art class. (46)

Marietta College developed out of the first academy in Ohio. (47)

The Ohio Institution for the Education of the Blind, 1878, Columbus. (48)

The Massillon Gazzette, August 14, 1844. (49)

The *Cleveland Herald* building, ca. 1875. (50)

the *Canton Repository,* the *Youngstown Vindicator,* the *Summit Beacon* later called the *Akron Beacon Journal,* and the *Toledo Blade.* Brilliant early editors like Charles Hammond and Samuel Medary kept the journalistic scene lively in a day when partisanship and contentiousness were regarded as virtues by newspaper readers.

The maturing of Ohio society allowed some citizens time to consider ways to ameliorate certain pressing social problems and concerns. In Ohio, as in portions of the East, many reform enthusiasms were supported by a small minority of citizens, most of whom were closely involved in the life of evangelical Protestant churches or with the Quakers. Among these causes were education, prison reform, missionary work, and care for the insane, the blind, and the deaf. Women's rights was an important concern. In 1850, two years after the famous Seneca Falls, New York, convention on women's rights, a group of Ohio women sponsored a similar meeting in Salem, a center of evangelical activity. Two years later, women meeting in Massillon formed the Ohio Women's Rights Association, which soon established branches throughout the state as part of a national movement.

Changes in the legal and economic roles of women were modest at best. In 1861 the general assembly enacted a law allowing married women to own real estate and to make contracts in cases where husbands deserted or neglected them, providing a court authorized this. A few women made careers in journalism—Josephine Bateham edited the ladies department of the *Ohio Cultivator,* Amelia Bloomer wrote for the *Lily,* and Columbus's Elizabeth Besbee edited the *Alliance.* Many were school teachers, usually working for less pay than men. In 1852 the Female Medical Education Society organized and promoted medical training for women. Most who were em-

Charles Hammond, editor of the Cincinnati *Gazette*, 1825–1840. (51)

ployed, however, labored in nonprofessional occupations in clothing and tailoring shops and factories, in printing and bookbinding establishments, and in cloak, mantilla, boot, and shoe works. The Civil War, with its consequent shortage of labor, opened opportunities for women in various areas of manufacturing, particularly in the clothing trades. Yet the vast majority of female wage earners were household servants. In 1870, of the 83,520 female employees, 51,310 were domestic help such as maids, cooks, and housekeepers. Clearly the movement for equal rights still had a long way to go.

Women's suffrage placard indicating that women were denied the vote as were idiots, convicts, Indians, and insane men. Frances Willard, temperance advocate, is the woman in the center. (52)

College girls of the late nineteenth century. (53)

A graduate of Oberlin, Lucy Stone was an early crusader for women's rights and other reform efforts. (54)

An Ohio Portrait

Demonstrating against whiskey, 1873, in Bucyrus. (55)

Temperance crusaders pray in front of a Howard
Street saloon, Akron. (56)

The Washingtonians attracted many of the "best"
people to the temperance cause in pre-Civil War
Ohio. (57)

The whiskey crusade, Mt. Vernon (Knox County),
1874. (58)

Temperance was another strong reform movement in Ohio. Early Ohio observers recognized chronic drunkenness as a great human waste and even as a sin. Crude practices such as throwing drunks in the canal, an experience that had "an instant sobering effect," did not really deal with the issue. Some reformers identified the problem as the ready availability of cheap, rot-gut liquor at militia muster, at camp meetings, at "socials," and at every grocery store where a dipper was hung by the whiskey barrel for the convenience of any thirsty patron. The amounts consumed were staggering—in more ways than one. In Licking County in 1820, some thirty-eight stills produced 97,000 gallons of whiskey, only 28,000 of which were exported, leaving 69,000 gallons to be consumed by fewer than 12,000 people! Similar statistics can be found for other Ohio counties. The Germans popularized beer and wine, which were not as potent as the hard liquor that poured from thousands of distilleries and home stills, but these beverages also came under attack.

Temperance attracted both men and women to its cause. Many, but not all, were strong church people. Many were also teetotalers themselves. Some eventually sought total prohibition, but early efforts were to restrict the availability of hard liquor to licensed taverns, where it would not be readily accessible to the young and indigent. Most vigorous in these early efforts was the Washingtonian Society, which pressed for licensing in Ohio. Success ultimately would come to these efforts and to legal prohibition, but in the 1840s and 1850s that time was still far in the future.

Success came sooner for the antislavery proponents. Like other reform efforts, the antislavery crusade was carried out by a determined minority who had to fend off the taunts and derision of those who were unsympathetic to the cause. Many Ohioans were comfortable with the work of the American Colonization Society, which sought to transport free blacks to Africa. Although the society's program of relocating large numbers of black people failed, it did result in the founding of Liberia on the West African coast. Eventually, one of Ohio's great industries, rubber, would have huge investments in Liberian plantations.

In 1815 the first abolitionist society in the state was formed in St. Clairsville by Benjamin Lundy, a Quaker. Two years later Charles Osborne, a Mt. Pleasant Quaker, started the nation's first abolitionist newspaper, the *Philanthropist,* and by 1821 Lundy was also in print with his *The Genius of Universal Emancipation.* Abolitionist activity represented the more extreme form of antislavery belief—slavery was morally wrong, a sin, and should be ended immediately without compensation to the slaveowner. Only a small minority of Ohioans concurred with this view, and most people were content to see slavery confined to its present borders. They believed that when the institution had run its course, it should be phased out gradually with fair compensation to the slaveowner for his property loss. More than any state of the West, Ohio contained a strong abolitionist element which grew in size and aggressiveness and had much influence in Ohio and national politics.

Some early antislavery activity was carried on in Cincinnati, which was in that part of the state least sympathetic to abolitionist doctrine. Lane Seminary, for the training of Presbyterian clergymen, opened in Cincinnati in the late 1820s at a time when that city harbored considerable anti-black sentiment. Cincinnati contained about one tenth of Ohio's blacks, most of whom could man-

age only a precarious existence. Some Lane students and faculty did welfare work among these people and sympathized with their plight. They also encouraged discussion of antislavery views. This was too much for the trustees, who voted to curtail further discussion of slavery. One trustee, Asa Mahan, and some students left Lane in protest and went north to Oberlin, which they promptly converted into a bastion of antislavery strength. At Oberlin the preaching of Charles Grandison Finney attracted a fervent band of young men, foremost among them Theodore Dwight Weld, who took up the antislavery cause with missionary zeal. One of Weld's converts to abolition was James G. Birney, a onetime slaveowner who became an antislavery advocate and moved to Cincinnati, where he published the *Philanthropist.* His press was destroyed by a mob. This threat to a free press in Ohio brought support to Birney and indirectly created sympathy for the antislavery position.

Shortly after the American Antislavery Society was formed in New York in 1833, chapters appeared throughout Ohio. As antislavery rhetoric intensified to the point where the Union itself seemed threatened, some anti-abolitionist societies were formed. In 1840 antislavery advocates formed the Liberty Party and chose James G. Birney as their presidential candidate, but to no avail. He received only 892 votes in Ohio. The Liberty Party merged with Free-Soilers, and ultimately antislavery advocates found their way to the Republican Party, newly formed in 1854.

In the Congress of the United States meanwhile, the antislavery forces had strong support from some Ohio legislators. In the House, Joshua R. Giddings of Ashtabula County was a staunch ally of former President John Quincy Adams in the fight against the infamous "gag rule" which prohibited presentation of antislavery petitions

The Underground Railway, by C. T. Webber (painted in 1893). (59)

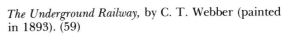

Sympathy for blacks forced some students and faculty to leave Lane Seminary at Walnut Hills (Hamilton County). (60)

Harriet Beecher Stowe (1811–1896), oil portrait by Alanson Fisher (1853). (61)

An Ohio Portrait

on the House floor. At the same time Thomas Morris fought vigorously against efforts to gag the Senate, saying resolutions to that effect were "the most daring attempt against American liberty, that has yet been brought forward in Congress, since the foundation of the Republic, and as such I oppose them." Morris's views on the slavery issue were too uncompromising for his fellow Democrats, who refused to renominate him.

Perhaps no aspect of the antislavery movement has attracted as much popular attention as the Underground Railroad. By this process escaping slaves were moved to freedom in Canada or isolated portions of the northern states. The degree to which this was accomplished by an extensive, tightly knit system of "conductors," "depots," and similar devices has probably been exaggerated. Nearly every town in Ohio claims an

Fugitive Slave Bill, 1850. Ohio abolitionists called it the "Kidnap Law." (62)

FUGITIVE-SLAVE BILL.

" All good citizens are hereby COMMANDED to aid and assist in the prompt and effectual execution of this law, wherever their services may be required."—*Sec. 5, Act approved by President Fillmore, Sept.* 18, 1850.

" THOU SHALT NOT deliver unto his master the servant which is escaped from his master unto thee: He shall dwell with thee, even among you, in that place which he shall choose in one of thy gates, where it liketh him best: thou shalt not oppress him."—*Deuteronomy* xxiii. 15, 16.

PLEDGE.

Whereas the late Act of Congress, called THE FUGITIVE-SLAVE BILL, makes a refusal to aid in the capture of a Fugitive a penal offense, the Subscribers, being restrained by conscientious motives from rendering any active obedience to the law, do solemnly pledge ourselves to each other, rather to submit to its penalties, than to obey its provisions.

old house or building said to have sheltered runaway slaves. In fact many escaping slaves did make their way across Ohio with the aid of white and black friends who fed, transported, and concealed them. Some, like Levi Coffin of Cincinnati and the Reverend John Rankin of Ripley, who kept a candle burning in his Ohio River home as a beacon for slaves escaping from Kentucky, were dependable and persistent in their aid, while many persons lent occasional assistance as fate and circumstance decreed. Presbyterians, Methodists, and Quakers predominated in this effort, with some of the Quaker towns and dedicated groups like the Oberlin people being especially active. By wagon, canal boat, and on foot, the runaways moved north toward Lake Erie ports such as Cleveland, known by the code name "Hope," or on into Michigan. The story of an escaping slave was told so poignantly by Harriet Beecher Stowe, who had witnessed the plight of blacks in Cincinnati, that her *Uncle Tom's Cabin* (1852) became an instant best seller and is credited with producing more converts to the antislavery cause than any number of abolitionist speeches.

A new federal Fugitive Slave Act, enacted in 1850 as part of the so-called Compromise of 1850, was deliberately designed to give the slavecatchers and their agents an advantage. When an alleged runaway was taken before a magistrate, the law prescribed that a judge who found in favor of the claimant would collect double the fee he would collect if he ruled against the claimant. No impediments were to be put in the way of those seeking to reclaim their slave property. Under this law legitimate free blacks were in peril of being claimed as runaway slaves. Reaction to this law was bitter among antislavery advocates, especially in the Western Reserve. In Akron, a former mayor, Lucius Bierce, told his fellow citi-

John Brown taking the oath to make Kansas a free state, 1857. (63)

zens, "I care not whether the order comes from a Judge or from the President himself, if it is to take a citizen of this state, from the protection of our laws, to a slave state, *I say resist it,* and let the South and her minions at the North know they sleep on a magazine that a spark from the North may at any moment ignite." The "Kidnap Law," as its enemies labeled it, was ignored repeatedly, and would-be slave catchers returned empty-handed on numerous occasions, especially from the Western Reserve.

The Oberlin-Wellington Rescue Cases of 1859 brought the issue to a climax. A group of thirty-seven citizens were indicted under the Fugitive Slave Law for aiding an Oberlin fugitive named John Price to escape from a United States deputy marshal at Wellington. Their cases were appealed to the Ohio Supreme Court, which was willing to rule on the constitutionality of a federal law which had been upheld in federal courts. By a three-to-two vote the Ohio court upheld the constitutionality of the Fugitive Slave Law. The prisoners were soon freed, but the issue did much to coalesce Ohio Republican sentiment along more militant lines.

The Kansas-Nebraska Act in 1854 had serious political repercussions in Ohio as elsewhere in the country. The opening of Kansas Territory on the principle of popular sovereignty led to a race between free state and slave state sympathizers to get there in sufficient numbers to capture control of the territorial legislature. Among those who went to Kansas from Ohio was John Brown, known locally in Summit and Portage counties for his antislavery zeal. One dark night in 1856 Brown and his band, including several of his sons, butchered five proslavery men in cold blood near the little settlement of Ossawatomie. These murders, characteristic of the savagery in "Bleeding Kansas," were decried by most northerners, but the more radical abolitionists hailed Brown as a righteous avenger—"Old Ossawatomie"—and responded to his requests for aid. Three years later, when Brown was hanged for his raid against the federal arsenal at Harper's Ferry, Virginia, many Western Reserve towns held days of mourning for "our old friend and neighbor, John Brown."

Brown may have died to free the slaves, but Ohioans in general were less interested in freeing slaves than they were in preserving an increasingly threatened Union. Soon the Union would be severed, and bloody Civil War would ensue. Ohio would play a central role in that conflict.

(64)

An Ohio Portrait

(65)

(69)

(70)

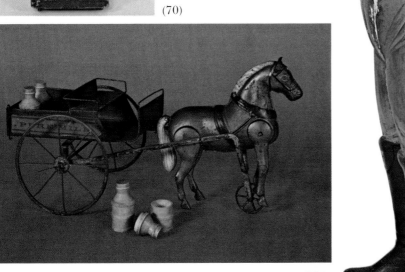

(71)

(73)

Throughout the nineteenth century, skilled Ohio craftsmen created both utilitarian and whimsical items of charm and style.

(72)

An Ohio Portrait

Politics and War

The political life of Ohio has been complex since territorial days when the Federalist governor and his supporters clashed with the Jeffersonian (Democratic-Republican) power in the territorial legislature. After statehood was achieved, the Federalists faded rapidly from the Ohio scene as they did nationally in the first decade of the nineteenth century. Ohio's first ten governors were Democratic-Republicans. Duncan McArthur, a National Republican, broke that tradition from 1830 to 1832. Since 1832 the governor's office has been held about equally by Democrats on the one hand and Whigs and Republicans on the other. Much more dramatic is the geographical split. Fifteen of Ohio's first sixteen governors came from the southern part of the state, as did practically all of Ohio's senators before the Civil War. The focus of political power was clearly in the southern counties in the antebellum period.

The first traumatic adjustment of the political power structure in Ohio came when Andrew Jackson appeared on the American political scene. He appealed to the western farmer and to some urban laborers as a man of the people. Henry Clay of Kentucky was popular in the West due to his strong support for internal improvements and his position on the tariff issue. In the 1824 presidential race, Clay received slightly more votes in Ohio than Jackson, but four years later Jackson won Ohio and the nation. Not all of Jackson's policies were pleasing to his supporters in the state. The Maysville Veto, denying federal support to internal improvements in Kentucky, caused particular concern among states such as Ohio which coveted federal aid.

In the Western Reserve, where Henry Clay was a longtime political favorite, a new influence developed about 1830. Concern grew among some Americans that secret societies, which were growing in number, were un-American and

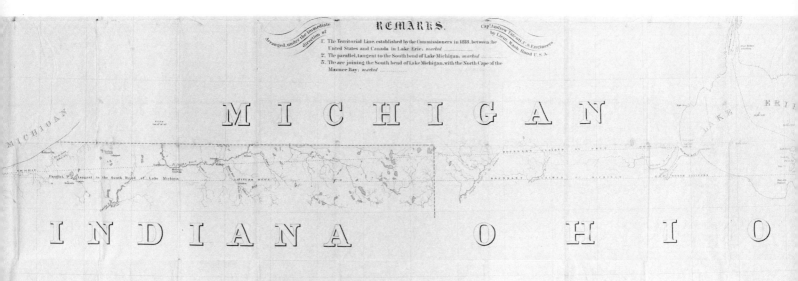

REMARKS.

Arranged under the immediate direction of

1. The Territorial Line, established by the Commissioners in 1818, between the United States and Canada in Lake Erie, marked
2. The parallel, tangent to the South bend of Lake Michigan, marked
3. The are joining the South bend of Lake Michigan, with the North Cape of the Maumee Bay, marked

Cap! Andrew Talcott U.s Engineer by Lieut. Wash. Hood U.S.A.

MICHIGAN

MICHIGAN

Parallel P tangent to the South Bend of Lake Michigan

INDIANA   OHIO

should be abolished. When a New York man was ostensibly murdered for revealing the secrets of the Masonic fraternity, feelings became so intense in parts of New York, Pennsylvania, and Ohio's Western Reserve that an Anti-Masonic party was formed. But in the presidential race of 1832, won by Andrew Jackson, the Anti-Masonic candidate William Wirt received only 509 Ohio votes. That same year Ohio elected its first Democratic governor — Robert Lucas of Pike County.

During his administration Lucas had to deal with the thorny issue of determining Ohio's northern boundary. A series of errors and misunderstandings led Ohio to claim more than its share according to the terms of the Northwest Ordinance. When the northern boundary of Ohio was surveyed in 1817, the line was run to the north cape of Maumee Bay, giving this valuable port location to Ohio. After much bluff and bluster between Ohio and Michigan interests (the so-called "Toledo War"), the Jackson administration, perfectly aware that Ohio had more political clout than Michigan, awarded the disputed territory to Ohio and compensated Michigan by awarding her the larger part of her present Upper Peninsula. In an ironic twist, the great mineral wealth of the Upper Peninsula, Michigan's consolation prize, was developed in large part by Cleveland entrepreneurs and carried in ships owned by Cleveland interests. Ohio thus benefited from being awarded the disputed territory and from reaping the economic benefits from Michigan's consolation prize.

An equally colorful but lesser-known affair during the same period was the invasion of Canada by members of a secret society called the Hunters, or Patriots, pledged to help Canadian rebels win independence from Great Britain. In 1838 at Cleveland, a gathering of Hunters elected General Lucius V. Bierce of Akron, a brigadier general in the Ohio Militia, as "Commander in Chief of Patriot Armies in the West." During the fall of 1838, Bierce commanded a motley force of about 400 volunteers encamped near Detroit. In December some 137 followed Bierce to the Detroit waterfront, where they appropriated a boat, crossed to Canada, burned the tiny settlement of Windsor, and burned a Canadian steamship in retaliation for the earlier destruction by Canadians of the American ship *Caroline* in the Niagara River. Surrounded by Canadian militia, most of Bierce's men were taken prisoner, but the commander and a few of his staff successfully recrossed the Detroit River. Two efforts to indict the popular Bierce for violating American neutrality laws failed. He returned to Akron and promptly was elected mayor.

In 1836 one of Ohio's best known citizens, William Henry Harrison, was an unsuccessful Whig candidate for the presidency of the United States, losing to Martin Van Buren, Jackson's political heir. His fellow Ohioans gave Harrison a majority, however, and supported him again in his successful bid in 1840. This famous "hard cider campaign" created a folksy image of the genteel Harrison through the use of frontier emblems and symbols, including bonfires, parades, and a catchy slogan, "Tippecanoe and Tyler too." The victory, after twelve years of Democratic control of the executive branch, brought less to the Whigs than they expected. Harrison, sixty-eight years old and the oldest man ever elected president, caught a cold at his inauguration parade. It turned into a fatal case of pneumonia only one month later.

The slavery issue entered Ohio politics with force in the 1840s. The antislavery Liberty party had little appeal at the ballot box, but the antislavery influence was felt within Whig and Democratic ranks. The admission of Texas to the

ap showing the area in dispute between Michigan
id Ohio in 1837. (1)

Campaign literature picturing the Whig, William
Henry Harrison ("Old Tippecanoe") as a simple
man of the people, 1840. (2)

(3)

Union in 1845 was of concern to antislavery elements. A provision of its admission was that as many as five states could be formed from Texas, and the possibility that such a number of new slave states might emerge caused alarm. Then, in 1846, expansionist sentiment led to the Mexican War. Ohio furnished more than 7,000 men to the armies led by the dignified Virginian, Winfield Scott ("Old Fuss and Feathers"), and by the unprepossessing Zachary Taylor ("Old Rough and Ready"). Ohio Whigs, especially those concerned about the expansion of slavery, were against the war. Senator Thomas Corwin's famous anti-war speech was the strongest statement of this sentiment, a feeling shared by a young representative from Illinois named Abraham Lincoln.

Under the leadership of Salmon P. Chase, a Whig and staunch abolitionist, the Free Soil party was organized in Ohio as the focus of antislavery interest. Claiming particular strength in the Western Reserve, it held the balance of power in the general assembly after 1848 and thus won concessions far in excess of those which its actual numerical strength might have dictated. Through its efforts the remaining Black Laws were repealed and both Chase and Benjamin F. Wade, a determined foe of slavery from Ashtabula County, were ultimately sent to the United States Senate. The Free Soilers also cooperated with the Democrats to secure a new state constitution for Ohio.

The Constitution of 1802 needed to be rewritten. It had placed too much authority in the legislative branch and had provided inadequately for the state's judicial needs. In 1849 the general assembly referred to the voters the question of holding a new constitutional convention. The voters favored calling a convention by nearly a three-to-one margin. The Democrats won an ab-

An Ohio Portrait

Flag carried by the 4th Ohio
Volunteer Infantry during the
Mexican War. (4)

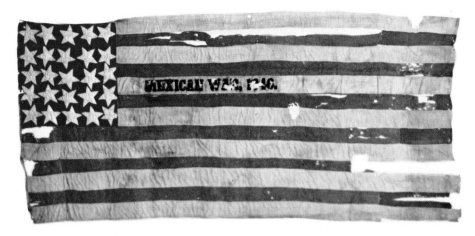

A field artillery unit in the
Mexican War, 1846–1848. (5)

The Quartermaster Department in action during
the Mexican War. (6)

Captain Hamilton's flag, 1st Ohio Volunteer
Infantry. (7)

solute majority of the delegates chosen. The convention met first in Columbus in May, 1850, adjourned due to a cholera outbreak, and reassembled in Cincinnati where it concluded its work in March, 1851. The voters ratified the new Constitution by a 125,564 to 109,276 margin, and it became effective September 1, 1851.

Under the new constitution the governor was still denied the veto. The number of supreme court judges increased to five, and all judges were to be chosen by the electorate rather than by the legislature. Limits were placed on the legislature's powers to create new counties and to contract debt. Taxation by the "uniform rule," in which all classes of property were subject to the same rate, was introduced and is still in effect in Ohio, as are the 1851 regulations on licensing traffic in intoxicating liquors. A requirement that in 1871 and every twentieth year thereafter the question of holding a constitutional convention should be submitted to the voters was also a provision of this basic framework of government by which Ohio is still operating a century and a quarter later.

Ohio's most radical political realignment since the Jacksonian surge occurred in July, 1855. The "Fusion" movement, made up of anti-Nebraska Whigs, antislavery Democrats, and Free Soilers, was joined by the anti-foreign, anti-Catholic, Know Nothings, who were more concerned about antislavery than nativism. The new coalition became the Republican party and nominated Salmon P. Chase for governor. He won over the Democratic incumbent, William Medill, and a die-hard Know Nothing, former governor Allen Trimble. The new party and its leader espoused antislavery doctrine and economic conservatism and, in 1856, gave the Ohio vote to the unsuccessful Republican presidential candiate, John C. Frémont. Frémont had helped open California,

Salmon P. Chase (1808–1873), governor of Ohio, senator, secretary of the Treasury and chief justice of the United States Supreme Court. (8)

to which thousands of Ohioans had rushed in 1849 and 1850 by prairie schooner and by ship to make their fortunes in the gold fields. Few "forty-niners" grew rich from gold, but a number, including many from Ohio, prospered in associated business ventures. Although Frémont, the popular "Pathfinder" of the West, was unsuccessful in 1856, some Ohio admirers had earlier renamed their city, Lower Sandusky, Fremont in his honor.

Ohio's role in the critical election of 1860 was disappointing because three native sons — former governor, then Senator Salmon Chase, Justice John McLean, and Senator Benjamin Wade — were under consideration as presidential candidates. However, they canceled each other out. The Republican's choice, Abraham Lincoln, was acceptable to the Ohio delegation, although he was still too "soft" on abolition to satisfy many Ohio Republicans. His wife's south-

ern family connections also worried others including one who thought that Lincoln's "bed partner" might tempt him to temporize with the South. Meanwhile, Ohio Democrats backed Senator Stephen A. Douglas over his rivals, John C. Breckinridge and John Bell. Lincoln won Ohio handily, running up an absolute majority over his three opponents.

Lincoln quickly demonstrated firmness in a time of crisis. After hostilities began in April, 1861, at Fort Sumter, his first calls for volunteers were oversubscribed in Ohio. In 1863, when the conscription law went into effect, it became a point of pride for the state and each of its counties to meet manpower quotas without having to resort to the draft. To assist in this effort Ohio paid bounties to enlistees, a small percentage of whom took the money and then deserted. Of Ohio's eighty-eight counties, only twenty-six finally succeeded in avoiding conscription. Strangely, the

A campaign poster of Stephen A. Douglas graces this scene of Newark in 1860. (9)

Camp Chase (Columbus) was one of Ohio's principal military establishments during the Civil War. It is the site of a small cemetery for Confederate soldiers. (10)

At no more than ten years of age, Johnny Clem of Newark became the "drummer boy of Shiloh." (11)

Camp Dennison, an important Civil War encampment near Cincinnati. (12)

Camp life for Civil War soldiers (above) was functional rather than glamorous. (14) The 126th "Colored Troops" assembled in Delaware (left). (13)

An Ohio Portrait

Pontoon bridge. (15)

The Battle of Stone River (1862) where Rosecrans'
federals won a costly victory. (16)

(17)

The "Guthrie Greys"
in front of
St. Nicholas Hotel,
Cincinnati. (18)

strongest antislavery region, the Western Reserve, could not escape the need to conscript, nor could the heavily German and Democratic counties just south of it. Conversely, the heart of southern influence in Ohio, the Scioto Valley and adjoining region, had an impressive record in filling its quotas with volunteers. Among the volunteers in the first two years were free Negroes from Ohio, but their offer of service was rejected. Some were finally enrolled in Massachusetts regiments. By 1863 however, Ohio accepted black volunteers. The 127th Ohio Volunteer Infantry was a black unit, and in all more than 5,000 blacks served in Ohio units; some fought effectively in the East during the last years of the war. Ohio contributed more than 346,000 men to the Union military forces. More than 11,237 of these were killed or died of wounds, 13,354 died of

disease, and more than 18,000 deserted or were conscripted men who failed to report. Ohio ranked third in the number of men in service and proportionately high in the other categories listed.

Initially no place suitable to quarter the enlistees was available. Governor Dennison and the legislature were forced to proceed on a trial-and-error basis, for the state had no experience in dealing with housing, clothing, feeding, training, equipping, and transporting such large numbers of men. Some Ohioans raised regiments privately and then delivered them intact to federal authorities. Camp Dennison near Cincinnati and Camp Chase near Columbus were the staging areas for Ohio troops called to federal service. State troops were billeted in a number of camps around Ohio. Supplying the troops was a monu-

Building breastworks. (19)

An Ohio Portrait

Lucy Webb Hayes (1831–1889) was one of many Ohio women who nursed injured and sick soldiers during the Civil War. (20)

mental task which lent itself to all sorts of confusion and profiteering. Slowly the organizational problems were controlled, but profiteers could not be prevented from milking the war for their own enrichment, and sometimes operated in cahoots with political and military associates. The selection of officers for Ohio regiments was another chronic problem. Initially the old militia practice of electing officers was used for the lesser ranks, but later abandoned. Governor Dennison had appointive powers for senior officers of state troops, and he exercised this prerogative by appointing a former regular army officer and Cincinnati railroad executive, George Brinton McClellan, to be major general in command of all Ohio troops.

McClellan reluctantly moved his Ohio troops in 1861 into western Virginia, where loyalist elements had received assurances of assistance from Governor Dennison. Occupying the line of the Baltimore and Ohio Railroad, the Ohioans drove off Virginia troops in one of the Union's first successful engagements of the war. In recognition of his services, McClellan was made a major general in the federal service, and Lincoln appointed him commander in chief, a move the president would shortly regret. Governor Dennison, meanwhile, planned to invade Kentucky but was restrained by Lincoln, who sought successfully to keep Kentucky neutral.

Ohio troops fought in every major theater of war and in most major engagements. They were present in large numbers at critical battles such as Shiloh in the West and Antietam and Gettysburg in the East. They were especially well represented in the western armies, fighting with Grant and with Sherman. They moved to Atlanta and from Atlanta to the sea with Sherman; they were with Sheridan and his precursors in the Valley of Virginia; they fought along the Atlantic Coast and in

northern Virginia; and some finished the war in the western theaters beyond the Mississippi. Thousands of Ohio boys sailed the rivers on gunboats and the high seas on naval vessels. Some wasted away in Confederate prisons like Libby in Richmond and the notorious Andersonville in Georgia.

The roles of women in the Civil War have not received the attention they are due. By the tens of thousands Ohio women found they must manage farms, keep businesses operating, maintain the institutional activities that hold life together, and provide education for the young. Some of the more visible services were rendered by nurses such as Maryanne Bickerdyke, Sister Anthony O'Connell, and Lucy Webb, who performed essential and rigorous service in the field hospitals. Many women assisted in the soldier relief work carried on by the United States Christian Commission with branches at Cleveland, Cincinnati, and Toledo. Cleveland women formed the nation's first soldier's aid society in April, 1861, which was later absorbed into a centralized relief agency called the United States Sanitary Commission.

The war touched Ohio directly in 1863. General John Morgan of Kentucky led 2,460 mounted raiders into Indiana and Ohio. Foraging through the countryside, Morgan was pursued by United States Cavalry units while units of the Ohio Militia attempted to intercept him. Crossing the state in an easterly direction from a point just north of Cincinnati, he reached the ford to Buffington Island in Meigs County. Morgan succeeded in getting part of his force across the Ohio before his pursuers forced the remainder of his men to dash away from the river for safety. A long northward pursuit ended on July 26 at West Point in Columbiana County, the deepest penetration into the North by any Con-

The United States Christian Commission was a soldier's relief organization that helped ease the rigors of war. (21)

Numerous Ohio prisoners died in notorious Andersonville (Georgia), prisoner of war camp. (22)

The raiders of Colonel John Hunt Morgan ride through Washington (Guernsey County), 1863. (23)

An Ohio Portrait

Johnson's Island in Sandusky Bay contained a prison camp for Confederate prisoners. (24)

federate military unit. This brief but costly venture gave Ohio a small taste of war, but residents were reassured when northern military forces responded so quickly and well to this challenge. Morgan was sent to the Ohio Penitentiary and charged as a common horse thief to divest his act of glamour, but he and six of his officers escaped in November, the only men to escape from the Ohio Penitentiary until well into the twentieth century. Ohio was also host to some unwilling Confederate guests, who were imprisoned on Johnson's Island in Sandusky Bay and at Camp Chase in Columbus. A quixotic scheme to free the Johnson Island prisoners was foiled. To this day, Daughters of the Confederacy decorate graves at these locations on Confederate Memorial Day.

Throughout the war Ohio was the scene of great disaffection for the Lincoln administration and its war policies. The political expression of this disaffection was found among the Peace Democrats, whose principal spokesman was Clement Laird Vallandigham, Congressman from Montgomery County. He and his "Copperhead" followers wanted the Union restored, but they were convinced that the Lincoln approach would create a great centralized despotism which would overawe the states and trample on individual liberties. Avid supporters of the Union war effort regarded Copperheadism as treason. General Orders No. 38 issued by General Ambrose Burnside, Commander of the Department of the Ohio, dictated arrest for anyone expressing sympathy for the enemy. When Vallandigham deliberately challenged them he was arrested, convicted by a military commission, and sentenced to confinement for the rest of the war. Lincoln, fearing Vallandigham would be regarded as a martyr, ordered him exiled to the Confederacy. Vallandigham was not pleased to be in the Confederacy, and at first opportunity moved to Canada and

Mr. & Mrs. Clement Laird Vallandigham. (25)

(26)

U.S. Grant and a favorite mount. (27)

William Tecumseh Sherman (1820–1891) of Lancaster was appalled when he first had to fight friends in the Confederate armies. His name was anathema in the South after his march from Atlanta to the sea. (28)

established himself at Niagara Falls. The Ohio Democratic convention, now controlled by the Peace Democrats, nominated him for governor in 1863 and waged a vigorous campaign on his behalf. Republicans and War Democrats, now joined in the Union party, tried to undercut Vallandigham's strength by dropping Governor David Tod, who had encountered animosity as he pursued a strong pro-administration policy, in favor of John Brough, a staunch Democrat of former times, now a Unionist. In a tense atmosphere which threatened deep schisms throughout the Northwest, Brough was elected by a margin of 100,882 votes. Ohio soldiers in the field, permitted to vote by a special act of the legislature, gave Brough their vote by an eighteen to one margin. A relieved Abraham Lincoln telegraphed Brough; "Glory to God in the highest: Ohio has saved the Union."

As one would expect from the third most populous state in the Union, Ohio's contributions of men and women, money (more than $10,000,000 for direct war purposes), industrial goods, and agricultural products were proportionately large, but in providing top-flight military leadership Ohio was clearly in front. Only Virginia, the key state in the Confederate cause, produced a group of military leaders approaching Ohio's in talent and accomplishment. Foremost among them was Hiram Ulysses Grant (accidentally appearing on army records, and ever after, as Ulysses Simpson Grant) who as commander in the West gave the Union its most striking successes of the early years. In 1864 Lincoln named him Commander in Chief of the Union forces, a role in which his talent for command coupled with good strategic insight allowed him to marshal superior northern manpower and material to wear down the South. Part of his effectiveness stemmed from his ability to write or-

Army wagons from Sherman's army in Zanesville, June 30, 1865. (29)

An Ohio Portrait

General James B. McPherson of Clyde, premiere artillerist of the Union armies, was killed near Atlanta in 1864. (30)

ders in clear prose, a quality he put to good use in his last years when he wrote his highly successful military *Memoirs*. William Tecumseh Sherman of Lancaster was one of the generals most admired by other professionals, but his name became anathema in the South after his armies cut a swath sixty miles wide across Georgia and the Carolinas. Philip Sheridan of Somerset, Perry County, was the preeminent Union cavalry leader late in the war. He was a fighter whose charismatic leadership inspired his troops to good effect. Lesser known than this triumvirate was the Union's best artillery tactician, Major General James McPherson of Clyde, killed at thirty-five in 1864 in the battle for Atlanta. Irvin McDowell, William Rosecrans, Don Carlos Buell, and numerous others deserve recognition, as do several men whose good Civil War records helped them gain political office — Rutherford B. Hayes, James A. Garfield, Benjamin Harrison, and William McKinley, as well as others.

Ohio civilians also played roles of great importance. Edwin M. Stanton of Steubenville was in the key cabinet position, secretary of war, and Salmon Chase was secretary of the treasury. John Sherman and Ben Wade wielded great influence in the Senate, though Wade was frequently impatient with Lincoln's policies. Democrats George H. Pendleton and S. S. "Sunset" Cox were able leaders in the House of Representatives. Chief financier of the North's war effort was Jay Cooke, a banker raised in Sandusky. The influence of these men on postwar events was modified by the death of President Lincoln. The complexion of the future changed when John Wilkes Booth's bullet removed Lincoln at this most critical time. Ohio mourned the dead president as his funeral train passed through the state. Cleveland erected an Oriental-style shrine, and in Columbus his casket was displayed in the state house.

The Civil War was the traumatic experience of America which has shaped national life to the present time. For years it remained the great reference point against which national affairs were measured. Certainly part of Ohio's national leadership and visibility in postwar political affairs can be traced to the attention focused on the state by her contribution to the successful effort to preserve the Union and by the activities of her people in the somewhat chaotic years of reconstruction.

The end of the war found the Union party in a quandary. Under its aegis Ohio ratified the Thirteenth Amendment abolishing slavery, but the Republican and Democratic elements within the party had no uniform view as to the role of the Negro and other pressing reconstruction issues. The Republicans harbored a "radical" group, of whom Ben Wade was most prominent, while the old-line centrists like John Sherman attempted to keep the party on a more traditional track.

On the national scene, Ohioans played prominent roles in the postwar adjustments. "Radical" Republicans like Stanton and Wade helped bring about a confrontation with President Andrew Johnson which led to his impeachment on the motion of Representative John Ashley of Ohio. Chief Justice Salmon Chase presided over Johnson's trial in the Senate, and sitting in the wings was the president *pro-tempore* of the Senate, "Bluff" Ben Wade, who missed becoming president of the United States by the margin of one vote, the margin by which Johnson was acquitted.

Within Ohio, debate about granting blacks the franchise was one of the most politically vital questions in the immediate postwar years. In the gubernatorial race of 1865, the Union party was silent on the subject, and the Democrats were staunchly opposed. General Jacob D. Cox of the Union party won the election. He believed that

John Sherman (1823–1900), brother of William, was one of the nation's outstanding legislators in the late nineteenth century. (32)

The catafalque prepared for Lincoln's body in Cleveland, 1865. (31)

(33)

An Ohio Portrait

George A. Custer (1839–1876) of New Rumley was a successful cavalry leader in the Civil War before suffering disaster at the Little Big Horn (1876). (34)

President U.S. Grant with Julia Dent Grant and friends. (35)

separation of the races was essential and favored setting aside portions of the southern states for America's blacks. Cox did support the Fourteenth Amendment, which was ratified in Ohio on a party vote. The Union party (or Union Republican party) came under control of the radicals, who pressed for an amendment to the state constitution granting the franchise to blacks. The party accepted this for its platform during the 1867 gubernatorial election. Their candidate, Rutherford B. Hayes, won over the Democrats' able Allen G. Thurman, who ran on a platform repudiating the reconstruction policies of the Congress and expressing hostility to Negro suffrage. Hayes won the governorship, but his party lost control of the general assembly, and the Negro suffrage amendment was defeated by 50,000 votes. Allen Thurman was given the senate seat formerly held by Ben Wade, thus repudiating Vallandigham, who was the Democrats' original choice for the position. The resolution of the Negro suffrage issue came in 1869. The general assembly by a narrow margin ratified the Fifteenth Amendment granting the Negro the franchise, and many thought that when this amendment took effect in 1870 the issue of Negro suffrage was settled. Nevertheless, Ohio did not bring its own constitution into conformity with the Fifteenth Amendment until 1923.

Ohioans were very much in the forefront of the Democratic party's national efforts following the war. "Gentleman George" Pendleton proposed the "Ohio Idea," sometimes called the "Ohio Plan," by which federal bonds were to be retired, where gold was not stipulated, in new issues of greenbacks. These greenbacks would have an inflationary effect on the currency, but the amount of paper in circulation would be controlled by eliminating bank notes from circulation. The "Ohio Idea" was a plank in the Democrats' 1868 platform, but with their defeat by the Republican candidate U.S. Grant, this plan was ignored. A second promising idea, Clement Vallandigham's "New Departure" — calling for acceptance of the war's verdict, universal amnesty, fiscal responsibility in government, a revenue tariff, and checks on the abuses of the spoils system — died with its originator, who accidentally shot himself.

General Grant had been a great success as a military leader, but he was inept in the political realm. He supported conservative and sometimes corrupt elements, although Grant himself was personally honest and circumspect, and these people wielded great influence in national affairs in the free-wheeling economic development of the postwar years. Reelected to a second term, he still failed to assert effective leadership. He is generally regarded as a failure in the presidency. The North's chief activity during Grant's administrations was to build on the expanded industrial base created before and during the late war, and no state was more tellingly involved in this expansion than Ohio.

(36)

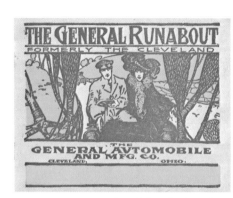

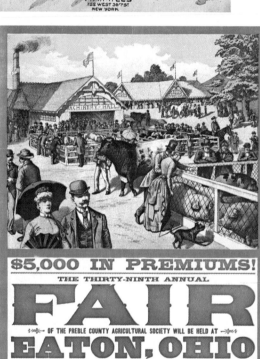

Ohio in the Era of Big Business

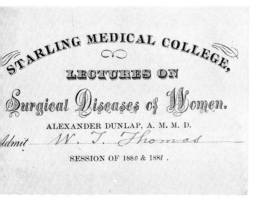

At the end of the Civil War Ohio was the nation's premier agricultural state, but her reign as queen of American agriculture was to be brief. The emergence of the great western farming states would have a profound effect on Ohio. Although the state's farms had increased in number from 143,807 in 1850 to 247,189 in 1880, the average size had shrunk during that same period from 125 acres to ninety-five. During the last quarter of the nineteenth century, however, agriculture continued to be Ohio's most important single industry, although by 1900 the value of all Ohio-manufactured products far exceeded that of her agricultural products.

The mechanization of the farm, which had started in halting fashion before the Civil War, gained great impetus because of that conflict, which made the use of machinery profitable and necessary. As mechanization progressed, Ohio prospered, for it was the nation's leading manufacturer of farm machinery until the end of the century. Mowers, reapers, seed drills, steel plows, cultivators, and binders dotted the rural landscape. Even the ordinary farmer had to become more capitalistic. In 1873 a Champaign County farmer raised a premium corn crop by methods that differed greatly from those of the pioneer farmer. The land, he said,

> was plowed about the first week in May, about twelve inches deep, with three horses and a steel plow; then harrowed and rolled well, and drilled with a Dickey drill, in rows about three and a half feet apart . . . Tended it by plowing with a double shovel and a Whitley [sic] plow, four times in all.

The new farming methods were necessary in part because Ohio had peaked as an area of virgin soil. The large, specialized corn, wheat, and hog economies of Illinois, Iowa, and other states to the west overshadowed Ohio. To compete successfully for markets, Ohio farmers began to seek out new cash crops like sugar beets; however,

An Ohio Portrait

Haggar's Corners near Bucyrus, late nineteenth century. (1)

Prize sheep at the Summit County Fair, 1885. (2)

corn remained the leading single crop. Some areas that had developed a type of specialization, such as the dairy industries of the Western Reserve, continued to practice their well-established specialties.

All those aspects of a modernized agriculture which had appeared tentatively in Ohio prior to the Civil War asserted themselves now in more thorough and pronounced fashion. Through journals, fairs, and organizations the farmer had access to improved techniques for practicing his arts and skills. In the late 1860s, Ohio took advantage of the Morrill Land Grant College Act to sell lands for the purpose of establishing an agricultural and mechanical college with the monies realized. In March, 1870, a charter was issued to the Ohio Agricultural and Mechanical College, a Board of Trustees was appointed, and within two years a campus site was selected on the old Neil farm two miles north of the center of Columbus. By the time the first students arrived in 1874, it had been decided that the college would be a comprehensive one rather than being confined solely to agriculture and engineering. Thus what is now the Ohio State University started operation.

By the 1860s, Ohio farmers were joining those of other states to form national organizations which could lobby effectively for farm interests. Many joined the Patrons of Husbandry, commonly called the Grange; this national body was founded in 1867 by Oliver H. Kelley, a government clerk in Washington D.C. The Ohio Grange was founded five years later by S. H. Ellis and within a year there were thirty local granges affiliated with the state and national organization. Farmers and their families gathered at regular meetings to socialize and to discuss ways of increasing their productivity and income. A majority of Ohio Grangers supported proposals

Frank McNeil's farm in Clermont County. (3)

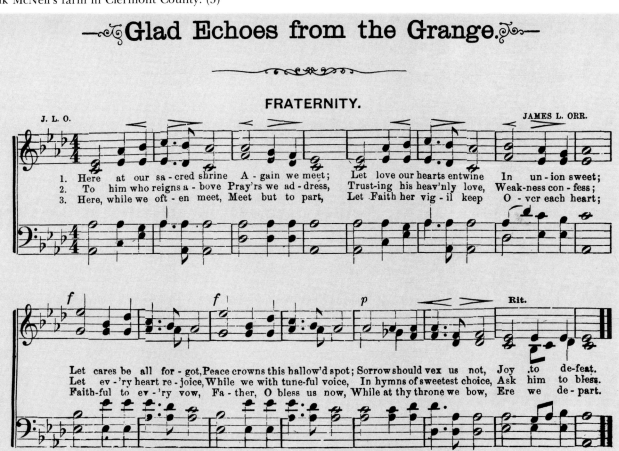

(4)

Children anticipate the first taste of new-made applebutter, ca. 1902. (5)

Threshing by steam power did not eliminate the need for considerable manpower on turn-of-the-century Ohio farms. (6)

The Henry Rutherford Johnston farm near New
Bremen (Auglaize County). (7)

Cuyahoga County, now almost entirely urbanized,
once had prosperous farms like this one
photographed in the 1930s. (8)

An Ohio Portrait

Contour plowing and planting help protect this
Muskingum County farm from erosion. (9)

to compel the railroads to reduce freight charges
and to stop those discriminatory practices which
enriched the roads at the farmers' expense. Ultimately both the state government and the national government would respond: the so-called
Granger Cases marked a turning point in state
efforts to control rates and associated consid-
erations, while an Interstate Commerce Act in
1887 was Congress' response to growing national
concern over the railroads' arbitrary practices. At
annual conventions, Grangers from across the
country passed resolutions to further regulate
railroads, tax railroad property, tax church
property and personal income, and reduce taxes
on farm lands. Much like the railroaders they
opposed, farmers were organizing to bolster their
position in the national economy.

    While these developments were moving
people into the modern age "down on the farm,"
an even more dramatic and visible development
was under way in business and industry. This
post-Civil War period was one of dramatic transi-
tions: from *laissez faire* to regulation; from water
and muscle power to steam and electric power;
from the candle, whale oil, and kerosene lamp to
electric light; from technologically primitive to
sophisticated machinery; from personally directed to corporately directed business; and from
local and regional arenas of operation to national
and even international operations. All of these
developments were gradual and not all of them
happened within any given business or industry,
so it is necessary to generalize about industrial
development with some caution, for there were
exceptions to every rule.

    As late as 1880, flour and gristmilling gener-
ated more income in Ohio than any other non-
agricultural industry; yet within a few years it

Billie Burke, the Fredericktown lamplighter, was still making his rounds at the turn of the century. (10)

A B&O Railroad train and crew, Bridgeport, 1898. (11)

Even small cities like Bucyrus were crisscrossed by power lines early in the twentieth century. (12)

An Ohio Portrait

Great manufacturing plants like the International
Harvester Company at Springfield dominated
Ohio's growing urban centers. (13)

would slip well down the list as iron, steel, machinery, clothing, oil, and a host of other rivals challenged it for the lead. Cincinnati was still the preeminent industrial center of Ohio in the immediate post-war period. It was the third most productive manufacturing city in America. Hundreds of manufacturing activities were located in the Queen City, and they still clustered around the big six that had made the city famous — clothing, foundries, furniture, distilleries and breweries, printing and publishing, and meat packing. These businesses accounted for more than half of the total capital invested in manufacturing and nearly half of the labor force in the city. Some of Cincinnati's industries such as meat packing were on a downhill slide, while others like soap products were in the wings, about to appear center stage when an effective national marketing apparatus had been developed.

Akron was more typical of Ohio's industrial

cities. It had boomed during the war until its 5,000 citizens qualified it as a city in 1865. Akron's population doubled in the next five years, and by the end of the century, it was a diverse manufacturing city of nearly 50,000 persons. In the 1880s Akron was a world leader in cereal milling, clay products (especially vitrified pipe and brick), matches, and farm machinery. In addition there was an iron company, a knife works, and a chain works, each of which served the farm machinery factories. An offbeat little industry, the manufacture of fishing tackle, had begun an operation that would make the city famous among anglers. By the end of the century Akron boasted the world's largest publishing plant. Breweries, carriage makers, machine shops, and a host of small entrepreneurial activities rounded out its industrial scene. Rubber, the item for which the city is internationally renowned, made its appearance in 1870 when Dr. B. F. Goodrich

Building automobile tires, Akron, ca. 1922. (14)

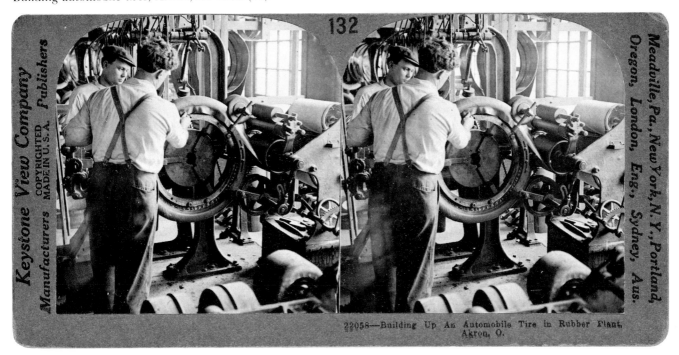

Cycling was an exciting pastime in 1885, but it also
helped create new business for the metals and
rubber industries. (15)

Women cycling enthusiasts and friends in the late
nineteenth century. (16)

An Ohio Portrait

A glassworks at Rossford, ca. 1922. (17)

By the early twentieth century, industrial complexes sprawled through Ohio's cities. Goodyear's Akron plants are located along the Little Cuyahoga River. In the background is the huge Goodyear Zeppelin Dock (1930s). (18)

An industrial company office. The White Sewing Machine Company, Cleveland, 1876. (19)

relocated his small rubber factory in Akron to take advantage of water, transportation, an available labor force, and the enthusiasm generated in a vigorous industrial environment. However, Goodrich's business was a tiny venture until the bicycle craze of the 1890s started to put America on rubber-tired wheels. Industrial expansion was equally visible in Dayton, Columbus, Toledo, Canton, and many other smaller cities which experienced great growth well into the twentieth century.

One reason Ohio's industrial life flourished at this time was its leadership in several of the great growth industries of that period — steel, oil, machinery, and later automobiles, rubber, industrial glass, business machines, and soaps. Since Ohio was in on the ground floor of these industries, its capital was invested in new plants as efficient as those found anywhere, its labor costs were competitive with those in similar industries elsewhere, and its proximity to raw materials and access to markets was excellent. Thus new money poured into the state's industrial coffers.

The city which profited most dramatically from the new growth industries was Cleveland, a key city in the expansion of the steel industry and oil refining. Its position as a port on the massive inland waterway of the Great Lakes; its service by trunk line railroads; and its nearness to coal, limestone, and oil had much to do with the emergence of Cleveland as Ohio's premier manufacturing city. These locational advantages would have been lost, however, had it not been for the ambition and insight of an impressive group of entrepreneurs who assembled the capital required to take advantage of business opportunities. Most dramatic was the lead taken by Cleveland capitalists in opening the rich iron ore deposits of the Lake Superior region and then building the Great Lakes fleets which carried this

Old skills were essential to the glass industry. (20)

A Lancaster glass factory, ca. 1890. (21)

The United States Shoe Corporation, Chillicothe, 1930s. (22)

Dayton's National Cash Register employees on the assembly line. (23)

An Ohio Portrait

The Maumee River at Toledo attracted heavy industries. (25)

Not all work was for hearth and home. This structure, reputed to be a floating bordello, was well known to some Lake Erie sailors in the late nineteenth century. (24)

Cleveland's steelmills (above) were served by lake freighters while Ohio Valley mills relied on rail and river transport (below). (26) (27)

Conneaut, one of Ohio's many small lake ports, ca. 1896. (28)

The old Standard Oil Company refinery, Cleveland, 1889. (29)

Lima was famous for the manufacture of locomotives. (30)

ore to northeastern Ohio and western Pennsylvania. There iron ore met the coal (coke) and limestone required for the smelting process. To this day, Cleveland names like Olgebay, Norton, Mather, Hanna, and Bradley are still associated with steel, coal, and lake shipping, although others who once figured prominently, especially Rockefeller, have disappeared from the contemporary scene.

Lake shipping brought jobs and reasonable wages to a host of small port towns like Conneaut, Ashtabula, Fairport Harbor, Lorain, Huron, Sandusky, and to larger cities like Toledo and Cleveland. Several profited from shipbuilding, especially Lorain where yards along the Black River gave birth to many giant ore carriers. The ores they hauled fed mills in Cleveland's "Flats," Lorain, the Mahoning Valley, the upper Ohio Valley, Canton, and Massillon. As the railroads converted to steel rails in the late nineteenth century and as wood and other materials increasingly gave way to steel, Ohio's economy boomed in response to the demand.

Geography and the availability of capital also played a part in Cleveland's rise as an oil refining center. The first commercially exploited oil field in America was located in the northwest corner of Pennsylvania about equidistant from Buffalo, Pittsburgh, and Cleveland. Each of these cities had several small refineries which processed barrels of crude, and each expected to exploit an ever larger part of the refining activity. A young wholesale grocery merchant, John D. Rockefeller, was responsible for bringing this rich industrial prize to Cleveland. He consolidated Cleveland's small refineries into a growing giant — the Standard Oil Company. Chartered in Ohio in 1870, Standard Oil was the prototype of that new form of business consolidation called a "trust." By controlling all aspects of the refining business,

John D. Rockefeller out for a spin. (31)

The Republic Steel Company's Warren plant. (32)

including sales, Standard Oil secured great clout which allowed it to buy or bully its competitors. Ultimately Standard claimed about 90 percent of the oil refining business in America and expanded into all facets of the complex petroleum industry. Jealous rivals and thoughtful citizens were concerned about Rockefeller's extraordinary power. An effort to limit this power under Ohio law failed in the late nineteenth century, but some years later, as the result of federal trust-busting activity, Standard Oil was ordered dissolved into component parts.

The name Rockefeller had become synonymous with enormous wealth. He and his associates, plus the larger business community of Cleveland, displayed a new-found elegance in palatial houses along "millionaires row" on Euclid Avenue as well as in their estates both in the Cleveland area and elsewhere in the country. This visible frosting was evidence of Cleveland's industrial prominence and power. Still primarily raw and untamed, vigorous and diffuse, Cleveland had passed Cincinnati as the metropolis of Ohio by the end of the century. Its maturing as a city with some amenities and culture had to wait until the great industrial machine was running well, as was the case with all other Ohio boom towns of the industrial age.

While new industries were flexing their muscles, many of Ohio's traditional enterprises were falling on hard times. Grain and cereal milling tended to move west closer to the source of supply. Meat packing deserted centers like Cincinnati for greater enterprises in Chicago, Omaha, and Kansas City. In large part the farm machinery business also went west to Chicago and Moline, for it was more economical to assemble these machines close to an increasingly western market. With the farm machinery industry went the supplier industries: the knife, chain, and binder twine factories.

Economic activity shifted within Ohio at times with the discovery of new potentials, such as the development of the oil and natural gas fields of western Ohio in the late eighties. Also important was the depletion of old sources of raw materials, such as coal or clay, and the opening of new fields elsewhere in the state. The locations of some of the newly developing businesses were transient, as various locales competed for them. Many Ohio towns appeared to be in the race to become important centers of the new automobile industry. Cleveland succeeded to a remarkable degree with Winton, Stearns, Packard, and scores of other firms, but eventually lost out to Detroit. Toledo was in the race briefly, producing a fairly limited number of cars. Toledo's contribution to the automotive industry was in supplying parts, such as glass, spark plugs, and hundreds of key components. Dayton became still another major automotive supply center. Toledo and Akron won out over the efforts of cities in other states to capture the glass and rubber industries. Thus the ebb and flow of industrial development dominated Ohio's economic life into the twentieth century.

The growth of business enterprise from a local to a national level was the result of many conditions working together. One of these conditions was the growth of science and technology. In the scientific realm only a number of Ohioans made major contributions during the nineteenth century. Earliest among them were men like Dr. Daniel Drake, the Cincinnati physician whose intellectual curiosity took him into many fields of investigation; Jared Kirtland, who helped found the Cleveland Medical College; Charles Whittlesey, an archeologist and geologist; William Sullivant, a practical engineer who excelled as a botanist; Ormsby Mitchell, a Kentucky-born astronomer who built an astronomical observatory in Cincinnati; and W. W.

Complex machines used by the American Steel Wire Company in the 1930s. (33)

F. S. Harmer in the automobile he invented, 1906. (34)

Charles Whittlesey (1808–1886) revealed to Ohioans the story of their land and of its prehistoric peoples. (35)

Mather, who established the Ohio Geological Survey in 1837. This survey, with its on-again, off-again history, was perhaps the state's chief contribution to science in the nineteenth century.

A considerable proportion of the early men of science had some training as physicians, and a number were associated with medical education. Not until 1900, however, did Ohio carefully regulate the quality of medical education required for a practicing physician, when it decreed that candidates for medical licenses must graduate from accredited medical colleges and also pass examinations given by the state board of registration. This law and succeeding modifications weeded out several medical schools and had the effect of affiliating medical and dental schools with large universities. In medical science, Dr. George Crile of the Cleveland Clinic was among those with well-deserved national and international reputations.

Another of Ohio's men of science, Thomas Mendenhall, defined the ampere, volt, and ohm, but his work in electricity was only part of his broad interest in scientific matters and practical administrative affairs. Another physicist, Arthur Compton of Wooster, was awarded the Nobel Prize in Physics in 1927. His brother Karl also was distinguished as a scientist. Both brothers served as university presidents, Arthur at Washington University and Karl at the Massachusetts Institute of Technology.

Perhaps better known to the public at large than the men who worked with the fundamental nature of science were those hundreds of inventors and technicians whose creations had obvious economic impact. Foremost among Ohio inventors, of course, is Thomas A. Edison. Born in Milan in Huron County, he accomplished his great work in electricity outside the confines of the Buckeye State. Charles Brush, another

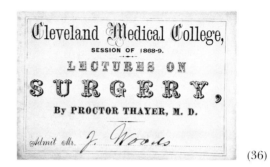

The Ohio Medical College, shown here about 1900, became the Ohio State University Medical School. (37)

(36)

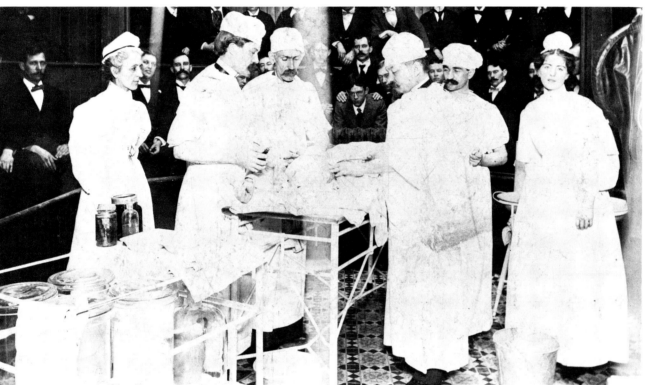

(39)

Park Street Medical School (Columbus), class in dentistry. (38)

An Ohio Portrait

Howard Chandler Christy's idealized Edison, and
(below) the inventor at rest. (40) (43)

Nela Park (Cleveland), a lighting research
laboratory in a campus setting, as it looked in the
1930s. (41)

The A. M. Allen Electric Company provided
services to early Akron motorists. (42)

Charles F. Brush (1849–1929) brought electric
lights to American streets. (44)

pioneer in the investigation of electrical phenomena, was a Clevelander who did much of his work there. In 1879 he demonstrated in that city the use of arc lights for street illumination. Benjamin Lamme, born near Springfield and educated at Ohio State, was foremost in the improvement of electrical machinery. Still another investigator of electrical devices was Elisha Gray of Belmont County, who contended with Alexander Graham Bell for recognition as the inventor of the telephone. Charles Hall, discoverer of an electrolytic process for separating aluminum from its ore, became the great benefactor of Oberlin College after his discovery made millions. Charles Kettering of Loudonville is said to have put the American woman in the driver's seat because he invented a self-starter for automobiles. He became the inventive genius behind General Motors and was long associated with the Dayton Engineering Laboratories Company (Delco), a chief supplier to the automotive industry. A seminal development that pioneered a whole new dimension of transportation and human interaction was the work of Wilbur and Orville Wright of Dayton. After years of trial and error, the brothers achieved powered flight in 1903 at Kitty Hawk, North Carolina, and a new era in human affairs began.

These names appear on everybody's list of Ohio innovators, but scores of other little-known inventors made contributions which enabled great industries to progress: Michael Owens in glass; Lewis Miller and William Whiteley in farm machinery; James Ritty and Theodore Schirmer in business machines; John Lambert, Alexander Winton, James Packard, and scores of others in gasoline-powered automobiles; Arthur Marks in rubber reclaiming; John Case in milling machinery; and Charles Harris in printing machinery. The list could go on indefinitely.

Charles F. Kettering (1876–1958), inventive genius of the automotive industry. (45)

Pearl Hopley driving the family car fitted out for her father's (State Senator James C. Hopley) campaign. (46)

An Ohio Portrait

Orville Wright flying a single propeller pusher, Dayton, ca. 1912. (47)

Katherine and Wilbur Wright in a plane, with Orville Wright looking on, ca. 1909. (48)

Alexander Winton (1860–1932) of Cleveland made the first reliable automobile. (49)

In many old railroad stations, passengers, baggage, and trains vied for space. The Union Depot, Akron, in the 1930s. (51)

Horsepower and steam power are both represented in this picture from Plymouth (Huron County). (50)

Contributing much to the expansion of Ohio business was a transportation system that increasingly tied various parts of the state together and connected Ohio with national markets. The railroad was still preeminent. A further consolidation of lines into through systems, the extension of branch lines into mining and rural regions, and diversification of equipment made the railroad the great transporter of goods and of people.

In the late nineteenth century the electric street railway and the interurban made their appearances. Horse-drawn carriages running on tracks were already a feature of many Ohio cities, but these "herdics" were slow, limited in range, and could not carry heavy loads. Electric power

James W. Packard manufactured his first automobile in Warren, 1899. (52)

An Ohio Portrait

Cincinnati's Vine Street and McMicken Avenue horsedrawn streetcar, ca. 1880. (53)

Street trolley in Bucyrus, ca. 1910 (54)

Street scene in Canton, ca. 1896. (55)

Cleveland's trolley system made a loop in Public Square in the early twentieth century. (56)

enabled cities to accommodate trolley systems which could effectively extend services to hitherto neglected areas and those undeveloped areas just beyond the city limits. Population expanded along the trolley lines in Cincinnati, Cleveland, Toledo, Akron, and most other Ohio cities. The owners and developers of these street railway systems often worked in close conjunction with real estate developers and with the owners of amusement parks or recreational facilities on the outskirts of the main population centers. Factory workers who had lived close to their places of employment — a necessity when everyone walked to work — could consider the prospect of locating farther away from the grime and filth surrounding most factories. The flight away from factory neighborhoods was modest and highly selective, however, since there were economic and social constraints restricting the movement of working men and women into new locations. The growth of trolley transportation cluttered the spaces over streets with a new set of wires to add to the web created by existing electrical services, and ultimately the trolley contributed to traffic congestion. On the positive side, however, trolleys brought mobility to the people and profits to the operators and the manufacturers of equipment. In a short time street railways became essential to the life of the larger communities, a fact that gave opportunity for some greedy owners and operators to gouge the public for whatever the traffic would bear. There were "traction wars" in Ohio and around the nation as competing operators strove to gain and preserve a monopoly in this potentially lucrative business.

The interurban is Ohio's child. Trolleys which moved between cities, connecting one settled area with another and with the hinterlands between, were a feature of the Ohio landscape from 1895 to 1940. In 1889 a car powered by an

electric motor traveled two miles between Alliance and Mt. Union (now a part of Alliance), but the first true interurban was the Akron, Bedford, and Cleveland (ABC) Line organized in 1895. Its cars ran over a twenty-seven mile route from Akron, through Cuyahoga Falls, to Newburg on the southern edge of Cleveland. From this modest beginning a great web of lines reached out from all the major population centers of the state and from most of the lesser centers as well. Ohio led the nation in the number of miles, 2,798, in its interurban system. Interurbans reached areas not served by the railroads; their passenger and freight services did much to end rural isolation. A Seville resident explained in 1913 that "shoppers can take advantage of Cleveland sales; farmers can expect their produce to arrive in city markets in good condition; and everybody can enjoy an outing to a motion-picture show."

The interurban also tended to create its own clientele. People moved into suburban areas that were formerly too distant from their jobs, and the land surrounding cities like Cleveland became urbanized for miles beyond the city limits. In the cities, traction terminals were busy places of fas-

Interurban car of the Lakeshore line at the Sandusky station, 1927. (57)

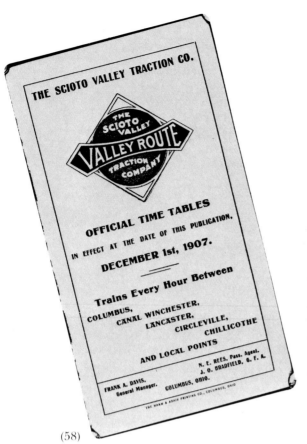

(58)

An outing on the trolley, probably near Bucyrus. (59)

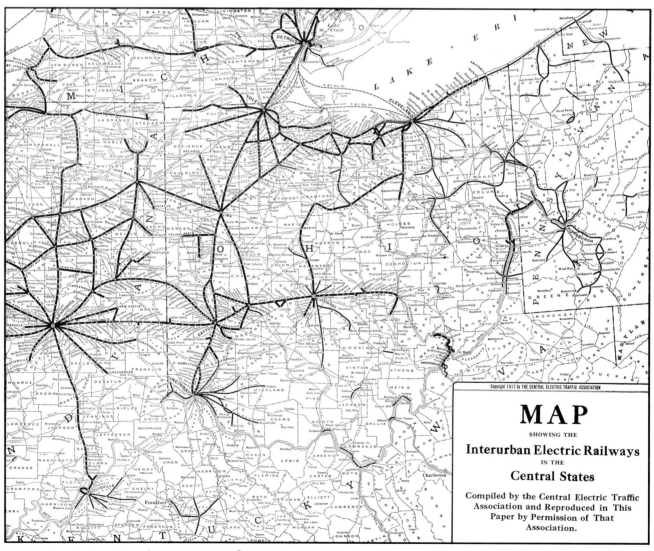

Ohio's interurbans were an important part of a
regional transportation network. (60)

Cincinnati's West Fifth Street, ca. 1898. (61)

Ohio in the Era of Big Business

Ohio River railroad bridge construction, ca. 1910. (62)

Rocky River Dummy Railroad connected West 65th Street Cleveland and Rocky River, ca. 1870. (64)

L.E. & W. Railroad station at Amsden (Seneca County), ca. 1908. (63)

(65)

An Ohio Portrait

The National Road at Linnville (Licking County) in
the late nineteenth century. (66)

Scene along Route 60, Erie County, 1924. (67)

cination to little boys and probably to grown men
whose sense of adventure and wanderlust was
stimulated by the "cars." Ironically, the fine service provided by some of these interurban lines
allowed a person to travel more quickly between
certain points than is now possible many years
after "improvements" — such as the automobile
and the highway — eliminated the electrified trolley and rail lines from Ohio.

Ohioans who remember the abysmal condition of so many of the state's roads in pre-World
War II days might be surprised to know that the
state was a pioneer in the business of paving
roads. Macadam pavement had been used for
generations, sparingly of course, but it was not
wholly satisfactory in Ohio, where the freeze-
thaw cycle of winter and spring damaged the
pavement almost as soon as it was laid. In 1892 a
new type of road pavement, concrete, was tried
near Bellefontaine, the first such experiment in
the United States. The possibilities afforded by
the new process seemed promising, and after the
advent of the automobile there was reason to
press ahead with it. Paving was a cumbersome
and expensive process in the days before great
earth-moving and paving machines mechanized
the process. Horse drags and manpower were
used to prepare roadbeds. The hilly portions of
the state required cutting and filling, while much
of Ohio's flat land was so wet that roadbeds had to
be graded up considerably. Most of the first roads
paved with concrete were paved on one side only.
Everyone wanted to drive on the paved lane, so
when two cars met, the one that had claim to the
pavement stayed on it while the other vehicle
moved off into the dirt lane.

Brick was a popular paving material in Ohio.
Readily available, it was therefore inexpensive.
The use of bricks kept Ohio kilns lighted and
provided income and jobs for local people. To

(68)

A 1908 Hupmobile. (70)

The use of mechanized equipment speeded the development of a modern highway system. A Cleveland tractor pulls a Galion scraper. (69) (71)

When motorbusses displaced interurbans, the bus
lines often took over the carbarns as well. (72)

Many Ohio highways were paved on one side only
in the early twentieth century. (73)

Busses stopped for passengers wherever they were
in 1924. (74)

Brick was an important paving material into the
1930s. These bricklayers are working in Alliance,
1936. (75)

The Cincinnati & Louisville railroad bridge spanned the Ohio River at Cincinnati. (76)

this day, especially in the eastern clay counties, one can find old brick roads that have survived the ravages of time, weather, and traffic even though they may swell and dip a little. Countless other brick roads have been paved with "blacktop," thus continuing to serve as a foundation for modern traffic.

The growth of big business and the evolution from local to national markets also must be considered from the perspective of the worker — the person whose skills and energies were harnessed to the impersonal demands of the industrial process. Well before the Civil War a small but active movement to organize labor had developed. The first "union" in Ohio emerged when the Dayton Mechanics' Society was formed in 1813. It was followed soon, especially in Cincinnati, by a number of other societies. In addition to improved working conditions some of the early societies promoted universal education, equal taxation on property, revision of the military system, and abolition of licensed monopolies, imprisonment for debt, and capital punishment. Every downturn of the economy affected these groups. Employers laid off workers, and the union was unable to bring effective action to the assistance of the worker. The Panic of 1837 almost wiped out Ohio's early labor movement.

In 1852 the general assembly passed a law to standardize the ten-hour working day and replace the old sunup-to-sundown limits. At the same time the legislature passed the nation's first law regulating working hours for women and children, but the law was not enforced and remained ineffective. During and following the Civil War a surge of new, essentially local labor organizations developed. In 1869 the new national organization, the Knights of Labor — a group that welcomed all working people except whiskey sellers, professional gamblers, lawyers,

Ohio River bridge under construction at Marietta. (77)

The Silver Bridge near Gallipolis, built in 1926, collapsed in 1967 with the loss of 46 lives. (78)

The Tom Greene and Betsy Ann race near Cincinnati. (79)

Child labor at the White Sewing Machine Company,
Cleveland, ca. 1880. (80)

The New Straitsville mine (Perry County) has
burned for nearly a century. Scene in the 1930s
near Plummer Hill. (81)

and bankers — moved effectively into Ohio, where it soon claimed thousands of members. The Panic of 1873, which endured for five years, temporarily demolished union influence in Ohio, but by 1885 there were 25,000 Knights of Labor in Cincinnati alone. Cincinnati has quite a history of labor violence. In the great railroad strike of 1877 the governor sent militia to that city and to Newark.

Other labor violence was most evident in the mining districts. Miners struck in Summit, Stark, and Wayne counties in the 1870s and 1880s, but the most traumatic of these strikes occurred in 1884 in the Hocking Valley where mining was the backbone of the economy. There a bitter contest ensued when strikebreakers were set upon by hungry miners who intimidated the strikebreakers, ruined mine property, and set mines on fire. Five mine cars loaded with burning coal were shoved down mine tunnels in New Straitsville in Perry County, and the fire that resulted has burned ever since, consuming uncounted millions of tons of coal. The importance of coal to Ohio's industrial expansion can hardly be overestimated.

In 1886 at a Columbus convention, some twenty-five unions combined to form the American Federation of Trades and Labor, with Samuel Gompers as president. This federation of craft unions became the most powerful labor voice in America, but first it had to weather many stormy years of inner turmoil and outer attack. A Cochocton schoolteacher, William Green, became its long-time president in the twentieth century. Also in Columbus in 1889, two groups representing miners joined to form the United Mine Workers of America, which ultimately came to dominate the mining industry and to be one of the most effective and innovative of American labor unions.

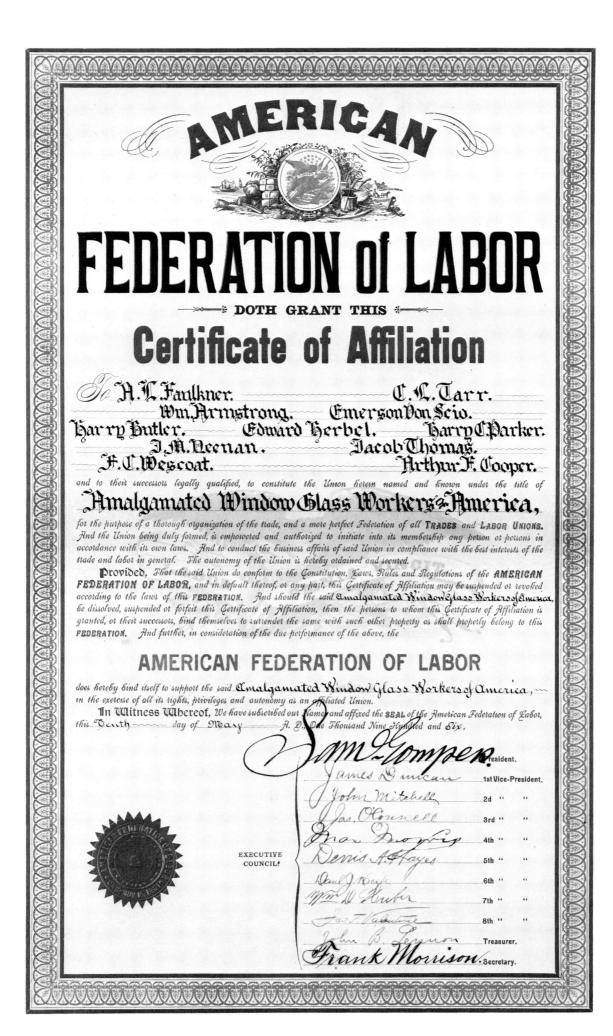

AMERICAN
FEDERATION of LABOR

DOTH GRANT THIS
Certificate of Affiliation

To A. L. Faulkner.   C. L. Tarr.
    Wm. Armstrong.   Emerson Von Scio.
Harry Butler.   Edward Herbel.   Harry C. Parker.
        J. M. Deenan.   Jacob Thomas.
    F. C. Wescoat.   Arthur F. Cooper.

and to their successors legally qualified, to constitute the Union herein named and known under the title of

Amalgamated Window Glass Workers of America,

for the purpose of a thorough organization of the trade, and a more perfect Federation of all TRADES and LABOR UNIONS. And the Union being duly formed, is empowered and authorized to initiate into its membership any person or persons in accordance with its own laws. And to conduct the business affairs of said Union in compliance with the best interests of the trade and labor in general. The autonomy of the Union is hereby ordained and secured.

Provided, That the said Union do conform to the Constitution, Laws, Rules and Regulations of the AMERICAN FEDERATION OF LABOR, and in default thereof, or any part, this Certificate of Affiliation may be suspended or revoked according to the laws of this FEDERATION. And should the said Amalgamated Window Glass Workers of America, be dissolved, suspended or forfeit this Certificate of Affiliation, then the persons to whom this Certificate of Affiliation is granted, or their successors, bind themselves to surrender the same with such other property as shall properly belong to this FEDERATION. And further, in consideration of the due performance of the above, the

AMERICAN FEDERATION OF LABOR

does hereby bind itself to support the said Amalgamated Window Glass Workers of America, in the exercise of all its rights, privileges and autonomy as an affiliated Union.

In Witness Whereof, We have subscribed our Names and affixed the SEAL of the American Federation of Labor, this Tenth day of May A. D., One Thousand Nine Hundred and Six.

Sam L Gompers President.

James Duncan 1st Vice-President.

John Mitchell 2d " "

Jas. O'Connell 3rd " "

Max Morris 4th " "

Denis A. Hayes 5th " "

Danl J. Keefe 6th " "

Wm D Huber 7th " "

Jos. F. Valentine 8th " "

John B. Lennon Treasurer.

Frank Morrison Secretary.

EXECUTIVE
COUNCIL:

South Sycamore Street barricade, Cincinnati riot, 1884. (83)

(84)

Ohio National Guardsmen near the Music Hall during Cincinnati's 1884 riot in which more than 300 persons were killed or wounded. (85)

The mining towns of southern and eastern Ohio were sometimes bleak and deprived of all amenities as in the case of this Hocking Valley homesite. (86)

The Blue Bell mine near Strasburg (Tuscarawas County). (87)

Again labor's cause was set back temporarily by economic disaster. The prolonged Panic of 1893 had a serious impact on Ohio. Many industries already weakened by shifting markets and raiding trusts were disappearing from the Ohio scene, and jobs went with them. Unemployment increased at an alarming rate. One citizen who had an imaginative scheme for retrieving the situation was Jacob Coxey, a Massillon businessman who organized a march on Washington by what was forever after known as "Coxey's Army," a group that included his daughter dressed in flowing gown and his son, "Legal Tender" Coxey. What Coxey advocated — using federal money to make work for the unemployed — was later used on a grand scale during the depression of the 1930s, but the scheme was hooted at by conservatives and got no real hearing. In Youngstown, however, an imaginative mayor secured funds to put unemployed steelworkers to work to create the beginnings of that city's great Mill Creek Park, an adornment to the entire community.

Several strikes in the early twentieth century brought the Industrial Workers of the World, the "Wobblies," to Ohio towns. Foremost among these were the Youngstown steel strike of 1905 and the Akron rubber strike of 1913. In the latter instance I.W.W. leader "Big Bill" Haywood himself came to town to lead the strikers. The rubber workers were disturbed by the steady encroachment of machines which replaced men on production lines. The workers were not well organized despite the I.W.W. When local citizens formed "peace" squads armed with billy clubs to counteract the marching lines of strikers, tempers were kept cool by a mayor who ordered all saloons closed. The strike fizzled out with only minor concessions to the workers.

Some progress had been made on the legisla-

The Hanna Coal Company, still one of Ohio's major producers, represents the modern counterpart of old-fashioned coal mining. (88)

This shot in a Hocking Valley coal mine may be the first "flash-light" photograph taken inside a mine. (89)

An Ohio Portrait

Coxey's Army passing the work house, Canton, March 25, 1894. (90)

"General" Coxey and his secretary arriving at camp. (91)

tive front in the late nineteenth and early twentieth centuries. Laws for minimum wages, safe working conditions, and workmen's compensation were established. The movement for the eight-hour day won a point when it became the standard for workers in government offices and on state payrolls. Children were finally out of the mines and off the production lines, although there were still children doing work that later generations would deplore. As elsewhere, Ohio women faced discrimination in the job market; however World War I provided jobs in many industries that had previously excluded them. They did not commonly receive equal pay for equal work, and society at large preferred to think that a woman's place was in the home or in some genteel occupation like schoolteaching.

After World War I, Ohio's industrial scene started a shift, almost imperceptible at first, that would eventually find it harboring an aging in-

dustrial plant, locked to a relatively high wage scale, and thus increasingly having to operate at a competitive disadvantage. Ohio would no longer enjoy the luxury of riding the great new growth industries to economic glory; instead, it would fight for its life in the economic markets of the nation and the world.

The great expansion of America's economic base in the period from the Civil War through World War I attracted new people into industrial cities and towns in unprecedented numbers. With mass production techniques and the mechanization of industry, unskilled workers could move directly into the labor force. Even before they knew the English language many newcomers with strong backs and willing spirits found themselves operating presses; assembling parts; stitching clothes, shoes, and leather goods; or burrowing into the earth for coal, clay, salt, and limestone. The most conspicuous portion of

Ohio in the Era of Big Business

Hungarians loading steel rails, Conneaut, ca. 1898. (92)

the new labor force coming into Ohio cities was of the so-called "new immigration," people from central, southern, and eastern Europe whose cultural inheritance set them apart from the early immigration dominated by persons from northern and western Europe.

Prominent among the new immigrants were Poles, Hungarians, Slovaks, Slovenes, Bohemians (Czechs), Italians, Greeks, Serbs, Croats, Jews from Russia and Poland, Ukranians, Romanians, Bulgarians, Macedonians, Montenegrins, and Albanians. By the tens of thousands they came to Ohio. The steel cities and mining regions in particular received large numbers of the newcomers. In Guernsey and Noble counties the "old immigrants" — the English, Scots-Irish, Scots, Welsh, and Channel Islanders — were joined in the late nineteenth and early twentieth centuries by Poles, Hungarians, Russians and various Slavic peoples. Some company mining towns in Hocking, Perry, and Athens counties were populated almost entirely by these new arrivals. In the early twentieth century more than half of Cleveland's people were foreign-born, and that bustling city was becoming a kaleidoscope of ethnic neighborhoods where street signs, advertising signs, and newspapers were in the language of the immigrants. Since the jobs were in the cities, people clustered there. Some groups, notably the Jews and the Italians, have been overwhelmingly identified with city life in America, while many other groups were ultimately represented in the small towns and rural areas.

Earlier immigrant concentrations, especially the Irish and German, were already well established by the time these newcomers arrived. The Irish displayed a talent for municipal politics, and in the larger cities they often formed the core of the police and fire departments. The Germans brought to Ohio a great deal of cultural baggage

including their churches, German language newspapers, singing clubs, athletic clubs, and social organizations. While they turned to business in the cities, tens of thousands settled on the land and became part of Ohio's agricultural scene. They were widely scattered throughout the state, but Cincinnati was possibly the city most visibly influenced by the Germans, and west-central Ohio the rural area most influenced. Even today towns, like Minster, New Bremen, and Maria Stein are reminiscent of their German origins.

In time, the new immigrants would compete successfully for recognition and for leadership in government and business. For the moment, however, they clustered together with their own kind in tight-knit ethnic communities. Here they found whatever comfort was available in the midst of an indifferent or openly hostile established society. Cleveland, the Ohio city most dramatically affected by this immigration, developed the classic pattern of ethnic neighborhoods. The Irish dominated "Shanty Town," "Vinegar Hill," "The Triangle," and "The Flats." Bohemian (Czech) settlements were "Little Cuba" and the "Cabbage Patch," the latter being close by an area south of Public Square called the "Haymarket," in which lived Italians, Negroes, and Jews. "Little Poland" and "Dutch Hill" would seem to be self-explanatory, but one might not guess that "Murray Hill" was Italian. Cleveland had no true Chinatown, only a "Dopetown," as the small Chinese district was called. The Chinese were not the only non-Europeans in Cleveland, for the city also received small numbers of Africans, West Indians, Mexicans, Japanese, and Turks. In all, more than forty-eight nationalities speaking more than forty different languages were found in Cleveland by the end of the century.

In 1914 about one-third of Cleveland's

An Ohio Portrait

Literacy and citizenship class, Mingo Junction
(Jefferson County), 1939. (93)

An Italian saloon, Cleveland, early twentieth
century. (94)

Orange Avenue, Cleveland, 1910. (95)

Palumbo Yard, Cleveland, 1925. (96)

people were Roman Catholic; others subscribed to the Eastern Rite or the Greek Orthodox faith. Nearly all of these church-going people were of recent immigrant stock. Their impact was profound in education. Failing to make the established public school system responsive to their wishes and desires, Roman Catholics and to a lesser extent Lutherans, established a parallel system of parochial schools. All of Ohio's large cities have substantial parochial school systems, usually organized into diocesan systems. One would have to look hard, indeed, to find any area of the modern state where parochial schooling is not available.

The swell of overseas immigrants to Ohio frequently conceals the equally large and significant internal migration, which brought hundreds of thousands of rural and small-town Ohioans to the cities and also great numbers of whites and blacks from Appalachia and the rural South. The intrastate migration is impossible to follow since it was and is constantly occurring on such a casual basis that it passes unnoticed. The more visible flood of people from outside Ohio tended to concentrate on certain target cities and was subject to much commentary while under way; hence people were aware of it.

Appalachian whites came in greatest concentration to cities such as Columbus and Dayton, whose period of expansion came at a time when overseas immigration was slowed by war or depressed economic conditions. Akron experienced the most dramatic influx during 1910-1920, when it was reputedly the "fastest growing city in America." The great rubber boom, fueled by the automobile and by the wartime economy, caused Akron to grow from a city of about 70,000 in 1910 to one of 208,000 in 1920; most of the newcomers were whites from Appalachia, including southern Ohio. Akron, it was said, was a

Before World War II, many workers still lived within walking distance of the industrial plants where they worked. (97)

A religious festival in Cleveland's "little Italy," 1930s. (98)

The R. A. Kelly Company, Xenia Machine Works, ca. 1895. (99)

Stevedores resting on the Ohio River waterfront. (100)

"hick-town" full of "hillbillies," and there were poor jokes made about it being the "capital of West Virginia."

The city outgrew itself. People with large lots living near downtown, assured of a quick sale, often built houses in their own backyards. Two or three story "duplexes" and apartments were crowded side by side on short, dead end "blind courts." Local landladies instituted a "warm bed" policy, often renting a bed for an eight-hour shift, three shifts every twenty-four hours. Not only were all city facilities overextended, it was difficult to secure taxes for relief because so many of the newcomers were not property owners or did not intend to stay in the alien environment of the city and could see no reason to pay taxes for schools, streets, and city services they probably would never need. To this day Akron is still trying to catch up with business left over from that period of overheated growth, including sewers, street paving, and mid-town recreational areas.

Cleveland, looking toward the heights, ca. 1870. (101)

Black migration into Ohio was also stimulated by the availability of jobs in the World War I era. Unlike southern whites, southern blacks were seldom recruited by agents of Ohio's expanding industries. They came on their own. Racist attitudes and assumptions still blocked opportunity, and in those businesses which employed black workers, only the least-skilled jobs were readily available to them. A chance to learn skills and to advance on merit was still in the future for most black working men. Black women sometimes found it easier to obtain jobs than did black men, but only because there was always a place for domestics. Despite the bleak picture for most blacks, a few were prospering in the professions, in newspaper, religious, and entertainment activities, and gradually in skilled positions in the machine trades and building trades.

City growth was accompanied by all the familiar kinds of urban growing pains, but one tends to forget how unbelievably squalid and violent the cities of an earlier time were. Examples of the filth and vice that were the daily lot of so many immigrants are readily available. A Cleveland newspaper report in the late nineteenth century described a "nest of Italians" located in a building on St. Clair Street: behind the "bar room" in the front of the building was a large room used as a dining room, kitchen, sitting room and store room, while a large calico curtain concealed ten bedsteads. The reporter found a woman cooking, an old man sleeping, and about fifteen younger men who were talking in the room at the same time, while just outside the door "lay a chubby little vagabond asleep in the sun covered with flies." Near him was "a heap of manure and a dead kitten." Generally this boarding house contained from twenty to forty individuals. The sight of all the miserable people seen in "the various low haunts" of the city, said the reporter, "excites

Substandard housing, a concommitant of social and personal malaise. (102)

in the visitor not only feelings of disgust but pity."

> They suffer in these hovels from every loathsome disease engendered by vice and filth, but equally as much from lack of ventilation and poor diet. The health officer may visit them and order them to change their style of living, but it is not sufficient to say: "Be thou clean" and then go your way without providing any means for carrying out the order. . . . The rent many of them pay for even the little room they now occupy taxes them severely. How then can their condition be alleviated? Certainly it cannot be done in their present location. They should be provided with small houses and cheap rent in the outskirts of the city, where they are not crowded together in one-fifth the space they ought to occupy . . .

Crowded conditions, poverty, ignorance, and disease were familiar problems for those who tried to manage the affairs of the burgeoning cities. Crime was another familiar problem. Contemporaries who think crime in the cities is a phenomenon of recent years are simply not acquainted with the record. In several Ohio cities in the late nineteenth and early twentieth centuries, concern over widespread crime inflamed public resentment into urban riots. Both Springfield and Akron suffered in this fashion, but the 1884

riot in Cincinnati outdid them in scope and violence. In the summer of 1883 Cincinnati experienced nine murders in nine successive days. Officials were not conspicuously successful in finding and punishing the criminals; of some fifty men tried for murder, nearly half were freed. Public denunciation of the courts was bitter. When a jury found two youths accused of murder guilty of manslaughter, public anger was intense, and leading citizens organized a group which forced the jailer to lynch the convicted men. The militia then arrived and fired on the heretofore orderly group, provoking three days of fighting. More than 300 men were killed and wounded; two of the dead were militiamen. The great courthouse was burned. All was in vain, however, since the crime wave intensified.

Steps toward improving the quality of life in Ohio's cities made faltering and tentative progress early in the twentieth century, when several of them, notably Toledo, Cleveland, and Dayton, provided healthy examples of good municipal government.

(103)

VOTE

IF YOU WANT TO FIGHT!

JOIN THE MARINES

Howard Chandler Christy, 1915.

McKINLEY'S WARD

FIRST WARD
REPUBLICAN
CLUB
CANTON, O.
1896.

FOURTH REG'T
OHIO VOL. INF'Y
MUSTERED MAY 19

OHIO
C

SMALL POX
WITHIN
KEEP OUT!
ANY PERSON REMOVING THIS CARD WITHOUT AUTHORITY WILL BE PROSECUTED
THE BOARD OF HEALTH

1908
WILLIAM HOWARD TAFT
JAMES SCHOOLCRAFT SHERMAN

GRAND OLD PARTY
1856 - 1908
STANDARD BEARERS

Leadership in National Affairs

In any selection of America's most representative state for the period from the Civil War through World War I, Ohio should be in the forefront. Not since the Virginia dynasty dominated the early years of the Republic had any state managed to maintain such a hold on high national office as Ohio did during these critical years. Seven native sons were elected president, and a number of others barely missed receiving their party's nomination. In 1920, at the end of this long period of political primacy, both major presidential candidates — Republican Warren G. Harding and Democrat James Cox — were Ohio newspaper publishers. Six native Ohioans sat on the Supreme Court during these years with both Salmon P. Chase and Morrison Waite serving as chief justices. Nineteen members of presidential cabinets were Ohio born. Several Ohio senators, including John Sherman, Allen Thurman, George Pendleton, Marcus Hanna, Joseph Foraker, and Charles Dick, wielded unusual influence in legislative affairs, as did a number of Ohioans in the House of Representatives.

One reason for Ohio's imposing record is that the Buckeye State was so diverse and yet so balanced that it required leading politicians to learn techniques and positions that appealed to broad spectrums of the electorate. From its inception, Ohio had both northern and southern points of view well represented in its body politic. When the Civil War began, Ohio's agriculture and industry were as well balanced as any other state as were its rural and urban populations. In Ohio the established institutional outlook of the East was tempered by the newer traditions of the West; Ohio was the westernmost of the eastern states and the easternmost of the western states. Of course other factors had more visible substance: Ohio was the third most populous state during much of this period, and it had propor-

An Ohio Portrait

tionately large delegations in Congress and in political conventions and caucuses. As one of the leaders among the industrial states, Ohio could find newly-rich men who were willing to bankroll political candidates. As noted earlier, the Civil War provided visibility to many Ohio military and civilian leaders, and these names stuck in the public memory for years to come. During this postwar period influential leaders came from the Republicans, who supported the victorious Lincoln administration, and the Peace Democrats who opposed it; among the latter were Clement Vallandigham, George Pendleton, and Allen Thurman. Although each of these factors has some merit, all are speculative to a greater or lesser degree. The definitive study which might explain Ohio's great influence during this period remains to be done.

Ulysses S. Grant was so obviously a war hero and proved so malleable in the hands of the politicians that his election in 1868 needs little further analysis. The tragedy of his two terms (1869-77) in the presidency was that his strengths while he operated in a military chain of command proved to be weaknesses when he operated in a political milieu. Despite his unsatisfactory record in office, Grant allowed himself to be nominated for a third term at the 1880 Republican convention. Both he and the nation were spared when the convention ultimately turned to another Ohioan, James A. Garfield. Grant's last years recaptured some of the nobility that had rubbed away during his presidency. Suffering from throat cancer, he raced against death to complete his military *Memoirs*. Grant won by the narrowest of margins and left to the nation one of the best personal accounts of command ever written. His clear prose suggests that one of his strengths as a commander was his ability to put orders in language so clear that they could not be misun-

President Grant and family at a New Jersey seaside cottage, 1872. (1)

The last photograph of U.S. Grant, 1885. (2)

Leadership in National Affairs

The Ohio Building is the only state structure of the Philadelphia Centennial Exposition, 1876, that still stands. (3)

A view of Main and Fourth Streets, Zanesville. (4)

An Ohio Portrait

James A. Garfield's
catafalque, Cleveland
1881. (7)

Garfield family portrait by DeScott Evans, Western
Reserve Historical Society. (5)

Garfield family at the home of Zeb Rudolph, Hiram
(Portage County), 1873. (6)

derstood. His family realized a handsome inheritance from sales of his works, which had been Grant's main objective for undertaking the task. While a great mausoleum was erected in his honor on New York's Riverside Drive, a Union reunited — if not emotionally restored — was his greatest and most enduring monument.

Final political restoration of the Union, and the last acts of the Reconstruction period, were presided over by Delaware-born Cincinnati lawyer Rutherford B. Hayes, who had served his nation as a major general and had served his state as congressman and governor. Nearly all of Hayes' political victories had been by the slimmest of margins, so it was consistent with previous experience that he should win the presidency by one vote in the electoral college, and that the one vote should be the result of unparalleled shenanigans. This famous "stolen election" of 1876 was so traumatic for Hayes, honorable man that he was, that he disclaimed any intention of seeking a second term — perhaps the only president in our history who said it and really meant it. Hayes and his energetic wife, the former Lucy Webb of Chillicothe, retired to their fine estate in Fremont, Spiegel Grove. There they are buried. The Rutherford B. Hayes Memorial Library and Museum — the nation's first presidential library building — is also located at Spiegel Grove.

Hayes' successor in the White House was James A. Garfield. Born in a log cabin in Orange Township, Cuyahoga County, young Garfield worked at many jobs to help his widowed mother. Years later he won political mileage from his service as a canal boy leading mules and doing odd jobs along the Penn-Ohio and the Ohio-Erie canals in northeastern Ohio. A graduate of Williams College, he was professor and later president of Hiram College. Garfield was also a minister in the old Campbellite (Disciples of Christ) denomina-

(8)

THE REPUBLICAN CANDIDATES FOR 1888.

GEN. BEN. HARRISON.   LEVI P. MORTON.

1888

(9)

For President: R.B. HAYES OF OHIO. For Vice President: W.A. WHEELER OF NEW YORK.

Lucy Hayes at Speigel Grove,
the family home in Fremont (left). Rutherford B.
Hayes (above) with 1876 campaign ribbon. (10)

An Ohio Portrait

William McKinley at Fernwood Camp near East
Liverpool, 1891. (11)

McKinley supporters were brought from miles
around in 1896 to greet the candidate on the front
porch of his Canton home. (12)

tion, a background that served him in good stead
when he debated religion with his Civil War
commander, William Rosecrans, a Roman
Catholic. While a major general in the Union
armies, Garfield was elected to Congress in 1863,
and resigned his commission to start a distinguished career in the lower house. Soon after his
inauguration as president in 1881, he was shot by
a disappointed office seeker and died in September. The Garfield tomb is located in Cleveland's Lakeview Cemetery; his home, Lawndale,
is preserved in Mentor.

Born at North Bend along the Ohio River
west of Cincinnati, Benjamin Harrison was the
grandson of William Henry Harrison and the son
of former Congressman John Harrison. A
graduate of Miami University at Oxford, he pursued his law career in Indianapolis; his mature
years are largely identified with this Indiana city.
While his one term as president included such
accomplishments as adoption of the Sherman
Anti-Trust Act (1890) and the annexation of
Hawaii, it was essentially bland and colorless, to
the extent that he is commonly remembered as
the man who served between the two terms of
Grover Cleveland.

Harrison left office just as the depression of
1893 plunged the nation into deep economic
trouble. Cleveland dealt with the critical period
from 1893 to 1897, when he was succeeded by
William McKinley. Born the son of a Niles iron
worker, McKinley was forced by illness and a lack
of finances to drop out of college. He then
studied law and moved to Canton to set up practice in this growing industrial city. McKinley married a banker's daughter, Ida Saxton, whose frail
health was overtaxed by the early death of their
two daughters. Throughout her life, Ida was
periodically a semi-invalid smitten by epileptic
attacks described as "nerves." During such attacks

Leadership in National Affairs

Ida Saxton McKinley seated by mementoes comprising her "shrine" to the assassinated president. (13)

A group of mothers from many states visit the McKinley home, 1896. (14)

An Ohio Portrait

The young Marcus Hanna of Lisbon developed into the wealthy and politically powerful Republican party boss, McKinley's friend and political mentor. (15) (16)

her husband provided the most effective calming influence. His great patience and forbearance were remarkable; he came closer than most to living his convictions, beliefs fashioned by the Methodist faith which was such a large part of his life.

McKinley first won political office as Congressman from the Canton district. He became the House of Representative's leading expert on tariff matters and consistently supported high protective tariffs which served the industrialists in his district well. It was a measure of his skill that McKinley convinced the laboring men in his constituency of the wisdom of a protective tariff. With the direction and support of the wealthy Cleveland industrialist, Marcus Hanna (called by some the man who came closest to becoming a national political boss), McKinley was elected governor of Ohio for two terms. Hanna then turned his organizing powers with great success toward securing the presidency for his friend. With McKinley contributing much to the effort, Hanna succeeded in arranging the Republican nomination. McKinley defeated William Jennings Bryan in the presidential election of 1896. Perhaps the best-remembered event of McKinley's presidency was the Spanish American War, which he initially opposed. To jingoists like Theodore Roosevelt it was "a splendid little war," which resulted in the annexation of Puerto Rico, Guam, and ultimately the Philippines. Ohio's contribution to the war effort consisted of some 15,345 national guardsmen, none of whom died in battle. Roughrider Teddy Roosevelt was a war hero and politically ambitious; Republican leaders put him on the ticket in 1900 as the vice-presidential candidate in an effort to keep him under control. Events frustrated this scheme. McKinley was shot in September, 1901, while attending the Pan-American Exposition in Buffalo.

The Stark County courthouse was draped in mourning for William McKinley's funeral in Canton, 1901. (17)

The 4th Ohio at Newport News, Virginia, enroute to Puerto Rico, 1898. (18)

Units of the Ohio National Guard departing from Portsmouth, April 26, 1898. (19)

An Ohio Portrait

A staunch advocate of the "social gospel,"
Washington Gladden of Columbus. (20)

This good man was mourned by the nation, and nowhere more than in Ohio, where the general assembly made his political good luck piece, the scarlet carnation, the state flower. Roosevelt moved into the White House to the discomfiture of Marc Hanna and other Republican regulars.

While McKinley was president, Ohio and the nation moved into the so-called progressive reform era. At the very end of the nineteenth century, a number of reform enthusiasms — improved working conditions for labor, banking reform, rate regulation for railroads and utilities, municipal government reform, consumer protection, and direct government — were just beginning to coalesce into the so-called progressive movement. Most of the reforms were aimed at curbing excesses and stopping abuses attributable to the great growth of monopolistic business enterprise. The area in which Ohio progressives made their most notable contribution was in providing the nation with several examples of enlightened municipal government.

That American cities suffered from corrupt and inept government can hardly be questioned. Indeed, one of the constants of the American urban experience was the lack of clean, honest and able administrations in larger cities. A number of Ohio cities were administered by corrupt and self-serving political organizations. George Cox, the Cincinnati tavern keeper, was almost the prototype of the nineteenth century urban boss. In Cleveland, nobody moved in city affairs without clearance from the Hanna machine or whomever happened to be the current dispenser of boodle and patronage. Canton was described by William Couch of the Cleveland *Plain Dealer* as "a lurid little city." Even in rural Adams County so many people admitted buying and selling votes that one quarter of the electors of Adams County had their ballots voided for voting improprieties during an early twentieth century election.

Early efforts at reform had been almost uniformly unsuccessful. Washington Gladden, minister of Columbus' First Congregational Church and proponent of the "social gospel," blamed state legislatures. "The Legislatures of many of our states," he wrote, "have tried . . . stripping the people of the cities of political power; the attempt has been made to take as many as possible of the functions of government away from the people and confer them upon outside commissions; and the result has been, in every case, disastrous. The weaker the municipal government is, the wickeder it is: is this not a universal rule?"

Among the first of Ohio's big city mayors to seize initiative in combating entrenched interests was Samuel "Golden Rule" Jones of Toledo. Having accumulated a substantial fortune, he left business for politics but found himself suspect among party regulars after he refused to play their game. Elected in 1897, Jones took the lead in establishing an eight-hour workday for city employees, and started free kindergartens, public playgrounds, and free concerts in the parks. He tried what proved to be too idealistic an experiment, sending police on their rounds unarmed; they did not even carry billyclubs. Jones fought monopolistic utilities and made himself accessible to the humble and needy. His former secretary and successor, Brand Whitlock, continued Jones's policies. Between them, Jones and Whitlock gave Toledo fifteen years of effective leadership.

In this same period, the remarkable Tom L. Johnson was making Cleveland into what Lincoln Steffens called the best-governed city in America. Johnson left his Kentucky home to become a multi-millionaire while still a young man. How-

On Tom L. Johnson's statue in Cleveland's Public
Square is his enduring tribute: He found us
leaderless and blind. He left a city with a civic
mind. (21)

(22)

An Ohio Portrait

ever, he found in the writings of Henry George a convincing critique of the system by which he had acquired his fortune. Johnson divested himself of much of his business property and set out to reorder society along lines later described as "people against privilege." After serving one term in Congress, he was elected mayor of Cleveland in 1901 on an independent ticket. During the next eight years Johnson worked to secure an honest police department and to provide street paving and lighting, clean water supply, parks, public amenities, and honest market inspection. His main goal — to revise the inequitable tax structure — eluded him as the courts consistently found in favor of those he challenged. His enemies even used their influence to get Cleveland's charter declared unconstitutional by the Ohio Supreme Court. The general assembly, manipulated by the bosses, then adopted a new municipal code designed to keep power out of the hands of reformers like Johnson. After his defeat in the election of 1909, Johnson passed from the political scene; his protégés, Newton D. Baker and Peter Witt, continued to have a healthy influence on Cleveland's political life. Cleveland finally got around to honoring its benefactor, and today a statue of Tom Johnson graces its public square.

Ohio cities were soon aided by a state constitutional amendment granting them charter government (home rule). This was part of an extensive package of reform legislation introduced by the constitutional convention of 1912. Delegates to that convention were influenced by the progressive spirit. Judging that any effort to rewrite the constitution would be defeated at the polls as the 1873 effort had been, they introduced forty-one amendments, each of which was considered separately by the voters. Thirty-three amendments passed, including charter govern-

ment for cities. A number of Ohio cities immediately voted on charter government. Salem, Canton, Elyria, Akron, and Youngstown rejected it initially; but Cleveland, Columbus, Lakewood, Springfield, Sandusky, and Toledo approved. Dayton adopted a charter which created the city manager plan of municipal government, the first large city in America to use this innovative structure. In later years every Ohio city of substantial size adopted charter government, although some did not succeed in obtaining it until long after World War II.

The last hanging at the Frankfort Street jail, Cleveland, 1876. (23)

Among other constitutional amendments accepted by the voters in 1912 were those establishing authority for workmen's compensation, wage and hour regulation, health standards in places of employment, preservation of natural resources, banking safeguards, speeding of court procedures, direct primaries, initiative and referendum, civil service reforms, and permission for the governor to veto selected items in appropriations bills. Among the eight defeated proposals were women's suffrage, abolition of capital punishment, and the use of voting machines. This period represents the zenith of progressive reform activity in Ohio.

William Howard Taft, Roosevelt's hand-picked successor, served as president of the United States from 1909 to 1913. While Warren Harding labeled him the "greatest progressive of the age," not all agreed as the capable Cincinnati lawyer and public official disappointed liberal Republicans by endorsing certain conservative programs. Although considerable progressive legislation was enacted during Taft's administration, Roosevelt challenged him for the Republican nomination in 1912 and failing, bolted the Republicans to become the candidate of the Progressive (Bull Moose) party, effectively splitting the Republican vote. Both Roosevelt and Taft were swamped in the Democratic landslide for Woodrow Wilson; Taft retired to private life until Harding appointed him chief justice of the Supreme Court in 1921. Taft, the only person to serve both as president and chief justice, is said to have preferred the latter job. In 1930 he was buried in Arlington National Cemetery.

Not all forward-looking legislation was initiated by progressives. A great natural disaster was responsible for one extraordinarily useful piece of legislation. In March, 1913, torrential rains

William Howard Taft and his wife, Helen Herron Taft, leave their cottage on Middle Bass Island, 1908. (24)

An Ohio Portrait

Rescue scene at Dayton, March 1913. (25)

caused floods of unprecedented magnitude throughout the state. Not only Ohio River towns, but many others were hit hard. The worst damage was at Dayton where virtually the entire central city was inundated, and fires fed by ruptured gas mains destroyed much property. The 428 Daytonians who died constituted the largest death toll from any natural disaster in Ohio. In addition to lives lost, some 20,000 Dayton houses were destroyed and nearly twice that number were damaged. Property loss was estimated in excess of $300 million. An experienced Cincinnati engineer, Arthur E. Morgan, was hired to recommend ways to prevent recurrences of this disaster. On his recommendation the general assembly passed the Ohio Conservancy Act in 1914. The main feature of Morgan's plan was to construct earthen flood control dams on the tributaries of those streams that converged at

Dayton. Costs were to be spread to all who would benefit in this Miami Conservancy District. This principle of cost-sharing was upheld in the courts, thus opening the way for the later creation of the even larger and more complex Muskingum Conservancy District, which added valuable concepts of conservation, reforestation, and recreation. Ohio's highly successful pioneering effort provided a model to be used by Morgan and others in the Tennessee River Valley in 1933 and by both federal and state governments.

The domestic focus of the progressive initiative was vitiated after war broke out in Europe in 1914. But wartime conditions had considerable effect on two great social reform movements which had commanded attention since well before the Civil War. The first of these, the temperance or prohibition crusade, had never really died. It was given new organizational strength in the postwar era by developments emanating from Ohio. In 1874 the Women's Christian Temperance Union (WCTU) was organized in Ohio by efforts of determined church women like Eliza Thompson of Hillsboro. WCTU campaigns against "demon rum" and liquor traffic have not stopped to this day. In 1893 the Anti-Saloon League was chartered in Ohio. From its national headquarters in Westerville it conducted literary and educational campaigns, organized support especially among the Methodist and other Protestant churches, lobbied in legislative chambers from Washington to the smallest communities, and generally forced public consciousness of it efforts. The Anti-Saloon League's most effective lobbyist was Wayne Wheeler, who had great success with the tactic of forcing political candidates to commit themselves publically on the temperance issue. The contest between "wets" and "drys" was intensely emotional and continually got in the way of rational discourse on other issues. Often "wets" opposed women's suffrage, fearing that if women voted they would tend to favor prohibition.

Ohio responded to the liquor problem by piecemeal legislation; "local option" by counties (the Rose Law, 1908) became a favorite device for handling it. In 1919 temperance leaders prevailed; the Eighteenth Amendment to the federal Constitution, as enforced by the Volstead Act, made the entire country legally dry. That "noble experiment," prohibition, had its dark side. The gang warfare and illicit "rum running" activities that marked this era were all too well represented in Ohio. A central location, a shared border with Canada (even though a watery one), and numerous small cities where hoodlums could cool off while police and federal agents sought them in New York, Detroit, or Chicago, all contributed to a troubled period for law-abiding citizens and the

The Taylorsville Dam, eight miles north of Dayton on the Miami River, is part of the Miami Conservancy District's flood control program. (26)

Lands controlled by the Miami Conservancy District (above) and the Muskingum Conservancy District are set aside for recreational use. (27)

An Ohio Portrait

Elliot Ness, Cleveland's Safety Director, at a youth development program, Hiram House, Cleveland, 1936. (28)

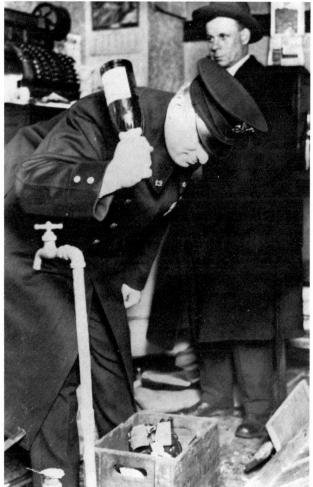

A familiar scene during Prohibition. (29)

officials charged with law enforcement. A number of Ohio fortunes and sullied civic reputations can be traced to this era of gangsterism, when city speakeasies were supplied by moonshiners and dealers in illegal "hooch."

The second great movement which achieved a major goal at the conclusion of World War I was the women's suffrage movement. The laws of Ohio, like those of other states, discriminated against women. Reformers were interested in the whole range of "women's rights," including such things as their right to control property, enter into contracts, and secure other fundamental economic privileges. Some of these rights were secured by state legislative action in the 1880s and 1890s. In the early twentieth century, the effort focused on securing the franchise or suffrage.

Before the turn of the century Ohio permitted women the right to vote in school elections, and some critics pointed out that only a tiny percentage of eligible women voters had taken advantage of the opportunity. In 1912, 1914, and 1917 (male) Ohio voters rejected proposals to grant women the franchise. Congress finally resolved the issue by passing the Nineteenth Amendment in 1919. Ohio was the fifth state to ratify the amendment, which took effect in time for women to vote in the all-Ohio presidential election of 1920. The idealistic arguments used to secure women's voting rights would soon give way to reality — women reacted at the polls much as did men. Unfortunately, the expected improvement in the moral and ethical tone of candidates did not materialize, but at least women had been granted equity. In 1923 the general assembly extended full civil rights to women, and when Cleveland attorney Florence Allen was elected to the Ohio Supreme Court, it appeared women's gains were assured. Ultimately, the women's rights movement would shift back to a

Leadership in National Affairs

Judge Florence Allen (1884–1966) of Cleveland, elected to the Ohio Supreme Court in 1922, was the first woman appointed (1934) to the United States Circuit Court of Appeals. (30)

Suffragists in Columbus, 1914. (31)

Support for Judge Florence Allen. (32)

broader and more fundamental set of objectives.

Meanwhile, America could not remain aloof from the European war. The vast, mechanized, impersonal nature of modern war — especially a war fought a great distance from home — divests it of the intense personalization of people and events that characterized the Civil War or the old Indian Wars. Only avid students of American military history or those American Legionnaires and Veterans of Foreign Wars who relive their own experiences in monthly meetings and annual conventions can remember much about America's participation in World War I.

Ohio's contribution was enormous. The Ohio National Guard was called into federal service and sent to Camp Sheridan in Alabama for training. Volunteers and draftees trained at Camp Sherman outside Chillicothe. Small units of soldiers trained elsewhere in Ohio, in factories and colleges. Many colleges had young men enrolled in the Student Army Training Corps, a forerunner of the later ROTC programs. In all, nearly a quarter of a million Ohio men served in the military; nearly 7,000 of them died or were reported missing on distant fields named Sedan, Meuse-Argonne, Compeigne and the St. Mihiel Salient. Some went down with ships torpedoed by the infamous German U-boats, while a few pioneer aviators died in air battles or plane crashes. Some emerged as heroes. Lieutenant Eddie Rickenbacker, for example, was a flying "ace" and a Congressional Medal of Honor winner.

Ohio women served as nurses; one of them, Mary Gladwin of Akron, compiled an extraordinary record in four years of difficult service in the most hazardous theaters of war. Nurses were needed at home too, where both military and civilian personnel died by the thousands in the 1918 influenza epidemic. At Camp Sherman alone, more than 8,000 men were ill of influenza or pneumonia and 1,101 died.

In 1919 most Ohio troops came home. The 166th Ohio, part of the famous Rainbow division, paraded through Columbus in May, 1919. The regiment had suffered 427 deaths, a fact that hit home with special force in towns like Marysville, Cardington, Greenfield, Circleville, London, Lancaster, Marion, Delaware, Washington Court House, and in Columbus itself.

Mary Gladwin of Akron had a distinguished career as a nurse in several wars. She spent four years in Serbia (above) during World War I. (33)

Leadership in National Affairs

Heroes of the air, Captain Eddie Rickenbacker and
Amelia Earhart, 1935. (34)

Red Cross canteen workers serving returning
troops, Defiance, 1919. (35)

Drill team at Columbus
Barracks, part of a readiness
campaign in the troubled
1930s. (36)

An Ohio Portrait

The World War I Martin bomber. (37)

Returning troops parade in Defiance, 1919. (38)

Victory loans generated financial support for
America's war effort. (39)

Manufacturing gas masks. (40)

Leadership in National Affairs

Red Cross parade, Defiance, 1918. (41)

Zanesville also had a Red Cross parade during
World War I. (42)

An Ohio Portrait

Temporary camps were established around the state
during World War I. Below is the camp at
Edgewater Park, Cleveland. (43)

As in the Civil War, Ohio's industrial capacity
played an important role in World War I. Not
only the quantity but the diversity of Ohio's industrial goods was staggering. Agricultural production peaked to provide wartime needs for soldiers, civilians, and overseas relief programs.
Ohioans, along with Americans elsewhere,
bought Liberty Bonds, observed "meatless Tues-
days," and made their individual contributions to
the war effort.

Some of these contributions were misplaced
and inappropriate, no matter how understandable. Ohio's massive German population became a
target for superpatriots and vigilantes who
seemed to believe that only by demeaning every-

thing German could the "Hun" be suppressed.
German language teaching was forbidden in
Ohio's schools. Even colleges terminated or at
least restricted instruction in German language
and literature. German street names were
changed to English names. German businessmen
were boycotted. All in all shameful conduct overshadowed efforts to maintain rationality. Soon
after the war the direct links of Ohio's Germans to
their old culture began to disappear rapidly. During World War II, when Germany was again the
enemy, few insults were directed at Americans of
German ancestry.

At war's end in 1918, Woodrow Wilson attempted to lead the peace negotiators along paths

CLEAR-THE-WAY-!!

BUY BONDS

FOURTH LIBERTY LOAN

(44)

Street markets in Dayton were heavily patronized in 1917. (45) (46)

By the 1920s, farmer's markets were becoming entirely motorized as in this Toledo scene (right). (47)

Market days were popular both in urban and rural
settings as seen in Dayton (above) and in the Amish
country (below) near Berlin (Holmes County). (48) (49)

An Ohio Portrait

President Warren G. Harding and wife Florence on way to visit the Lincoln Memorial, 1923. (50)

Harding supporters in Marion on notification day. (51)

that European leaders like France's Clemenceau and Britain's Lloyd George found too idealistic. Ironically, while Wilson won his battle to have France, Britain, and other allied powers accept his covenant of the League of Nations, a program for a rule of reason in world affairs, a coterie of American senators blocked its acceptance in the U.S. When Wilson was succeeded in 1921 by Warren G. Harding of Blooming Grove and Marion, Ohio, the league issue was still unsettled. America never did accept the league, although it participated in a number of league-sponsored activities.

Warren Gamaliel Harding scarcely seemed the man to handle great public issues. After winning the Republican nomination as a last ditch compromise candidate in the famous "smoke-filled room" in Chicago's Blackstone Hotel, Harding went on to a smashing victory over James Cox of Dayton, a victory Harding said would result in a "return to normalcy" for the nation. Ill-prepared by training or temperament to be president, Harding was a kind, amiable man who presided over an administration that proved to be corrupt to the core, although Harding in no way profited from the misdeeds of his appointees. Scandal so blackened his administration that it was not until President Herbert Hoover consented to perform the honors, that a highranking Republican could be persuaded to dedicate Harding's tomb in Marion.

Recent studies of Harding as president depict him in a more favorable light than earlier treatments of his career. Scholars working with the extensive Harding papers assert that he initiated or supported policies that helped segments of the nation, and that his posture in foreign relations was constructive.

Ohio was affected by all the opportunities and tribulations of the Roaring Twenties. The

Leadership in National Affairs

Harvey S. Firestone, Henry Ford, and Thomas A. Edison at the King residence while attending the funeral of their friend, Warren G. Harding, in Marion, 1923. (52)

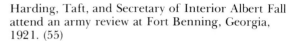

Harding, Taft, and Secretary of Interior Albert Fall attend an army review at Fort Benning, Georgia, 1921. (55)

(53)

President and Mrs. Harding on the president's last trip, to Alaska, 1923. (56)

Harvey S. Firestone and Warren G. Harding on a Maryland camping trip, 1921. (54)

An Ohio Portrait

Amy Kankonen, purportedly the first woman in America to be elected mayor, Fairport Harbor (Lake County), 1921. (57)

brief depression of 1920-21 hit some industries hard. More than 40,000 rubber workers left Akron in those years, but their replacements and more poured in as prosperity increased late in the decade. Relatively new industries like the automotive, trucking, aircraft, dirigible, electrical appliance, new machine tool, and metal fabricating plants were among businesses headed for what appeared would be great accomplishments in the late twenties. Things did not go so well on the farm, however. Hundreds of thousands of acres of agricultural land were taken out of production following a collapse of farm prices which brought hard times to rural areas, especially to the proprietors of small family farms. A modest recovery in farm prices was evident by the end of the decade.

No one can ignore basic economic conditions, but the twenties provided plenty of diversion. On the serious side was a swelling of nativist and racist sentiment. In part this was directed against certain foreigners, as in the "Red Scare" and Palmer Raids of 1919 and 1920, and the Sacco and Vanzetti case which extended over most of the decade. In part nativism was an effort to maintain what many people thought of as old patriotic, American, Protestant, Christian virtues. One manifestation of the rise of nativism — the Knights of the Ku Klux Klan — was especially visible in Ohio. Indeed, Akron and Dayton, each of which had experienced rapid growth from an influx of rural and small town southerners who often found cities alien and threatening places, had klan groups that were among the largest in the nation. Foreign Catholics, with their presumed "un-American" influences, were more the target of invective and intimidation than Jews and blacks, who were neither numerous nor visible enough to be considered much of a threat. The Akron Board of Education was controlled by

avowed klan members in 1923-25. They hired as superintendent a klansman who had been fired from a similar position in Springfield. Many other public officials, in Akron and Summit County — the mayor, several county commissioners, the sheriff, and some local judges — were klansmen. Internal squabbles, jurisdictional disputes, money problems, and the discrediting of a prominent Indiana klan leader all contributed to the decline of klan activity.

The klan was not the only manifestation of reactionary thinking. In Dayton, Tennessee, the nation watched William Jennings Bryan and Ohio's Clarence Darrow square off at each other in the Scopes "Monkey Trial." Though John Scopes was convicted of violating Tennessee

Clarence Darrow (1857–1938), born in Kinsman (Trumbull County), was a skillful advocate in many dramatic trials including the 1925 Scopes "monkey" trial. (58)

Young followers salute Charles E. Ruthenberg (1882–1927), first secretary general of the U.S. Communist party. He was a leading Cleveland Socialist in the era of World War I. (59)

Ruthenberg speaking in Market Square, Cleveland, October 28, 1917. (60)

Ku Klux Klan parade, Springfield, 1923. (61)

Crosses burn at a KKK rally in Dayton, 1923. (62)

Port Columbus dedication, 1929, showing
Trans-Continental Air Transport (TAT) tri-motor
airplanes. (63)

The old-time confectionary store,
fondly remembered by
generations of Ohioans. This
scene is at Dellroy (Carroll
County). (64)

Leadership in National Affairs

A view down Sycamore Street, Cincinnati, 1930s. (65)

For many years the fifty-two story Terminal Tower in Cleveland was the tallest building between New York and Chicago. (66)

Cincinnati's Union Terminal was one of America's finest passenger facilities. (67)

Workers at Kahn's Packing House, Cincinnati, 1938. (68)

statutes forbidding the teaching of Darwinian evolution, his cause ultimately prevailed. Darrow's attacks on Bryan's fundamentalism, meanwhile, made him a champion of intellectual and religious liberals.

For many Ohioans, diversion was of a less serious nature during the twenties. During the "Jazz Age," clubs and road houses featuring dancing and illegal drinking were found in every city. Commercial radio made its appearance in 1922 with stations WLW in Cincinnati and WHK in Cleveland leading the way; before the year was out Ohio had thirty-four stations. Movies became talkies in the 1920s. Every town boasted its movie theaters, with massive and elaborate structures impressing the citizens in the major cities. Sports heroes — "Babe" Ruth, Lou Gehrig, Bill Tilden, Gertrude Ederle, Helen Moody, and Bobby Jones — thrilled the country, as did a young aviator named Charles Lindbergh. But the automobile was perhaps the most radical development of all in its social implications. This new mobility changed Ohio and the nation in fundamental ways; the process of adjustment to the car culture still goes on, with the ultimate questions it raises still unanswered.

The face of Ohio cities changed in the twenties. Cleveland's Terminal Tower complex in the public square is a monument to financial wizards Oris and Mantis Van Sweringen, railroad entrepreneurs and the developers of America's most luxurious suburban community at that time, Shaker Heights. Public buildings graced Cleveland's mall and a great stadium was begun on the waterfront. Cincinnati welcomed its new customs house, post office, and Union Terminal. Toledo built a new university campus, established huge new commercial facilities, and extended its excellent art museum. Dayton, Youngstown, Canton, Akron, and smaller cities like Lima, Mansfield,

and Hamilton also experienced the building boom. Columbus began to look more like a state capital. New state office buildings, civic center improvements, commercial buildings, and the development of the Scioto shoreline gave Columbus the appearance of the big city it was becoming. Presiding over much of this vigorous period was "Veto Vic" Donahey, a Democrat from Tuscarawas County, who clashed frequently with the legislature as Ohio, like the rest of the nation, moved unknowingly toward the great social traumas of the depression thirties.

The decade of the 1930s marked a turning point in American history. Not only did the severe economic and social depression of the time set it apart, but the federal government moved into people's lives with massive programs of aid which eventually directed America away from its state capitals toward Washington.

In Ohio, some Democratic and most Republican party leaders resisted this move, exaggerating in the process the state's ability to take care of its own people while declaiming against the wastefulness of federal programs, especially the various "relief" programs. Democratic Governor Martin L. Davey said of these programs that he proposed "to stand firmly as the protector of the taxpayers of Ohio against waste and inefficiency and loose management." His successor, Republican John W. Bricker, told a 1939 New York audience that he had "the high privilege" of assuring them "that Ohio is still there! We have not been taken over by the White House or the Department of Interior."

Ohio, like other states, was unprepared for the disaster that followed the 1929 stock market crash. As the downward economic spiral gained momentum, workers were laid off by the tens of thousands. Those who retained jobs were often able to work only a few days a week or a few hours

A Lithuanian neighborhood on Star Avenue, Cleveland, 1940. (69)

a day. Some employees, especially public employees, were paid in script. Many workers agreed to reduce their hours in order to spread the shrinking number of jobs among as many people as possible. The mining industry collapsed in the eastern and southern counties.

Farmers too felt the pinch. Only 15 percent of Ohio's people lived on farms in 1930, and they experienced a farm income drop of 42 percent between 1929 and 1930. Prices dropped so drastically that crops sometimes cost more to make than they sold for. Severe summer droughts in the mid-thirties contributed to the developing rural disaster. Unemployed farm hands wandered to cities, where they intensified already severe unemployment. Hobo jungles proliferated and Hoovervilles, improvised dwellings made of junk, crates, boxes, and sheets of scrap metal, sprang up in major cities.

In 1931 some 125 Ohio banks failed. All kinds of financial institutions were in deep trouble. Cleveland's greatest bank was in difficulty; in Toledo seven of ten banks closed by 1933. The pattern was repeated around the state. This depression discriminated less between the rich and the poor, the skilled and unskilled, the production worker and the manager than did most business recessions. The national and state economies had been dealt such a savage blow that nearly everyone suffered, whether from loss of job and income or from loss of savings and investments.

The loss of income was reflected in a loss of tax revenue. There were insufficient funds for cities, counties, and the state itself to make more than a small dent in their needs. The Ohio General Assembly responded to the crisis in a halting, piecemeal fashion, trapped perhaps by the difficulty of grasping the scope of the crisis and unwilling to accept drastic new initiatives in government assistance programs. Voluntary charitable organizations exhausted their resources early, as did cities, counties, and school districts which had supplied clothing, medicines, and shoes to needy children. Although the legislature permitted counties, townships, and cities to issue bonds to finance relief, insufficient monies were realized to meet the need.

By 1932 the relief effort was collapsing under the weight of this need. In Cleveland, city relief agencies were caring for 20,500 families, and one-third of the working force was unemployed. Similar plights were characteristic of Youngstown and other steel cities; of Toledo, where the automotive industry was in trouble; and of Akron, whose rubber plants had cut back production severely. In smaller towns and cities desperate citizens pressured helpless public officials. More than 1000 families in Zanesville demanded assistance from the city council. Petty thefts increased as persons who were scrupulously honest under normal circumstances stole food or clothing for their families. A Toledo paper's headline read, "Girl Shot Stealing Food for Children. Pleaded Guilty. Freed."

The halting and modest efforts of the Hoover administration to channel emergency aid to the states were too little and almost too late. By mid-1933 Ohio had received about $19 million. In the presidential election year of 1932, Americans entrusted management of the crisis to the Democrats, from whom they sought — and received — a more adequate level of assistance. Franklin D. Roosevelt and his Democratic Congress pressed a comprehensive relief and recovery program which helped the nation survive and led it toward an economic recovery that was ultimately assured by the full production economy of World War II. In 1932 Ohioans gave Roosevelt a modest majority; they also placed Democrat George White in the governor's chair and sent a

An Ohio Portrait

The inner-city, Toledo, in the 1930s. (70)

Store on Woodland Avenue, Cleveland, 1940. (71)

Democratic majority to the general assembly. For the first time in nearly fifteen years, Ohio's lower house was controlled by Democrats.

The most urgent business of the new legislature was to secure revenue for relief and for schools. After a bitter battle with the state's business interests, a 3 percent sales tax took effect January 1, 1935. This kind of regressive tax would lose favor with liberals in later years, but, at the time, at least the people paying the tax were people with spendable income, however modest. Soon after Martin L. Davey succeeded White in 1935, the general assembly enacted the School Foundation Program, designed to equalize educational opportunities and to force the closing of outmoded, uneconomical school facilities. The new program gave a great boost to the creation of consolidated school districts, in which children were bussed in from outlying areas to central schools of adequate size; this created an adequate population base to pay teachers better salaries. A host of other concerns — old age pensions, unemployment insurance, minimum wages, the plight of property owners with delinquent taxes — confronted legislators in the early thirties.

In retrospect, it is clear that Ohio desperately required the federal assistance that poured in through various relief "make work" programs. The Works Progress Administration and the Public Works Administration put the unemployed back to work, while the Civilian Conservation Corps not only salvaged many young men from despair but also brought income to their families. Ohio is dotted with buildings, roads, stadiums, and other lasting public improvements built by WPA or PWA labor. One might cite, from hundreds of examples, the 520-unit Lakeview Terrace in Cleveland, the Brand Whitlock Homes in Toledo, Fremont's Sandusky County Courthouse, Akron's Rubber Bowl, and the

Listening to a game, Scovill Avenue, Cleveland, 1940. (72)

United States Post Office and Courthouse in Columbus. In September, 1938, more than 25 percent of the families in twelve Ohio counties had some member employed by WPA. At the WPA's peak strength in Ohio, more than 287,000 people were employed and an additional 38,000 were eligible and awaiting assignment. One unusual feature of employment programs under the WPA was the hiring of people for artistic, musical, and writing projects, one of the latter being the useful *Ohio Guide*. Ohio's parks and conservation projects were built in large part by the CCC. Largest of Ohio's public works projects was the Muskingum Conservancy District development, completed in 1938 under direction of the Army Corps of Engineers, at a cost of $43 million.

The enduring value of most federal work projects in Ohio is only part of the story. In Cleveland by 1938, 70,000 people on federal work relief were supporting not only themselves but also their families. The money channeled into Ohio by work relief projects was but a part of the federal contribution. In direct relief, the federal government spent $175 million in Ohio; state government spent $97 million; local governments spent $40 million. The critics of federal programs were both wrong and right: wrong in the short run about the state being able to care for its own, and right in the long run that more and more of the state's old responsibilities would be assumed by the federal government, putting Ohio into a sort of vassalage to Washington. But neither the nation nor the state remains static. They are forced on occasion to break new ground in their relationship, and the process is usually painful.

Despite the crisis in employment, the depression years were fraught with violence, as organized labor flexed new muscles provided by section 7(a) of the National Industrial Recovery

A class in secondary education, Hamilton, 1936. (73)

An Ohio Portrait

The Sandusky County courthouse at Fremont was expanded through a public works program in the 1930s. (74)

Lakeview Terrace, Cleveland, constructed by WPA labor. (75)

Urbana sidewalks were improved by a federal work relief program. (76)

A new home meant new play areas for these children in Lakeview Terrace. (77)

Young men of the CCC worked on outdoor
projects across the state. Scene in Butler County. (78)

The WPA sponsored self-help projects throughout
Ohio during the depressed 1930s. (79) (80)

Artists and writers also were employed by the WPA.
A picnic near Dayton, 1936. (81)

An Ohio Portrait

Norman Thomas, six-time Socialist Party candidate for president, once was a paperboy for Warren Harding's *Marion Star*. (82)

Strike at the Fisher Body plant, Cleveland, 1939. (83)

Act and later by the Wagner-Connery Act of 1935, which guaranteed labor the right to bargain collectively. Unions had been active in Ohio during the crisis of the early thirties. More than .800 strikes marked the years from 1929 to 1936. In Toledo, the 1934 Electric Auto-Lite strike portended unionization of the automotive industry.

The formation of a new industrial union — the Congress of Industrial Organizations (CIO) — under the resourceful and aggressive John L. Lewis, brought on new organizing wars which led to major strikes in Ohio. One of the first was the Goodyear strike of 1936. Like many Ohio corporations, Goodyear had long had a thorough program of employee benefits; but paternalistic management, however well-intentioned and operated, still kept all the options to itself. When Goodyear workers struck for recognition of the CIO as bargaining agent and refused to vacate their posts, the "sit-down" technique, first used in

a General Tire strike, was perfected. By the early 1940s Goodyear and the other major rubber producers were successfully organized by the United Rubber Workers (CIO). In 1937 the CIO turned its attention to the steel industry. The steel owners and managers were anti-union and fought a determined battle to keep the CIO out of Republic Steel, Youngstown Sheet and Tube, and other members of "little steel." Several strikers were killed and many were injured in the resulting violence in the Mahoning Valley. The Ohio National Guard was called to duty, and under their protection workers returned to their jobs. Ultimately the union prevailed and "little steel" was organized. Similar contests on a lesser scale were fought all over the state, until World War II put a damper on labor organizing activity.

The impetus which the New Deal gave to federal involvement at all levels of American life was reinforced and extended in some ways by

World War II. When bombs fell on Pearl Harbor in 1941, America had taken only halfway measures to prepare for a war which many citizens still hoped could be avoided. Some Ohio boys were already in the service, having been drafted under terms of the Burke-Wadsworth Act of 1940. Once actual hostilities broke out, Ohio and her sister states made quick and extensive adjustments to wartime conditions.

This statistical summary conveys some idea of the scope of Ohio's involvement: More than 600,000 Ohio men and women served in the armed forces, on land, sea, and in the air. As in previous wars, black Ohioans served in proportion to their numbers. Ohioans predominated in some units, including the 37th Division, the old Ohio National Guard unit. In early 1941 its 9,000 guardsmen were augmented by 10,000 conscripts, bringing the unit to full division strength. The 37th performed with distinction in the southwest Pacific and in Luzon. Its accomplishment was representative of many other essentially Ohio units.

On the homefront, a total effort went into supplying food and equipment to sustain worldwide military operations. In a move reminiscent of the first World War era, tens of thousands of farm workers were imported from Mexico, the West Indies, and the American South to provide agricultural labor. German and Italian prisoners of war were also used as agricultural laborers and in food processing plants at places like Bowling Green and Defiance. These efforts helped provide a 30 percent increase in Ohio's agricultural production between 1940 and 1945, even though the number of acres under cultivation actually declined. Home consumption of food supplies was lessened by the success of "victory gardens," in which Ohioans used marginal lands to produce vegetable crops worth more

Instruction in a World War II defense training school, Delaware, 1942. (85)

Assembly line at the Westinghouse plant, Lima, (86)

Corsair fighters, built by Goodyear Aircraft in Akron, on duty in the South Pacific. (87)

than $150 million.

In industrial production Ohio's record was awesome. Through V-E Day (April, 1945) Ohio industries had received war contracts totaling nearly $18 billion, with aircraft, ordnance, and shipbuilding predominating. Only Michigan, New York, and California produced more for the war effort. Among Ohio cities, Cleveland led the way with contracts valued at $5 billion; Cincinnati had $3.4 billion; Akron had $2.1 billion and Dayton $1.7 billion. Ohio's production of coal increased 82 percent between 1939 and 1945. Overall employment in Ohio was up 55 percent in 1943 over the 1939 level, and average earnings of industrial workers increased 65 percent.

The labor void in industry was filled by

Troops of Ohio's 37th Division on reconnaissance duty in the Solomon Islands. (88)

southern blacks, who migrated to Ohio in record numbers; by white women, those "Rosie the Riveters" of the wartime song; and by the young, who were not yet eligible for the draft. By 1945 blacks constituted 8 percent of Ohio's skilled workers, up 6 percent from the 1940 figures. Black workers joined the CIO with little difficulty, but the old AFL craft unions still largely denied them entry.

Gross statistics conceal as much as they reveal, dealing as they do with percentages, averages, and totals rather than with individuals. Civilians complained about inconveniences — gas and tire rationing, food shortages, power dimouts, crowded public facilities, and similar problems. Colleges became overwhelmingly female and most abandoned varsity athletics, except for the numerous Ohio colleges with military training programs. Many people lived with intense anxieties, fearful of their own predicament and those of their sons, husbands, daughters, and friends. But to a greater degree than in any previous war perhaps, Americans were united, agreed upon the need to press victory against archenemies about whose villainy there was little doubt. The internal divisions that marked Ohioans during the Civil War and the intense, anti-German harrassment campaigns of World War I had no counterpart in this great struggle.

War's end found Ohio with a vast pool of veterans to be absorbed into the economy. This was accomplished with considerable effectiveness, given the enormous scope of the problem. By the tens of thousands, Ohio veterans took advantage of the G.I. bill, an educational benefits package which trained men and women in everything from nuclear physics to mortuary science. Great numbers of women left their wartime factory jobs, many of which were taken up by returning veterans. Unemployment compensation, G.I. loans for easy term house purchases, and a generous state bonus assisted veterans in this transition period. The long-term effects of the war were many, but the major ones were: the end of the depression; a redistribution of population; the education of a whole generation to America's place in a world society; a liberalization in thinking about women's roles; an expanded industrial base that largely underwent quick reconversion to civilian needs although some tank plants, ordnance plants, and military installations were not readily convertible; and, one may surmise, a temporary sense of national accomplishment in a great cause.

(89)

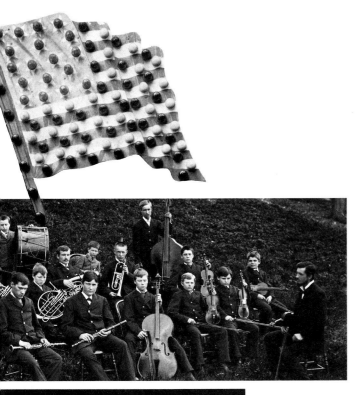

Ohio and the Arts

The development of cultural refinements is directly related to leisure time. Those who write, paint, and compose must be free to exercise their creative talents; those who admire their works must have at least marginal time and energy for this pursuit. Clearly, in a pioneer state not many can spare the time or energy for cultural pursuits. The country fiddler and the homestyle poet reciting doggerel verse are the products of an environment where the arts are marginal to the main business at hand — making a living. However, from Ohio's earliest days small numbers of people were engaged in creative artistic endeavors. It is not surprising that the focus of this activity was in the towns, especially Cincinnati, for traditionally town dwellers have more leisure to cultivate the arts than do an essentially rural people.

As Ohio matured, one might expect a native literature to develop, but this did not happen. Ohio gathered in people of many different traditions — New England, Pennsylvanian, and Southern — and from this amalgam emerged no single tradition or style that would be peculiarly Ohio's. Those characteristics people share and recognize as part of their common heritage were not so focused in Ohio as perhaps they were in old Connecticut or Virginia. Indeed, one of Ohio's most pronounced traits was — and is — its "typicality;" it has always lacked a sense of uniqueness.

When creative artists did emerge in Ohio they frequently moved elsewhere to do their work — to New York, or Boston, or even to Europe. There they could find like-minded people who shared their enthusiasms, and there were located the publishers and much of the art-buying public. Nevertheless, the artists and writers who spent their formative years in Ohio were as much the product of the state as were glass, tires, roller bearings, vacuum cleaners, cash regis-

An Ohio Portrait

William D. Gallagher (1808–1894), poet and journalist. (1)

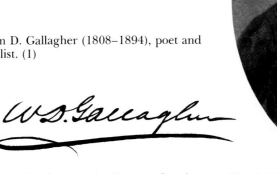

ters, scales, soap, or playing cards. Years after he left his native state, Sherwood Anderson acknowledged that his Ohio experiences still molded his outlook.

Among the arts, it was in literature that Ohio made its most impressive contribution to the national culture. Some who came into the Ohio Country at an early time left journals describing the wilderness and the efforts made to tame it. Dr. Daniel Drake, the versatile Cincinnati physician and man of many talents, wrote valuable descriptions of his city while also composing useful works in the natural sciences. The principal man of letters in early Ohio was perhaps William D. Gallagher, who came to Cincinnati when he was ten years old and, as a poet and journalist, tried to do something for the literary character of "this Transmontane world." Another early contributor to literature was the Reverend Timothy Flint, whose subjects ranged from local ones to more exotic locales such as Mexico. Much of early Ohio's literary energy went into periodical publishing. The foremost magazines included the *Ladies' Repository, and Gatherings of the West;* along with the *Western Review, Western Messenger,* the *Cincinnati Mirror,* and the *Western Monthly Magazine;* all of which were published in Cincinnati, the literary center of the entire West. Early Ohio newspapers often featured poetry on the front page; this literary form was surprisingly popular 150 years ago.

Women contributed a large part of Ohio's pre-Civil War literary efforts. The Cincinnati sisters, Alice and Phoebe Cary, wrote saccharine verses which were widely read and admired. Sarah Morgan Piatt was another early writer of lyric poetry. Most notable among women authors was Harriett Beecher Stowe, a Connecticut native whose residence in Cincinnati provided her with material for her famous and influential novel,

Uncle Tom's Cabin. Other successful women writers of the time included the novelists Maria Collins, Mrs. E. D. Livermore, and Martha Thomas.

Two Ohio writers who were extraordinarily successful in the decades before the Civil War were Emerson Bennett and Ned Buntline (E. C. Z. Judson), whose adventure stories were best sellers. Both concentrated on Indian tales and western adventures, although Buntline occasionally looked farther afield for topics.

William Dean Howells was Ohio's first native son to earn a literary reputation of the first magnitude. Born in Martin's Ferry, he spent his youth in a variety of Ohio towns from Hamilton to Ashtabula as his father, a newspaperman, moved from place to place. Howells wrote frequently of his early years in Ohio; he left the state in 1872 at age thirty-five. Perhaps the best of these efforts was his autobiography, *Years of My Youth.* Of the scores of volumes he produced, *The Rise of Silas Lapham* is most often cited as a work of enduring literary merit. Some of his most important work involved editing a number of influential eastern magazines. For these activities, and because of his prominence among literary figures, he became known as the "dean" of American letters.

Late nineteenth century authors include Brand Whitlock of Urbana, whose public career was as well known to contemporaries as his writings. Ambrose "Bitter" Bierce of Horse Cave, Meigs County, wrote fine Civil War stories but was best known perhaps for his *Devil's Dictionary,* filled with caustic social commentary. Charles W. Chesnutt, a black Clevelander, wrote the *Conjure Woman* at century's end. Widely recognized fictional characters created by Ohio authors of this period were Elsie Dinsmore, the heroine of a series by Martha Finley of Chillicothe, and Nick Carter, defender of the law, the creation of Thomas Harbaugh of Casstown.

Ohio and the Arts

The poems of Phoebe Cary (1824–1871) and her sister Alice were widely admired in mid-nineteenth century America. (2)

William Dean Howells (1837–1920) supported the "new realism" in literature. (3)

Paul Laurence Dunbar (1872–1906) at home in Dayton. (4)

Ohio's foremost poet at the turn of the century was Paul Laurence Dunbar of Dayton. As a Negro, Dunbar repeatedly experienced personal frustrations, but he was persistent in his art and ultimately received wide acclaim shortly before his early death at age thirty-four. He is best known for dialect poems such as "When the Co'n Pone's Hot" and "When Malindy Sings," but he was equally effective in literary English. Today his Dayton home is maintained as a property of the Ohio Historical Society.

Among writers of historical romances one might include Delaware's Mary Catherwood (*Romance of Dollard*), and Malta's James B. Naylor (*In the Days of St. Clair*). One of the most famous of Ohio's historical novels is *Betty Zane*. Its fame rests less on its literary merits than on the fact that author Zane Grey thought that this account of his heroic ancestor, the savior of Fort Henry during the Revolution, would be his most famous work. It could not begin to compete in popularity with his enormously successful westerns such as *Riders of the Purple Sage*.

In the twentieth century a number of Ohio-born authors achieved literary eminence. Sherwood Anderson of Camden described the hidden side of small town life in his famous *Winesburg, Ohio*. Louis Bromfield of Mansfield was an important novelist who won the Pulitzer Prize for *Early Autumn*. But his more enduring fame will forever be associated with books describing his restoration of worn-out Ohio farm land by the application of natural restorative techniques. Malabar Farm, his 400-acre spread in Richland County, is the subject of much of his later writing.

Hart Crane, born in Garrettsville, wrote *The Bridge*, a work that placed him among the best of modern poets. Crane ended his difficult life prematurely at thirty-two by leaping from a ship which was bringing him home from Mexico.

Sherwood Anderson (1876–1941) used people of Clyde (Sandusky County) as models for his characters in *Winesburg, Ohio*. (6)

Part of Langston Hughes' productive career was spent in Cleveland. (5)

Zane Grey (1875–1939) of Zanesville forsook dentistry for writing and became a master teller of western tales. (7)

Louis Bromfield (1896–1956) excelled in his twin loves, writing and agriculture. At Malabar Farm. (8)

The poetry of Hart Crane (1899–1932, shown at right with his father, combined good technique with experimental daring. (9)

(10)

'For Heaven's sake, why don't you go outdoors and trace something?'

A relaxed James Thurber (1894–1961) and a familiar Thurber cartoon.

(11)

(12)

Another poet and novelist from northeastern Ohio, Herman Fetzer, wrote for an Akron paper under the name Jake Falstaff. His zestful and nostalgic pieces reveal a love for life and for Ohio people and the countryside. Other early twentieth century poets of note were the "hard luck" writers, Jim Tully and Harry Kemp, and also Ridgely Torrence of Xenia, Jean Starr Untermeyer of Zanesville, and the one-time Clevelander, Langston Hughes, black poet and writer.

James Thurber of Columbus was one of America's most accomplished humorists. He described his early years in Columbus in *My Life and Hard Times*. His simply executed cartoons with captions of off-beat whimsy were popular features of his work. Thurber was identified with the Ohio State University. A number of other writers with some university connection or identification are Dorothy Canfield Fisher, Ludwig Lewisohn, Rollo Brown, Harlan Hatcher, Walter Havighurst, and Gustave Eckstein.

The buckeye state was the birthplace or residence of a host of important writers of history, biography, and other non-fiction, but there is not space for a roll call. Ohio's literary contributions today are noteworthy both for quality and quantity. The Martha Kinney Cooper Ohioana Li-

brary Association does much to both encourage and recognize contemporary Ohio writers. Until its recent demise, the *Kenyon Review* was an outstanding periodical which frequently published emerging writers. Several university presses provide outlets for serious works, most of which have limited general sales appeal. Economic realities have forced several such presses to close, but the Ohio State, Kent State, and Ohio University presses continue to publish. The Ohio Historical Society maintains a scholarly journal, *Ohio History*; a popular publication, *Echoes*; and publishes a great assortment of useful material dealing with the state's people and places. The Cincinnati and the Western Reserve historical societies also publish much material of value. A number of smaller local or regional journals of history, the arts, and commentary on contemporary issues also help to provide outlets for Ohio writers.

In the visual arts as in literature, the early years in Ohio were not conducive to major accomplishments. Indeed, until very recently Ohio has not been a center of major importance for painters and sculptors. Although many fine artists were Ohio-born or spent their creative years in the buckeye state, there has never been a concentration of talent and method that could be

An Ohio Portrait

Fountain Square, Cincinnati, May art exhibit in the 1930s. (13)

identified as an Ohio "school." Early Ohio painters were likely to spend their time at practical tasks like decorating furniture or painting signs. Some of the most creative artists earned their livings by painting chinaware. Pioneer society could be a limiting environment for one who wanted to earn a living painting landscapes or portraits. There were a few, however, like George Beck who came to Cincinnati in the late eighteenth century as a soldier and stayed to paint landscapes and portraits. John I. Williams, Godfrey Frankenstein, and Thomas Cole also achieved recognition at an early time, especially the English-born Cole, who later won fame as one of the Hudson River School of painters.

Among early Ohioans who went to Europe for training and inspiration was sculptor Hiram Powers, who got his first training in the short-lived Cincinnati Art Academy in 1826. Under the patronage of Nicholas Longworth, he moved to Florence, Italy, where his talents matured. Perhaps his best known work was the *Greek Slave*, which caused a furor when it arrived in Cincinnati in 1849. The Queen City survived its shock at seeing this undraped female form, and Powers' work won acclaim throughout America. Ohio's foremost sculptor, however, was John Quincy Adams Ward of Urbana, who concentrated on American themes such as the well-known *Indian Hunter* in New York's Central Park and the statue of General George H. Thomas, "The Rock of Chicamauga," in Washington, D. C.

Cincinnati dominated the Ohio art scene in the nineteenth century even as it dominated the literary scene. Here the first art gallery was established prior to the Civil War, and here worked Frank Duveneck, a native Kentuckian who sharpened his skills in Europe before returning to Cincinnati in 1888. A highly talented artist in his own right, he was also most influential in his role

as Dean of the Faculty of the Cincinnati Art Academy and as an adviser to the Art Museum. Duveneck was accomplished in oils, etching, and sculpting. Other artists associated with Cincinnati in the mid and late nineteenth century were Joseph Twachtman, an impressionist, and Robert Henri who, while born along the Ohio, spent much of his career abroad before returning to America to become the leader of the "Ashcan School" of early twentieth century realists.

Not all of Ohio's artistic action was in Cincinnati. Archibald Willard of Wellington did much of his work in Cleveland, and he practically made a career out of his one great painting that struck the fancy of the nation, *The Spirit of '76*, which he painted again and again so that several places today claim originals. Cleveland was also the home of one of the state's premier etchers, Otto Bacher. Perhaps the best recognized Ohio painter is George Bellows of Columbus. His love of action and sports is reflected in his subjects. Movement and occasional vivid colors give vitality to his paintings. His most widely reproduced painting, *Stag at Sharkey's*, which depicts a prizefight in a smoke-filled room, hangs in the Cleveland Museum of Art. Charles Burchfield of Ashtabula was among the first to paint realistic pictures of small towns, including many in Ohio.

To assess Ohio artists of the last forty years would require a study well beyond the scope of this survey. It is a shame that this cannot be done, for Ohioans should know of the many skilled painters, sculptors, etchers, engravers, potters, weavers, jewelers, and similar artists and craftsmen who worked in relative obscurity. The artistic life of Ohio has never been so vital as it is today. Every community of any size has its local art circles whose members support and encourage one another and organize shows that put their creations before an ever larger, appreciative

Cleveland Museum of Art. (14)

public. Prices paid for original art works have risen to the point where many artists can now earn all or a significant part of their livelihood from sales. Art shows and art galleries have proliferated throughout the state, not only in the cities but in little towns like Peninsula in Summit County, restored Roscoe Village in Coshocton County, and Roseville in Perry County. It is true that much of the contemporary production and display is of the "artsy-craftsy" style, but in the visual arts, as in music and literature, those things that appeal to a broad public audience are not always the creations considered most worthy by expert critics and assessors.

Ohio's major resources for the visual arts are impressive. The Cleveland Museum of Art has one of the nation's finest collections, housed in superb buildings, and managed in a highly professional manner. The Toledo Museum of Art boasts an outstanding collection of glass among its many other treasures. The Cincinnati Art Museum, with many valuable works including those of Ohio artists, is of major importance. The Butler Gallery in Youngstown, the Columbus and Dayton museums, and a number of smaller galleries — Oberlin College, Taft Museum, Johnson-Humrick-House Museum at Coshocton — have important collections. Canton, Akron, and numerous smaller cities are constantly developing their galleries. The Ohio Historical Center, the Western Reserve Historical Society Museum, the Cincinnati Historical Society, and numerous county historical groups have art treasures hanging in their properties and museums.

One of Ohio's major art resources is to be found in its uncommonly large number of college and university art programs. Here in departments of art and fine arts are concentrated tremendous reservoirs of talent which would astonish the man-in-the-street, who generally does

not know of their existence. Their influence in educating the public, especially the students who are training to become art teachers in the secondary and primary schools of the state, will have a great deal to do with the future vitality of artistic endeavor in Ohio. To a large extent these schools have replaced the art schools formerly associated with galleries. There are still, however, a few outstanding art schools around the state, including Cleveland's Institute of Art, one of the best known of these institutions. Still another evidence of the current vitality of art in contemporary Ohio is the presence of art critics on the staffs of leading daily newspapers. The critics' views may have more influence on the opinions of professionals than on the buying habits of the public; nevertheless, their presence is evidence of the maturity achieved on the Ohio scene. This abundance of artistic endeavor and accomplishment bodes well for the future of the visual arts in Ohio.

Ohioans' contributions to music represent various levels of sophistication. As with literature and the visual arts, Ohio is associated with an impressive level of musical accomplishment. Few

Dayton Art Institute. (15)

An Ohio Portrait

Riverfront No. 1, oil by George Bellows (1885-1925). (16)

Columbus Before the Council of Salamanca, by Frank Duveneck (1814-1919). (18)

Midsummer Day, watercolor by Alice Schille (1869-1955). (17)

Several Ohio galleries own works of important Ohio artists. These works represent a variety of periods, media, and styles.

Dancer in a Yellow Shawl, oil by Robert Henri (1865-1929). (21)

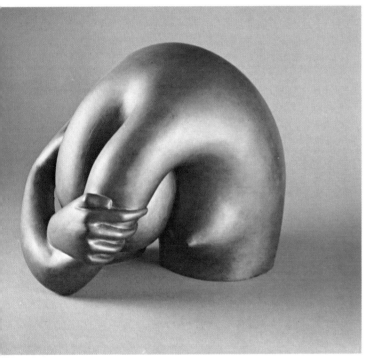

Figure in Grief, bronze sculpture by Hugo Robus (1885-1964). (19)

Winter Solstice, watercolor by Charles Burchfield (1893-1967). (20)

Shake Hands? or *The Cook,* oil by Lilly Martin Spencer (1822-1901). (22)

An Ohio Portrait

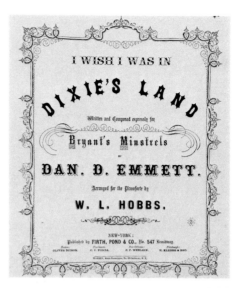

(23)

Ohioans are aware of the major musical talents associated with their state; more, perhaps, would recognize Ohio's contributions to popular and church music. Certainly in its early years Ohio was better represented in the popular ranks than in the so-called "serious" or classical musical traditions.

Folk visual art had its counterpart in folk music during the pioneer period. The laments, work songs, and drinking songs of various groups of settlers were brought to Ohio. Gospel hymns were popular everywhere; people liked to sing them even when there was little evidence that they took the words as seriously as they might. Ohio composers contributed many of the best-known and best-loved of these hymns, among them *The Old Rugged Cross* by George Bernard, *Softly and Tenderly Jesus is Calling* and *Bringing In The Sheaves* by William Thompson, *Jesus Lover of My Soul* by R. E. Hudson, and *Brighten the Corner Where You Are* by Homer Rodeheaver. Among Ohio composers of popular secular songs are Benjamin Hanby (Rushville), *Darling Nellie Gray*; Daniel Decauter Emmett (Mt. Vernon), *Old Dan Tucker*, and *In Dixies Land*, which he wrote for Bryant's Minstrels with whom he performed. *Dixie* became a favorite in the North and was adopted by the Confederacy as its rallying song. Tell Taylor (Findlay) wrote *Down By the Old Mill Stream*; H. D. L. Webster (Zanesville) wrote *Lorena*, a Civil War favorite; Oley Speaks (Canal Winchester) wrote *On The Road to Mandalay* and *Sylvia*, both much favored of concert singers; Ernest Ball (Cleveland) wrote the sentimental *Mother Machree* and *Let the Rest of the World Go By*.

The early singing traditions of Ohio were related strongly to the presence of German and Welsh immigrants. Both formed singing societies and encouraged systematically the perpetuation of their rich musical traditions. The German

Maennerchors, Liedertafels, and Saengerfests brought a vital musical tradition to many Ohio cities and towns. The Welsh organized annual singing competitions. The Eisteddfod has long been a tradition at Jackson (Jackson County) in the coal district where Welsh miners were employed. Immigrants from many other countries brought their musical and dance traditions with them to Ohio in the late nineteenth and early twentieth centuries.

Sangerfest buildings in Cleveland above ca. 1875, and Cincinnati (below). (24) (25)

The Halka Singing Society of Cleveland, 1937. (26)

For over a century, Cincinnati's May Festival has been a great cultural attraction. (27)

Cincinnati dominated early Ohio's serious music efforts; organized musical groups appeared there as early as 1811. Five years later a band was formed, and shortly after that the Haydn Society came together to sing the great oratorios. Thanks to the Germans, good string orchestras were playing in Cincinnati by 1825. By mid-century, many Ohio cities and towns had musical societies and organizations; they supported concerts, brought visiting artists like the "Swedish Nightingale" Jenny Lind, Ole Bull, and Adelina Patti to perform in the local opera house or music hall; supported private music teachers, termed the "professor" in many nineteenth century novels, and began music instruction in public schools. Musical organizations of all kinds, especially bands and singing societies, proliferated in the late nineteenth century. Touring minstrel shows brought "blackface" entertainment to generations not yet embarrassed by racial stereotypes.

Permanent musical societies organized to perform or sponsor formal music date from the post-Civil War period. In Cincinnati the Theodore Thayer orchestra concerts led to an annual May Festival starting in 1873. Great excitement was generated by the annual festival. Henry Howe described the scene in the 1880s:

> The streets are gay with flags, the hotels and public buildings resplendent with artistic adornments, illustrative of music and musical celebrities, and at night illuminated. Multitudes come, some from hundreds of miles away, to attend these festivals; from Missouri, Illinois, Michigan, and other Western States; and it is said that once there was a man who came all the way from Boston, but we never believed it.

By the early twentieth century, fine symphony orchestras were playing in Cincinnati and Cleveland. The Cincinnati Symphony (1895) rose to the first rank under Leopold Stokowski. Many other fine musicians, among them Fritz Reiner, Eugene Goosens, and Thor Johnson have served as its conductors. The Cleveland Orchestra became a permanent organization in 1918 under the direction of Nikolai Sokoloff. A permanent home for the orchestra was secured with the construction of Severance Hall in the University Circle area. Under great conductors such as Artur Rodzinski and George Szell, the Cleveland orchestra became the best symphony ensemble in the world, in the opinion of many informed observers. In recent years, goodwill trips overseas by these two great orchestras have spread their fame far beyond the nation's borders. They are

Sangerfest in a contemporary setting, Columbus. (28)

Cleveland Orchestra in rehearsal. (29)

Cleveland Summer Symphony Orchestra at Public Hall, 1940. (30)

Blossom Music Center, Summit County, the summer home of the Cleveland Orchestra. (31)

A band concert on the village green at Medina recreates a favorite diversion of earlier times. (32)

University Circle, Cleveland, with Severance Hall in the foreground and the Museum of Art in the background. (33)

clearly among Ohio's prime cultural assets. The Cleveland Orchestra has a new showcase summer home, the Blossom Music Center, located in a pastoral setting in the hills of Northampton Township, Summit County.

Ohio claims a number of other symphony orchestras whose performances reach a high level of achievement, even though their players are not full time performers. The Akron, Canton, Dayton, Columbus, and Youngstown symphony orchestras fall in this category. Hamilton, Lima, Mansfield, Middletown, Newark, and Springfield also boast symphony orchestras.

The colleges and universities of Ohio support impressive, comprehensive music programs. Oberlin Conservatory (1867) was the first collegiate music school in the nation. From the colleges and universities come symphony orchestras and bands, chamber groups, all sorts of small ensembles, extremely talented solo performers, vocalists, choirs, glee clubs, and of course, the great razzle-dazzle marching bands. Ohio State claims the first all-brass marching band; Akron had the first rolling bass drum, encased in a huge rubber tire; Wooster's Scots march in kilts; and out in front of every band are scores of majorettes contributing to the visual attraction. The Cincinnati Conservatory of Music and the Cleveland Institute of Music are highly regarded independent schools. Faculty members of these schools are often symphony orchestra musicians.

Opera, oratorios, and choral music have long been a part of the Ohio music scene. Opera has traditionally been located principally in Cincinnati and Cleveland. The Metropolitan Opera makes an annual one-week appearance in Cleveland each spring. Now, thanks largely to the concentration of talent in various schools of music, opera groups can be found around the state, especially in Cleveland, Columbus, Springfield,

An Ohio Portrait

Phillegan's Brass Band, Cleveland. (35)

A dance orchestra entertains in front of Cincinnati's
Union Terminal, 1936. (34)

With his everpresent top hat, cane, and clarinet, Circleville's Ted Lewis won millions of fans with his rendition of "Me and My Shadow." (37)

and other metropolitan areas. Various Ohio composers have written operas, such as Henry Lawrence Freeman's *Voodoo* or Francesco De-Leone's *Alglalla*, an attempt at American opera first performed in Akron by Metropolitan Opera stars. Among Ohio's operatic and concert singers one might mention Rose Bampton, Helen Jepson, Cecil Fanning, and Evan Williams as representative of an impressive array of talent.

One often overlooks those people whose financial support and organizing ability made possible the great musical organizations. Henry Abbey of Akron became the nation's premier talent organizer in the late nineteenth century through his work with New York's Metropolitan Opera Company. Augustus Julliard established the Julliard Foundation, which supports one of America's fine music schools. Many dedicated women played significant roles. In Cincinnati Mrs. Maria Longworth Nichols, Miss Helene Sparrman, and Mrs. Charles Taft made it possible for that city to enjoy much of its fine music. In Cleveland Mrs. Adella Prentiss Hughes and Mrs. Dudley Blossom are among many who helped bring the best in music to the Forest City. Today's enormous costs have forced music organizations to look toward a broader base of support involving large numbers of donors. If costs and labor problems can be reconciled, the future of Ohio's professional musical organizations seems very bright indeed.

In the field of contemporary popular music Ohio has been a major producer and consumer of talent. Among native sons and daughters who have received national recognition are band leaders Ted Lewis, Sammy Kaye, and Henry Mancini; singing groups like the Mills Brothers; vocalists like Dean Martin, Vaughn Monroe, Nancy Wilson, and Jane Froman.

Ohio has never been a true mecca for jazz or

Dixieland enthusiasts, but it has done somewhat better with country music which has always had a wide appeal in the buckeye state. Ohio shares a little of the Appalachian tradition, but the southern hill people who came by the hundreds of thousands in the war years of the twentieth century provided impetus to what was once called hillbilly music. It is all-pervasive on scores of radio stations. The Paint Valley jamboree at Bainbridge is an indication of the vitality of this musical style as is the Country Cavalcade in Columbus. Today on every college campus and in hundreds of clubs and lounges, home-grown groups are playing good quality jazz, rock, and country music. Soul music and gospel music rank high in listener appeal on many Ohio radio stations with several stations geared almost entirely to the listening tastes of black citizens. Latin and mariachi styles are universally popular but are particularly featured by stations that reach Ohio's Mexican, Puerto Rican, Cuban, and other Latin groups.

Related to the musical arts is dance. Again one must distinguish between professional, classical dance and the kind of tap and toe dancing that graced endless grade school and high school stages. Serious students of the dance generally

An Ohio Portrait

The Paint Valley Jamboree, Bainbridge, Ross County. (38)

Square dancing, a popular pastime for thousands of enthusiasts. (39)

left Ohio to learn their art in one of America's few dance centers. But today the situation has changed. A growing popular appetite for professional dance has led to the formation of numerous dance programs affiliated with a college or community. Older groups in Dayton, Cleveland, and Cincinnati have been joined in recent years by talented new groups like the Ohio Chamber Ballet.

Perhaps the best way to discover the variety and vitality of current musical art forms in Ohio is to peruse the local newspapers and magazines, which feature the arts and schedules of their performances. The magnitude of musical activity of high caliber is impressive. One must conclude that Ohio is alive and well in the musical arts.

One can escape most art forms if a particular expression is not pleasing. There are few times, aside from school assignments, when one is compelled to read a particular novel, listen to certain music, or study a painting or sculpture. With architecture, however, it is different. We cannot avoid seeing the architect's work about us, every day, in every condition of light and in every mood. Only the all-prevailing Muzak piped into the dentist's office or the atrocious painting hung in our line of vision at the office approaches the assault on our aesthetic senses that characterizes our daily view of buildings. Whatever constitutes charm to the eye and spirit of the beholder is generally lacking in Ohio towns and cities. Few have been able to protect themselves from strip development, urban sprawl, and the loss of softening trees to Dutch Elm disease, oak wilt, or various other natural disasters. A few Ohio towns retain some sense of self-contained integrity. Hudson, Westfield Center (Leroy), Granville, Mount Pleasant, Burton, and Oxford are some of the towns that remain essentially intact. Others that once had great beauty and charm — Norwalk, Marietta, and Lancaster, for example — are still above average in attractiveness, but newer buildings and the deterioration of previously attractive areas detract from the congruence they formerly displayed. Something happens to the spirit of a town when fine old homes have store fronts attached to them or gas stations built alongside them.

Not all of the burden can be laid at the feet of the architect. Most buildings never see the fine hand of a professional designer, and as for the destruction of the integrity of a town or city, blame the city fathers for a lack of intelligent code and zoning enforcement.

In architecture as in other art forms, Ohio has been eclectic from its early days. First settlers built log cabin houses and slightly larger log structures which served as barns. Within a very few years, however, many had abandoned their initial dwelling for a frame house built of lumber cut in nearby mills. At this point distinct regional styles became evident. Wherever New Englanders settled, one would find the one-and-a-half cottage or its later variation, the Cape Cod cottage, the Central Chimney Colonial, and the two-story Double Pile (Georgian) house, featuring on both floors a central hallway with two rooms on either side of it. Throughout northern Ohio, the gable-front house with sidewing was popular. In the Western Reserve, houses were often painted red. Henry Howe, who traveled this way in the 1840s, was reminded of old Connecticut by the structures, their color, and arrangement. When Howe traveled the same country forty years later, most houses were painted white or a neutral color; many were the ornate creations of architects; porches and various adornments had been added.

In southern and central Ohio considerable variety appeared in early house styles. The En-

Downtown renewal programs are changing the face of Ohio cities as in Akron's "superblock" development. (40)

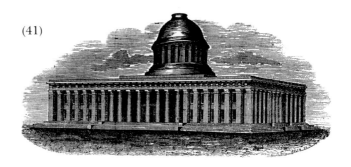

(41)

(42)

glish "I" — two and a half stories high, one room deep, with center chimney and side gables — was a common form. Frequent additions were made to the basic structure. The Log Pen cabin and the Double Southern style house were also relatively common. Southern influences were seen in high ceilings and in the frequency with which brick construction was used. Areas settled by Pennsylvania Germans contain stone houses so sturdy that many are only slightly changed today. Wayne County, especially, has many handsome examples of stone structures. Many farm houses in Seneca County were constructed of brick, and to this day they dot the rural landscape around Tiffin.

At a surprisingly early time some quite elegant houses were built, especially in the larger towns and emerging cities. By the mid-nineteenth century Ohio was able to boast communities like Lancaster, Warren, Painesville, Chillicothe, Marietta, and many more which had streets lined with houses of architectural interest and distinction. Much of the interest derived from the introduction of newer styles such as the Greek Revival and the Jeffersonian Classic. The post-Civil War period brought the elaborate Gothic Revival and the Victorian Mansard styles to cities and towns. On farms and in small communities the same period saw the large-scale introduction of the pyramid roof style. Both a southern and a midwestern variety of this basic pattern exist in the state.

Many excellent books, some beautifully illustrated, detail the development of architectural styles in Ohio and in certain sections of the state. Only a few of the state's structures that are of special interest either because they typify a particular form or style or because they are unique can be mentioned here. The Ohio State House must be noted first. Situated in a ten-acre park in

The Ohio State House was designed with a dome (top), but the Greek Doric structure was completed in 1861 without it. At the turn of the century (middle) the grounds were less developed than at present (bottom). (43)

Tyler Davidson Fountain, Cincinnati, ca. 1876 (44)

Dayton Public Library building, late nineteenth century. (45)

Cincinnati's Union Terminal is one of many Ohio public buildings displaying artistic murals. (46)

The classical lines of the old Montgomery County Courthouse, Dayton, as they appeared, ca. 1870. (47)

The Licking County courthouse in Newark is rather typical of the monumental architecture favored for such structures. (48)

Public Square, Mansfield, in the late nineteenth century with City Hall (center) and the Richland County Courthouse. (49)

the middle of Columbus, the capitol building is a splendid and dignified example of the Greek Revival style with its great Doric columns setting off a severe facade. The cornerstone of this massive structure was laid in 1839, but the building was not completed until 1861 since disputes, disease, and delays hampered its progress. A compromise with the original plan resulted in the planned full dome giving way to a flat-topped cylindrical dome. Beloved by many Ohioans for its uniqueness, the effect caused some early observers to call the building a "cheesebox on a raft." An annex built in the early twentieth century detracts from the symmetry of the original building.

Many other public buildings are of note in the state: The old Montgomery County Courthouse in Dayton, started about 1850, is an outstanding example of the Classic style. The older State Office Building in Columbus is a good example of an institutional style much favored in the 1920s and 1930s, while the new, forty-one-story State Office Tower represents contemporary thinking about proper form for large public office structures. Cleveland's new Justice Center, still under construction, is an example of how difficult it is to construct large public buildings. The changes and compromises required by cost overruns, political squabbles, and interest group pressures often result in a building that is different in important ways from that originally projected, but such has always been the case with public buildings.

Churches provide one of the best showcases for architectural skills. Though most are simple or predictable structures, many in Ohio are of unusual interest. The 1825 Congregational Church on Tallmadge green has long been recognized as an outstanding example of the New England style, although the death of surrounding elms and the nearness of heavy traffic now

Octagon House, Monroeville, represents a
nineteenth century architectural fad. (50)

Interior of Stan Hywet Hall, Akron, one of
America's finest tudor style residences. (51)

Affluent Ohioans built striking homes. The Dudley Blossom residence (right) in Cuyahoga County, and *Glamorgan* (below) the H. W. Morgan mansion, Alliance. (53) (54)

The Wescott House, Springfield, designed by Frank Lloyd Wright. (52)

Residential housing on Hillsboro's North High Street in the late nineteenth century. (55)

deprive it of some of its former impact. An unusual innovation in church design is credited to Lewis Miller, farm machinery inventor and manufacturer and a founder of Chautauqua. His "Akron Plan," first employed in the First Methodist Church destroyed by fire many years ago, featured an auditorium-style sanctuary. In some churches the sanctuary was located side-by-side with another pie-shaped room of similar size which was partitioned into Sunday school rooms. Often this area could be isolated from the sanctuary by closing huge doors which telescoped into the walls when in the open position.

Many older churches like the Old Stone Church on Cleveland's Public Square have long been focuses of community sentiment. This 1855 structure of simplified Romanesque design now sits in the shadow of nondescript commercial buildings. The neo-classical Avondale Synagogue of Cincinnati represents fine design and detail. Toledo's Our Lady Queen of the Holy Rosary Cathedral is unique in that its Spanish Plateresque architecture was designed to represent the community's affinity for its overseas sister city, Toledo, Spain.

Countless new church buildings in a modern or contemporary mode have sprung up throughout Ohio. Lutherans and Roman Catholics in particular have built in a modern mode. Heaviness has given way to light and color. In fine suburban and exurban locations, park-like settings enhance beauty and effect. Ohio also has the modern counterpart of the old revivalist tabernacle. A striking example is the Cathedral of Tomorrow, a huge, circular structure in Northampton Township (Summit County), which is designed to take maximum advantage of television; indeed the congregation maintains the adjacent elaborate, modern TV studio. Clearly Ohioans cannot be of one mind about church architecture. For every

modernistic or functional structure rising in the state, a traditional style church may also be found under construction, although it is unlikely that the great elaborate buildings of a half-century ago will make a comeback.

Among the great houses of Ohio only a few can be mentioned. The Baum House in Cincinnati (now the Taft Museum) was built in 1820. Designed by James Hoban and Benjamin Latrobe, it is a fine example of Federal Period architecture. Even earlier, Thomas Worthington built his splendid Adena, a southern style country estate whose gracious stone mansion sits on a hill overlooking Chillicothe. Most of the great houses built by the industrial barons of the late nineteenth and early twentieth centuries have been razed or converted to other uses. Cleveland's "Millionaires Row" along Euclid Avenue is no more. The spread of the urban core destroyed fine houses in Toledo, Dayton, Cincinnati, and most smaller places like Chillicothe, Hamilton, East Liverpool, New Philadelphia, Findlay, and Tiffin. A few examples of these fine mansions remain — Hower House and F. A. Seiberling's Tudor mansion, Stan Hywet, in Akron; W. H. Morgan's Glamorgan in Alliance; Charles King's Kingwood in Mansfield; the Frank Lloyd Wright designed Westcott House in Springfield — but businesses, apartments, and condominiums now occupy the site of many gracious old houses. A recent development that is catching on across Ohio is the planned community. Here the architect and the landscape architect combine talents to create a controlled living environment such as one might find in the attractive Walden near Aurora in Portage County.

A number of Ohio structures merit special mention. Among them is the old National Cash Register plant in Dayton, America's first "daylight" factory building, whose walls are 80 per-

The Goodyear Zeppelin Dock, Akron, no longer houses the great dirigibles it was built to accommodate. (56)

Buildings and grounds of Dayton's National Cash Register Company. (58)

The University Hospitals of Case-Western Reserve University represent early twentieth century institutional architecture. (57)

cent glass. The Goodyear Zeppelin Dock at the Akron Municipal Airport is the world's largest building (in floor area) without interior supports, so immense that it rains inside the building when water vapor condenses. Older structures like Cleveland Municipal Stadium and the Ohio State University Stadium, each of which seats more than 80,000 fans, stand in contrast to the new Riverfront Stadium in Cincinnati. The Cleveland Coliseum, seating more than 20,000 people, is a good example of the modern indoor arena. Among commercial buildings the most impressive new developments are the great shopping malls, whose covered walkways are the modern urban substitute for the small town main street of years ago. Ohio, long in love with the automobile, has a vast number and assortment of these commercial centers which cater to a motorized public. They may lack the uniqueness of the Cleveland Arcade, the shopping mall of an earlier era, but they bring in the customers.

Much new construction graces Ohio's numerous college campuses. Many schools, including university branches and community colleges, are almost entirely new. Sinclair Community College recently built an entirely new campus in downtown Dayton. The Stark County Branch of Kent State University and the Stark Technical College share a new campus overlooking the huge new Belden Village shopping mall, where encroaching residential and apartment construction assure that in the near future it will be surrounded by a substantial new population base. Most construction at state campuses is clean, functional, and on the whole attractive, but little of it has the unusual or monumental quality that will set it apart in time to come. It is safe to speculate that there is no single building among those recently constructed that will retain the architectural appeal of Ohio University's Cutler Hall (1817) or Kenyon's Old Kenyon Hall (ca. 1827).

Cleveland Arcade. (

A scene in German Village, Columbus. (60)

Interior, Akron's E. J. Thomas Performing Arts Hall. (61)

A fine example of contemporary library construction, Taylor Memorial Library, Cuyahoga Falls. (62)

The cultural facilities of Ohio have been upgraded in the last two decades through construction of new, architecturally pleasing facilities for the arts and for literature. The old Carnegie Libraries that graced so many Ohio towns and cities are giving way to more open, well-lighted, and inviting structures like the Taylor Memorial Library in Cuyahoga Falls, where local artists provided paintings, sculptures, and artifacts to create a most pleasing effect. To the great cultural centers of Ohio — Cleveland's University Circle complex and Cincinnati's Eden Park, Music Hall, and other facilities — one can add a growing number of new centers designed to enhance the arts. Canton's Timken Cultural Center provides rooms for a theater, art gallery, and musical performances, all in a handsome structure, well-landscaped and located within easy access of the area's population. Akron's E. J. Thomas Performing Arts Hall, with its computer-controlled ceiling that can be adjusted to fit the auditorium to the size of the audience, has been widely praised as one of the nation's best facilities of its kind. The contemporary form of the Ohio Historical Center in Columbus caused some anxiety to traditionalists who associate historical societies with less modernistic building styles, but visitors enjoy its display areas.

Today the physical restructuring continues. Most Ohio cities have developed urban renewal programs. Cleveland's Erieview helped the Forest City start on a much-delayed and still incomplete redevelopment of the downtown area. Akron increased its tax revenues by converting a semi-slum into an attractive business development, the Grant-Washington project. Canton used urban renewal to create room for an industrial park. Cincinnati remade its Fountain Square area to emphasize a community focus. Lima, Newark, Middletown, and other small manufac-

Pegasus, in Canton's Timken Cultural Center. (63)

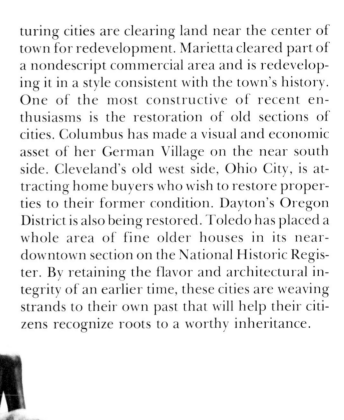

turing cities are clearing land near the center of town for redevelopment. Marietta cleared part of a nondescript commercial area and is redeveloping it in a style consistent with the town's history. One of the most constructive of recent enthusiasms is the restoration of old sections of cities. Columbus has made a visual and economic asset of her German Village on the near south side. Cleveland's old west side, Ohio City, is attracting home buyers who wish to restore properties to their former condition. Dayton's Oregon District is also being restored. Toledo has placed a whole area of fine older houses in its near-downtown section on the National Historic Register. By retaining the flavor and architectural integrity of an earlier time, these cities are weaving strands to their own past that will help their citizens recognize roots to a worthy inheritance.

(64)

Leisure, Recreation and Sports in Ohio

A society reveals much about itself in the way its people spend their leisure time and their marginal money. Once the necessities of life are provided, certain options remain; people will find some way, be it public or private, boisterous or quiet, to spend their surplus time and money. While many of Ohio's early settlers came from a Puritan tradition, they did not work all the time. The preachments of clergymen and church elders, who called attention to the serious and earnest sides of life, should not lead us to assume that this outlook was typical of the people at large. Quite the contrary is true. Though limited by isolation, poverty, illness and other circumstances, most Ohio pioneers seemed to believe that "all work and no play makes Jack a dull boy!"

Recreational activity in pioneer Ohio was often a cooperative work effort. Husking and quilting bees, barn raisings, and the like brought people together for the social and emotional release they needed. Similar release came from occasional militia musters or religious camp meetings, where copious amounts of raw whiskey often accelerated conviviality to the detriment of the serious purpose at hand.

Sporting contests involved tests of strength and skill in activities that were essential to the development of a pioneer society. Shooting at a mark, log-chopping contests, foot races, and wrestling were outlets for competitive spirits. These contests and, of course, horse racing also provided the chance to make a wager, an act that intensifies anxiety and stimulates interest in the outcome. Hunting and fishing were practical necessities for supplementing the pioneer diet, but they often doubled as sporting or recreational activities. The great community hunts, organized to reduce the population of varmints that destroyed crops and livestock, were as much social as practical. Indeed, from a practical point of view they were

Hockey on the Ohio-Erie Canal, Newark, ca. 1900 . (1)

almost too effective since such mass slaughters hastened the premature disappearance from Ohio of several wildlife species.

The earthiness associated with activities of the earliest period gave way to a more constrained and sedate type of leisure activity later in the nineteenth century. This was true, at least, for the middle and upper class population influenced by the formalisms and delicacies that were thought to represent good manners during the Victorian era. However, the formal conduct and mannerisms of this part of society should not be confused with the more relaxed attitudes prevailing in the larger society. Nevertheless, since it was the class most influenced by Victorian mores that tended to control much of the business and political life of the state, the sedate and genteel element sometimes succeeded—as with the introduction of Sunday blue laws—in building constraints around the options of those who did not share their sense of propriety.

Though some barriers were placed in their way, people still had fun. Among the organized activities popular in the mid-nineteenth century were dances (with folk or square dances probably more common and popular than ballroom dancing), picnics, church and Sunday school outings, boating, excursions to picnic groves or amusement parks, festivals, and parades. Many Ohio communities organized mass sleigh rides during which scores of sleighs would drive to and through a nearby town. It was then a matter of pride for the town thus visited to organize an even larger return visitation. The crisp air created hearty appetites, and a sumptuous spread of food and drink was a perfect way to end the trip. In March, 1856, Cuyahoga, Medina, and Summit counties competed in a grand contest in Richfield. Only four and six-horse teams counted, and on the big day 462 sleighs came into

Richfield "with horses prancing, bells ringing, and horns blowing." Some 12,000 persons witnessed the gaiety and color of the day's events. The victory banner went to Summit County, which had 171 teams, but a few days later Summit relinquished the banner to Medina when that county made a surprise descent on Summit with 182 teams. Similar competitions flourished in later years, except that horses and sleighs gave way to bicycles or still later, to automobiles. In 1916 some 1,100 Zanesville residents motored to Newark to celebrate the paving of the National Pike, and the next year nearly 1,500 Newark residents rode in 500 automobiles to Zanesville to return the visit.

The picnic grove, the lakeside pavilion, and the amusement park were to be found nearly everywhere in Ohio by the late nineteenth century. An extended transportation system was partly responsible for the proliferation of these recreational spots. People arrived by boat or power launch at river and lake locations, by railroad excursion train, by horse and buggy, but above all by trolley and interurban car. Street railway and traction companies promoted recreation areas to stimulate business. A ride to the park on the "cars" was nearly as big a thrill for youngsters as the allurements of the park itself. Many picnic groves and amusement parks were transient, flourishing for a few years and then disappearing as housing or commercial developments encroached upon them or as economic difficulties pressed them.

The small, informal parks of earlier days gave way to much larger, diverse, and commercially oriented parks. One could not begin to name even the famous amusement centers in Ohio without the risk of leaving out some that were much loved by generations of youngsters who, now grown considerably older, still associate

Leisure, Recreation, and Sports in Ohio

Annual Charity Ball, Cleveland Association of
Colored Men, Cleveland Chamber of Commerce,
1914.(2)

Swimming pool, Zanesville, ca. 1910 (3)

Buckeye Lake Yacht Club,
1902. (4)

An Ohio Portrait

Coeds clear hurdles under the coach's watchful eye, 1922. (5)

Scott Pool, Toledo, in the 1930s. (6)

Modern knights improvise recreation in a city park in the 1930s. (7)

Entrance to Buckeye Lake Park in the 1920s. (8)

them with halcyon days. Some of the more representative amusement parks of note were Cedar Point outside Sandusky, Coney Island on the Ohio just east of Cincinnati, Cleveland's Euclid Beach Park, Idora Park in Youngstown, Meyers Lake in Canton, Olentangy Park in Columbus, Summit Beach in Akron, Chippewa Lake in Medina County, Russell's Point on Indian Lake, and Buckeye Lake.

In the post-World War II era, only a small number of amusement parks still flourished. Increased costs of operation, competition for the entertainment dollar, television, and other factors help explain their demise. The parks that flourish today tend to be much more comprehensive and elaborate than earlier ones. Families now drive long distances to spend the day at modern and attractive parks like King's Island north of Cincinnati; Cedar Point; Geauga Lake and Sea World, both near Aurora southeast of Cleveland; Fun 'N Sun near Hillsboro; LeSourdsville Lake in Butler County; and Gooding Amusement Park north of Columbus. Some commercial enterprises, including those at Port Clinton, Sandusky, Cedar Point, Kings Mills, and Aurora, feature animals or fish as their central attraction.

People who enjoy the entertainment or instructional value of zoos are well served in Ohio. The Toledo Zoological Park and the Cincinnati Zoo are among the country's best. Cleveland, Columbus, Akron, and Mansfield have less comprehensive parks which feature "children's zoos."

For the outdoor lover, Ohio offers a variety of seasonal attractions. The development of means for making artificial snow and ice has greatly extended the season for skiing and ice skating. Ice boating attracts a limited number of enthusiasts as does ice fishing. In the warmer months outdoor activities proliferate. The state and other governmental units have made

A fast ride at Euclid Beach, Cleveland, 1950. (9)

An Ohio Portrait

Coney Island Park, Cincinnati, 1968. (10)

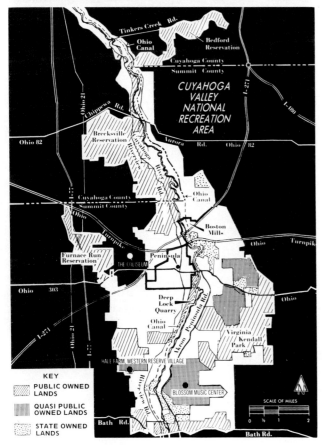

KEY

PUBLIC OWNED
LANDS

QUASI PUBLIC
OWNED LANDS

STATE OWNED
LANDS

Thousands of acres in Summit and Cuyahoga
counties are embraced in the new Cuyahoga Valley
National Recreation Area. (11)

enormous strides in recent decades in providing
pleasant and accessible facilities.

Governmental responsibility for creating recreational areas extends well back into the
nineteenth century. The creation of Mill Creek
Park in Youngstown during the 1890s affords an
early example of government aiding in the creation of recreational areas. During the 1920s a
magnificent system of metropolitan parks was
begun near Cleveland, surrounding the Forest
City with an "emerald necklace" of inestimable
value. A similar development in the Akron area
in 1923 led to the Akron Metropolitan Park District which, like others in Ohio, has the power to
generate tax support. Many of these park systems
were put into good operating condition through
the work of the Civilian Conservation Corps during the 1930s.

Ohio's best example of governmental responsibility for recreation is the impressive state park
system developed as a comprehensive program
within the last forty years. The pace of this development has accelerated as population pressures,
coupled with diminishing amounts of open land,
spur recognition that there is never a better time
than the present to secure land. Today Ohio has
well over fifty state parks, most of which offer
camping, swimming, boating, and hiking—
nearly the whole span of outdoor activities. Some,
like Crane Creek and Headlands Beach on Lake
Erie, were started as swimming beaches; others,
like Hocking Hills and Nelson's Ledges, evolved
around interesting and scenic natural sites. Finley, near Wellington, is an example of a park
developed around an artificial lake in a region
where there is no outstanding natural attraction.

Also in the postwar era, the state built beautiful
rustic lodges at Punderson, Mohican, Salt Fork,
Burr Oak, Lake Hope, Shawnee Forest, and
Hueston Woods. The Muskingum Conservancy

Power boating off South Bass Island, with Perry's
monument in the background. (12)

District maintains a popular lodge at Atwood
Lake. These facilities are full all year. Families
also find attractive, functional cabins available at
these sites for modest rents. Much credit for ac-
celerating the development of state parks belongs
to Governor James Rhodes, who saw not only the
recreational value of a comprehensive park system, but also emphasized that parks created jobs
in areas where people had few other job prospects.

Most recently the federal government has
made efforts to preserve Ohio lands and to develop them for recreational use. For many years
the United States Forest Service has managed
extensive timber resources in southeastern Ohio,
especially the Wayne National Forest. Within the
past two years, the Cuyahoga Valley National
Recreation Area was established by Congress. Ultimately the National Park Service will develop a
comprehensive park in this largely "unspoiled"
area lying in the heart of a population of more
than four million people.

Another leisure-time activity which Ohioans
have enjoyed for over a hundred years is the
excitement and socializing associated with fairs,
festivals, and parades. The Ohio State Fair,
started in large part to encourage better agricultural practices, is now one of the nation's largest.
Today big name entertainment is as much a feature as are displays and contests. Nearly every
county has an annual fair, generally held late in
the summer or fall. Throughout the year various
localities sponsor festivals to celebrate some local
product and to bring money into the community.
Among them are festivals featuring grapes at
Geneva, pumpkins at Circleville, bratwurst at
Bucyrus, poultry at Versailles, sweet corn at Mil-
lersport, maple products at Chardon, apples at
Jackson, apple butter at Burton, tomatoes at
Reynoldsburg, and honey at Lebanon. Others

A day's catch (above) in a 1954 Toledo park
contest. (Below) An Ottawa River marina, Toledo,
reflects the popularity of boating.

(13)

(14)

Scene at the Toledo Zoo. (15)

The lodge at Burr Oak, Athens County. (16)

State park beaches attract enthusiastic crowds. (17)

Skiers at Snow Trails, near Mansfield. (18)

celebrate a variety of themes: the Ohio Hills Folk Festival at Quaker City, pottery at Crooksville, clay at Urichsville, Canal Days at Canal Fulton, cherry blossoms at Barberton, an International Festival at Toledo, Antique Festival at Millersburg, and Wonderful World of Ohio Mart at Akron.

Parades are a feature of every festival, and Ohioans have always loved them. Parades became a feature of early Fourth of July celebrations and of political campaigns. But the great surge in their popularity can be traced to the post-Civil War era when many featured units of the Grand Army of the Republic (GAR). In 1888 some 70,000 veterans marched through Columbus streets. Every town brought forth its local band and marching groups on every suitable occasion. When the cornerstone was laid at Buchtel College in 1872, the parade included twenty-two units: the GAR, Masons, Odd Fellows, Knights of Pythias, city officials, clergy, citizens, many bands, and even the Father Matthew Temperance Society, a group which must have felt needed when two drunken men crashed their carriage through the parade lines.

The large urban parades of recent years appear to have fewer lodges, military and veterans' units among the marchers while attracting more floats, bands, and special drill units. Cleveland must hold the record for parades, since its many ethnic and other special communities favor this activity. In ethnic communities in the early 1900s a parade would be but part of a daylong celebration which usually included a High Mass, sumptuous food, drink, and dancing. Typical of such gatherings still much in evidence today was the September, 1974, observance of "Slovak Day" at St. Josephat Church in Parma: parishioners and friends attended High Mass, and then consumed an assortment of food and drink. Singing and

The Cherry Blossom Festival parade, Barberton, 1969. (19)

Ringling Brothers circus calliope in Columbus. (21)

Chillicothe, decorated for the Ohio Centennial celebration, 1903. (20)

Elephants in Zanesville circus parade, early twentieth century. (22)

Crowd on Government Square, Cincinnati, just after the Grand Army of the Republic parade had passed, 1898. (23)

Thanksgiving day parade in Dayton, 1935. (24)

July 4th parade, Cleveland, 1910. (25)

The only photo that shows the entire Sells Brothers Circus, winterquarters, Columbus, 1891. (26)

An Ohio Portrait

Liberation takes a step forward as these young ladies play baseball with the boys. (27)

Cleveland's Wambsganss executes the only unassisted triple play in World Series history against Brooklyn, 1920. (29)

Professional baseball began with the 1869 Cincinnati Red Stockings whose first year record was 57 wins and 0 losses. (28)

Denton "Cy" Young (1867–1955) of Gilmore, Tuscarawas County, spent much of his great career with the Cleveland Indians. The Cy Young Award is given annually to the major leagues' outstanding pitcher. (30)

dancing were important parts of the celebration, as was a talk by Cleveland's mayor on the importance of maintaining ethnic customs.

The advance of the industrial age with its clustering of people into cities and towns gave impetus to the development of team sports. Ohio has made notable contributions to many of them. Perhaps the emergence of baseball as a national pastime best illustrates the state's role in this process. Baseball, which evolved from cricket and rounders, was played long before the Civil War. Following that war, however, baseball enjoyed wide acceptance; returning veterans started community ball clubs in which they took great pride. A local Cincinnati team was a focus of such pride, so players and fans alike were humiliated when their team suffered defeat at the hands of the barnstorming Washington Nationals, who operated on what appeared to be a semi-professional basis. In the summer of 1869, Harry Wright, a jeweler who headed the amateur Cin-

Action in Cleveland's Lakefront Stadium. (32)

Cleveland's Larry
Doby, the
American
League's first
black player. (31)

Catcher Johnny Bench addresses a Fountain
Square crowd celebrating the Cincinnati
Reds world championship, 1975. (33)

Lou Boudreau (left) and Joe Gordon of Cleveland's 1948 world champions. (34)

Frank Robinson, star player with the Cincinnati Reds and current manager of the Cleveland Indians. (35)

cinnati club, organized America's first professional baseball team. Supporters paid him $12,000 to organize, manage, and play center field for the Cincinnati Red Stockings. Wright recruited talent so successfully that his professional players won fifty-seven games without defeat in 1869–70. Not until the Red Stockings were beaten 8–7 by a Brooklyn, New York, team were the escalating salaries and other procedures questioned.

The Red Stockings temporarily disbanded in 1870, but eleven years later they joined the Cleveland Forest City and several other teams to form the National Association of Professional Baseball. In 1886 this association formed the National League, the first of the modern baseball leagues. The second major baseball league also had Cincinnati origins when, in 1892, Bancroft Johnson and Charles Comiskey, manager of the Cincinnati Reds, formed the Western Association, which evolved into the American League.

Coincident with the rise of professional baseball in Ohio was a growing enthusiasm for football. In the 1890s colleges were playing scheduled games, and shortly after the turn of the century semi-professional football was common. Famous teams like the Columbus Panhandlers, Akron Indians, Dayton Triangles, and Canton Bulldogs attracted large crowds, because of their professional performances. Outstanding college players were recruited by the St. Patrick's Catholic Church team in Youngstown, but the Canton Bulldogs got the recruiting prize when Jim Thorpe joined that team in 1915. In 1920 the American Professional Football Association was formed in Canton, and an effort was made to bring order and respectability to the game. Recently, professional football has been well represented in Ohio. The Cleveland Rams moved to Los Angeles in the mid-1940s, but the

With coach John Heisman playing quarterback, the Buchtel College team won this 1894 game against Ohio State at the Ohio State Fairgrounds. (37)

Cleveland Browns of the All-America Conference took up the slack with championship teams coached by the peerless Paul Brown, whose earlier reputation was earned in Ohio high school and college ranks. Today both the Browns and an expansion team, the Cincinnati Bengals, also coached by Paul Brown, represent the state in the Central Division of the National Football League.

Football and college are inseparable in the twentieth century. Ohio schools were among the earliest to compete in this sport on a regular basis. From student-managed club efforts, the sport has grown to phenomenal size. Among major college powers, Ohio State University's Buckeyes are perennial contenders for conference and national honors. The Mid-American Conference, featuring Kent State, Miami, Ohio University, Bowling Green, Toledo, and some out of state teams, is a major conference. The old Ohio Athletic Conference boasts excellent small college teams like Wittenberg, Muskingum, and Heidelberg. Football is also taken seriously on the high school level. For years the outstanding program at Massillon's Washington High School was the prototype of high-powered high school play.

The Heisman Trophy for football excellence is named for John W. Heisman, coach of Oberlin and Buchtel College teams in the 1890s. (38)

Professional Football Hall of Fame, Canton. (36)

An Ohio Portrait

Paul Brown's unparalleled coaching career includes Massillon High School, Ohio State University, the Cleveland Browns and the Cincinnati Bengals. (39)

Cleveland Browns, playoff victors over Dallas. (40)

Charles "Chick" Harley, Ohio State football star of the World War I era. (41)

Davis Cup tennis match, Cleveland, 1969. (42)

Basketball is another team sport long popular in Ohio. On the professional level the Cincinnati Royals and the Cleveland Cavaliers have represented the state. Among university teams Cincinnati, Dayton, and Ohio State have won major national titles, while many other Ohio colleges and universities have strong teams each year. The annual Ohio high school state tournament in Columbus features the best in high school basketball.

Another sport played on the professional level is ice hockey, a relative newcomer to Ohio except for the now-departed Cleveland Barons. The Cincinnati Stingers and the Cleveland Crusaders play in the World Hockey Association. Ohio also has several minor league franchises and a growing number of college and high school teams.

Boxing is a sport that has roots in Ohio's history. Bare-knuckle fisticuffs are apt to be prevalent everywhere and at any time when boys and young men are together for any length of time. Today Golden Gloves competition offers a select few amateur fighters the chance to move into national and international competition. It also starts some talented fighters on the road toward the elusive big money earned by successful professionals. Ohio produced a number of professional champions such as James J. Jeffries of Carroll and Johnny Kilbane of Cleveland. Ohio has also been the scene of great fights like the 1919 Dempsey-Willard fight at Toledo. However, today the majority of fans prefer to watch boxing, and professional wrestling on TV where they can see all the action at less cost.

Contrary to the predictions of some social commentators, America has not become a nation of spectators who satisfy their athletic interest vicariously through radio and television broadcasts. If anything, the popularizing of sports through extensive television coverage has

Many experts consider Columbus' Jack Nicklaus the greatest golfer of all time. (43)

An Ohio Portrait

Cleveland Air Races. (44)

brought thousands out to participate and enjoy sports suited to their skills, pocketbooks, and physical condition.

Golf, tennis, and bowling, long the pastime of the exclusive few, became widely popular as new facilities sprang up everywhere in the state. Akron with its World Series of Golf, its PGA tournaments, and the American Golf Classic is a mecca for professional golfers. And for bowlers too. The Professional Bowlers Association, which was founded and is still located in Akron, annually hosts the pro-bowlers major tournament. Many other Ohio cities have hosted major professional tournaments in golf and bowling. Cleveland, Toledo, Akron, Columbus, and Cincinnati have active tennis programs and sponsor professional tournaments. Many players of national stature were raised in Ohio, among them Jack Nicklaus and Tom Weiskopf in golf; Tony Trabert, Clark Graebner, and Shirley Fry in tennis; and Jim Godman and Dick Hoover in bowling. But it is not the stars who matter so much as the widespread participation in healthful activity by millions of people whose lives are more interesting and stimulating as a result of their involvement in sports and recreation.

One can always attract a crowd with a race. Ohio has numerous outlets for speed enthusiasts, whether their preference runs to horse racing, trotters, speed or sail boats, motorcycles, autos, or dragsters.

Track meets are gaining in popularity, but they are still largely confined to school meets. Few track stars become well known, but among the immortals of track and field one must include Cleveland's Jesse Owens, whose brilliant performance in the 1936 Berlin Olympics inspired a nation. Other sports featured in Ohio high schools and colleges are soccer, hockey (both field and ice), wrestling, gymnastics, swimming (Ohio

Jesse Owens of Cleveland and Ohio State put on a sensational performance at the 1936 Olympic games in Berlin. (45)

Wrestling has grown in popularity in Ohio's secondary schools and colleges. (46)

Annie Oakley
(1860–1926),
"Little Miss
Sure Shot."
(47)

Miss Annie Oakley

Trotters racing; a popular Ohio pastime. (49)

The All American Soap Box Derby draws throngs
to Akron's Derby Downs. (50)

The 1930s when soap box derbies were run down
Tallmadge Avenue hill, Akron. (51)

The Grand American Shoot, Vandalia,
Montgomery County. (48)

State was long a national power in this sport),
cross country, and riflery. Shooting scarcely
seems a sport to many people, but for thousands
of target shooters the great contests at Camp
Perry and Vandalia are a magnet. Who can forget
the greatest shooter of them all, Annie Oakley of
Darke County, Ohio's foremost representative in
that skill.

The participation of women in every kind of
sporting and recreational activity, Annie Oakley
notwithstanding, is a recent development. Ohio
shared a fundamental conservatism with other
midwestern states about women's place in society.
Women were allowed to compete in a select few
sports—golf, swimming, tennis, and field
hockey—and then only with other women.
Changing social values, new fashions, and the
women's rights movement of the 1960s and 1970s
broadened women's opportunities in athletics.
Colleges and universities are responding by sharing facilities, money, and opportunities for par-
ticipating with male students. Women professionals hold golf, bowling, and tennis tournaments which are as well attended as many of the
men's events. At the other end of the sports spec-
trum, girls now join teams formerly composed
entirely of boys—Little League baseball, for
example, or college tennis teams.

Girls participate, and very successfully too, in
the Soap Box Derby. This "greatest amateur racing event in the world" was started in Dayton in
the early 1930s by an enterprising newspaper
man. Since 1935 Akron has been the home of the
derby, and each August champions from around
the country and from various foreign nations
compete at Derby Downs for college scholarships
and other prizes.

Other group sporting activities are sponsored
by the physical fitness clubs of various ethnic
groups. The Sokols, Turnvereine, and athletic

An Ohio Portrait

When downtown theaters were still alive, Lima, 1922. (52)

Old vaudeville days. The "country store," Princess Theater, Youngstown, 1915. (53)

A crowded house for "No Mother to Guide Her," Captain Billy Bryant's Ohio River Showboat, ca. 1938. (54)

Cotton Blossom showboat. (55)

festivals that were traditions in European countries were transplanted to America and took root in ethnic communities in the larger cities. To this day, many such organizations maintain their vitality and reveal to the larger society the dedication and the discipline that controlled athletic participation brings to a people.

Any account of recreational and leisure time activities in Ohio must include the theater. From one point of view, the theater can be described as an art form, but from another it is a form of popular recreation. It is in this latter sense the theater has had its most marked impact on Ohio, at least until relatively recent times.

As in so much of Ohio's early record, Cincinnati looms large in the history of theater. The first play known to have been performed in Ohio was O'Keefe's comic opera, *The Poor Soldier*, presented in 1801 by the Thespians at Fort Washington. By 1815 a professional company from Pittsburgh was giving plays in Cincinnati; its fare, like most early productions in the West, was ribald enough to discourage attendance by genteel folk. Many of the best known performers of pre-Civil War America—Edmund Kean, Tyrone Power, Junius Brutus Booth—came to the Queen City.

Outside of Cincinnati, only Columbus seems to have made an effort to support regular theater offerings in the early days. The Columbus Theater, opened in 1835, was described in some detail by a local newspaperman who also observed that the bar in the rear of the building was its most popular feature. The theater was closed as a public nuisance.

Perhaps the most romantic form of pre-Civil War theater was the showboat. The earliest boats were not fancy; they were generally towed from town to town, and their stay in any one port was apt to be brief. Their performances were

shunned by so-called respectable people, who thought that the theater encouraged sinfulness and sloth; they feared the corrupting influences of plays on young minds.

By the late nineteenth century, showboats had become floating palaces which appealed to young and old, to "proper" people as well as to those of lesser social pretension. Brilliant lights, steam calliopes, and other allurements packed customers in. One observer described the annual visit of a showboat: "It was irresistible;" even "local church elders, Sunday school superintendents, and their families, usually denied such luxuries, found their way to its moorings, so that the children might have an opportunity to hear the 'music.'" Often these boats made one-night stands, but in the more populous towns they remained for a week. In either case, they returned annually to rekindle excitement and anticipation.

Akin to the showboats on the major rivers, a few canal boats were apparently fitted out for stage performances in the antebellum period. They toured Ohio's canal system, but their influence was far less pronounced than that of the larger, gaudier, and longer-lived showboats.

Rehearsal at Player's Guild Theater, Canton. (56)

An Ohio Portrait

Elsie Janis, "Sweetheart of the A.E.F." (57)

Members of the cast, Godman Guild performance, Columbus. (58)

The Gene Gordon band plays for the 1941 spring fete of the Friendly Inn, Cleveland. (59)

The era of the showboat was also the era of blackface minstrel shows, a very popular form of entertainment in the nineteenth century. Dan Emmett of Mt. Vernon, an organizer of such shows, performed with Bryant's Minstrels and others until late in his life. Tent shows were also popular in this period. Some were simple carnivals with barkers, "wonders," music and dancing, animals, a sideshow, and other attractions. In time Ohio became the home of several of the nation's leading traveling carnivals, tent shows, minstrel troupes, and circuses.

Permanent facilities for popular entertainment were found in every sizeable town. Some of these were elaborate, like Pike's Opera House which opened in 1859 in Cincinnati. That city had five theaters and Toledo, new city that it was, boasted three theaters in the Civil War era. Columbus, Cleveland, Dayton, and Akron had halls, theaters, or opera houses, as they were variously called in the late nineteenth century.

During the late nineteenth, and well into the twentieth century, Ohio experienced its golden age of live theater. The great stage performers of the day—Sarah Bernhardt, Maude Adams, Anna Held, Ethel Barrymore, and Eva LeGallienne—performed before Ohio audiences. New buildings accommodated enthusiastic audiences for legitimate theater, vaudeville, and minstrel shows.

By the 1920s the importance of the theater as a public entertainment medium was seriously undermined by the growth of the motion picture industry. The excitement and scope of screen fare, coupled with its low prices and ready availability to a mass market, made the movies America's most popular form of theatrical entertainment.

Perhaps the most important aspect of Ohio's recent theatrical history is its indigenous efforts to support local repertory companies and the tremendous swelling of amateur "little theater" activities. Early efforts at repertory theater were given a boost in the depressed thirties when the Federal Theater Project supported companies in Cleveland and Cincinnati. Cleveland had its Repertory Theater, a marionette unit, and a Negro unit which performed several plays, including *Conjure Man Dies* and *Noah*. The Cleveland unit produced eighty-seven performances and the Cincinnati unit 191 before the federal program was phased out in 1939.

Among Ohio's earliest little theater groups was the Cleveland Playhouse, organized in 1915. It specialized in experimental work and in the revival of old plays and has long had its own facilities. Today every Ohio city, large and small, boasts its little theater groups. Many of these have developed a tradition for excellence which ranks among the best in the land. Summer theater has proliferated to the point that one must choose among a great number of competing attractions in the larger urban areas.

As with other art and entertainment forms, Ohio colleges and universities contribute much to the current health of theater. Many schools have fine theaters in which they train generations of student performers and to which they bring some of the country's most accomplished theatrical talent for special performances or for resident visits. Experimental theater is a special province of the collegiate groups. Through their efforts the usual theatrical fare has been widely extended to include much more variety in plays and staging.

Today, there are few places in the United States where it is possible to find as much high quality entertainment as one can find in the regions surrounding Ohio's two great cultural and sports centers, Cleveland and Cincinnati. But the spread of this activity around the state is so general that Ohio can no longer be thought of as backwater for cultural and recreational pursuits. Within an easy drive from any part of the state one can find such a wealth of amusement, recreation, and cultural activity as to have astonished earlier generations.

(60)

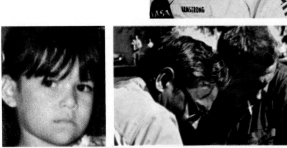

Contemporary Ohio

Ohio, like the rest of the nation, has experienced profound change since the end of World War II. Although much of this change has had a positive impact, negative results or implications have developed from some. In many significant areas—the economy, population trends, and political life, for example—the record is mixed and only time will tell whether the outcome has helped or hurt Ohio. In discussing contemporary Ohio, we are dealing with a story whose complex plot suggests but does not assure the action yet to come.

In every decennial census since 1800 Ohio has shown population growth. Within its first fifty years the new state shot up to become the third most populous member of the Union. By 1890 it had been displaced by Illinois. California was even with Ohio by 1940 and well ahead by 1950. Texas also moved ahead of Ohio in 1970 leaving the Buckeye State sixth in population. Its 9.7 percent rate of population growth between 1960 and 1970 was the lowest among the five states of the Old Northwest and almost four percentage points below the national average. Estimates indicate that Ohio has done little more than hold its own in the five years since the last census.

A redistribution of people within the state has taken place in the postwar period. Every major city except Columbus and Toledo has lost population; those two owe their continued growth, in part, to the annexation of large tracts of surrounding land. Early in the postwar period Ohio experienced a great swelling of population in the suburbs of its major cities, but that trend has slowed. The United States Census Bureau's estimates of growth from 1970 to 1975 indicate that of the thirteen Standard Metropolitan Statistical Areas (SMSA) wholly within Ohio, only five—Columbus, Toledo, Canton, Lima, and Springfield—experienced any growth. This

An Ohio Portrait

Plans for urban development have been
commonplace since World War II. Toledo drafted
this Master Plan in 1951. (1)

suggests that the loss of people from the central
city is enough to offset the modest gains made by
the older suburbs which are considered part of
the SMSA. This apparent lack of growth also may
be attributed to the development of new suburban areas lying too far away from the central city
to be included in its SMSA. Portage County, for
instance, grew more than 34 percent and Medina
County nearly 30 percent from 1960 to 1970 and
have continued to grow in the last five years. Yet
both were essentially rural counties and thus lay
outside the Cleveland SMSA and the Akron
SMSA, although those two central cities provide
many services and jobs for residents of these
counties. In the last decade and a half, twenty-one
Ohio counties have lost population. The great
majority of them are located in that southeast
portion of Ohio which is part of Appalachia. Vinton County, which lost 9.5 percent, was hardest
hit. It is now the state's least populous county with
fewer than 10,000 inhabitants. The strip-mined
counties of eastern Ohio also lost population.

In spite of the pessimistic implication of some
of these population figures, Ohio has much going
for it. A recent national trend for retired people
and young marrieds to return to smaller towns
could serve Ohio well, for the state has an abundance of locales of appealing size. Though it is the
most densely populated state of the Old Northwest with an average of 260 people per square
mile, the wide distribution of population centers
throughout the state spreads its people across the
land more equitably than in sister states like Illinois, with its Chicago complex, or Michigan,
with Detroit the dominant force. Cleveland,
Ohio's largest Standard Metropolitan Statistical
Area with 2,064,194 people, is only the fourteenth largest in the nation. Metropolitan Cincinnati, with many of its 1,384,851 people in Kentucky and Indiana, ranks second in the state and

twenty-second in the nation.

Ohio's farm population appears to have
stabilized in recent years after suffering a prolonged decline. From the halcyon days a century
ago, when Ohio ranked first in the value of her
agricultural products, the state has slipped to
fourteenth position nationally. Yet the
$2,098,000,000 (exclusive of government grants)
earned as farm income in 1973 makes agriculture
Ohio's largest industry. That total is about 20
percent of the value of all Ohio products in
1973.

Redirection of agricultural effort is evident
since the immediate postwar years. Ohio farmers
produce less fruit, wheat, hay, and seed crops, but
more feed grains, vegetables, and above all soy
beans. Total crop production has risen more than
fifty percent and livestock and poultry production has held its own. Some 750,000 Ohioans
presently work in agriculture.

Life on the farm in postwar Ohio is no longer as
isolated or self-sufficient as it used to be. A good,
comprehensive highway system puts major
shopping and service facilities within easy range
of most farmers. Television, daily papers, radio,
and even that most recent communications
phenomenon, citizen's band radio, have ended
rural isolation. Walking down Broad Street in
Columbus today, one could not pick out the country folk from the city folk by dress, appearance, or
mannerism. Indeed, a short distance away on
North High Street there is a good chance that the
Ohio State University students wearing blue
denim bib overalls are the sons and daughters of
big city doctors, insurance salesmen, and brokers.

While agriculture appears to have stabilized at
a respectable and profitable level of productivity,
the picture is less clear with respect to Ohio's
tremendous industrial activity. Since World War
II, the picture has shifted from the optimism that

Ohio History publishes articles dealing with the history of the buckeye state. (2)

A modern Toledo glass factory demonstrates big industry's need for extensive land for plant, parking, and settling pools conveniently located near railroads and highways. (3)

accompanied the growth period of the 1950s and 1960s to the more cautious outlook of the 1970s. The question now is not so much a concern for the near future as for the more distant time when Ohio must participate more fully in current growth industries if it is to remain near the top in industrial production.

Ohio was fortunate to be among the leaders in several of the great growth industries of the late nineteenth and early twentieth centuries. Iron and steel, petroleum products, rubber, industrial glass, electrical machinery and appliances, metal fabricating, non-electrical machinery, and household products were the focus of its strength. Much of the industrial plant which was built to produce these goods is now too old-fashioned and inefficient to compete successfully with the modern, single-process plants located around the nation. Ohio has its share of these new plants, but the state has not built them fast enough nor plentifully enough to keep some industries from moving to what they consider to be more favored locations. Many companies that remain Ohio-based have built new manufacturing plants across the nation and the world to be near their markets and to take advantage of local conditions elsewhere.

A 1973 survey of sixty-one Ohio companies employing more than 500 workers each as reported in the *Bulletin of Business Research*, published by the Center for Business and Economic Research at Ohio State University, revealed that 21 percent of Ohio's industrial plants are considered obsolete, compared with 12 percent nationally. The degree of obsolesence ranges from 44 percent in primary metals to 6 percent in transportation. Among Ohio's industrial centers the study shows Cincinnati to be in relatively healthy condition, Cleveland facilities slightly less obsolete than the Ohio average,

The modern Rockwell International plant is situated adjacent to the airline services of Port Columbus. (4)

An Ohio Portrait

An effort to develop new energy sources. NASA's sophisticated windmill at Plum Brook, near Sandusky. (5)

Columbus slightly above average in plant obsolescence, and the Youngstown-Warren area considerably above average.

Obsolete plants are not the only consideration in industrial relocation. Many of Ohio's traditional centers of industry are so surrounded with commercial and residential building that there is no room to expand. Real estate costs are high and real estate taxes are also rather high in some of the older industrial areas.

Still another consideration militating against expansion of industry in its old locale relates to labor. This is a volatile subject on which feelings run high. Management claims that certain union locals in the older, established industrial centers of Ohio have secured such a high wage scale, such good benefits, and such restrictive work agreements as to make them uncompetitive with labor costs in some other areas of America and the world. Akron rubber manufacturers, who have built extensively in states like Alabama, Oklahoma, Virginia, and Tennessee, make this argument. Labor has responded by attempting to negotiate industry-wide contracts, but this has led to internal conflicts because members of the older locals, being themselves older on the average, are interested in retirement benefits to an extent not shared by the generally younger membership of the newer locals, who are more interested in current earning power and working conditions.

Ohio has profited from heavy investment in new or modernized plants in some of its older industries, at the same time attracting new businesses which have built modern plants in the state. The automotive industry has invested so heavily in Ohio in recent decades that Ohio is now a close second to Michigan, the traditional leader in this business. From the giant General Motors complex at Lordstown and the huge Chrysler stamping plant at Twinsburg, to the Ford assem-

bly plant at Lorain, this investment can be seen across the state. Foundries, stamping plants, and assembly plants are supported by a bewildering array of supplier industries, so that nearly every Ohio city of fair size makes a contribution to the industry.

Strenuous efforts have been made during James Rhodes' former and present terms as governor, to attract new industry to Ohio. Some of Ohio's attractions are: a relatively low state tax rate, a central location for securing raw materials and for supplying markets, a mature and experienced labor force, a comprehensive and varied transportation network, and the goodwill of state officials. "Rhodes' Raiders," as they are dubbed, scour the nation, Japan, South America, and Europe looking for prospects. The slogan, "Profit is not a dirty word in Ohio," sums up the administration's philosophy. Yet the implications of that phrase are a source of concern to many residents who fear that business will receive advantages that might work against a broader public interest in areas like the equitable sharing of the state tax burden and effective environmental control.

A little-appreciated fact which tends to modify the loss of some production jobs to Ohio is the replacement in some industries of blue collar workers by white collar workers. Ohio cities which have the headquarters and the research and development facilities of major industries report that an increase in white collar and management personnel at company headquarters has helped offset the loss of production jobs to other areas of the nation. This phenomenon has contributed to a healthy social mix within some Ohio cities which are no longer the "mill towns" of former times. This condition is not exclusively the result of activity within major companies. To a considerable extent it also reflects the growth

Huge coal-burning plants like this one along the Ohio River continue to supply most of Ohio's electrical power. (6)

Part of Ohio's commitment to the space age: NASA's Lewis Research Center at Cleveland Hopkins International Airport. (7)

An Ohio Portrait

The "towboat" *Advance* handles barges on the Ohio River. (8)

nationally of service industries and public employees, and the proliferation of workers classified as professional.

Traditionally Ohio has been well supplied with energy from water, steam (coal), natural gas, and electrical sources. At a time when energy resources are a matter of intense public concern, it is reassuring to Ohio business to recognize the long-term potential of its energy resources. There are still enormous coal reserves within the state. These are now being developed more effectively than at any time in the past half century. Strip mining is the chief source of commercial coal, and the devastating scars left by that extraction method will be eliminated as more stringent reclamation controls are applied in conformance with recent laws. Scrubbers and other smoke controls allow many Ohio industries and utilities to burn coal with a sulphur content which formerly created pollution problems. Local natural gas wells are being tapped to allow some industries a degree of independence from supplies piped into the state from the southwest. Most controversial of current developments is the construction of several enormous nuclear power plants along Lake Erie and the Ohio River. Environmentalists fear the overheating of nearby water supplies, but an even more vital consideration is the possibility of radiation leaks, failures, and the disposal of waste materials.

The revival of the coal industry has been good news to southeastern Ohio counties which are the chief beneficiaries. A long-term economic depression could be reversed for some areas by this revival. Small towns in this region look forward to securing industrial plants which are attracted to places where overcrowding is minimal and the bureaucratic maze is not quite so complex. The more rural areas of this part of Appalachia may continue to attract income from tourist travel as the Appalachian Highway and the interstates make access easier and as the state continues to develop recreational resources.

It is easy to look at certain gross figures and conclude that the industrial life of Ohio is in trouble and that the state's days as an industrial leader are numbered. A 1972 study, for example, reveals that the Gross Ohio Product (GOP) as a part of the Gross National Product (GNP) rose from 5.7 percent in 1949 to 6.1 percent in the period 1953-56. After 1956 it declined rather steadily to 5.3 percent in 1970. Such figures conceal the fact that while Ohio's total industrial output continues to climb, it is not increasing as fast as that in some other sections of the nation. There is reason to suspect that Ohio will remain one of the nation's leading industrial states. Its current position as the second largest exporter of manufactured goods to foreign consumers is one hopeful sign in a day when American business activity is increasingly part of an international web of interdependence.

A special feature of the business climate that has always been important is the transportation network. Ohio has experienced the same evaporation of passenger rail traffic which has characterized the rest of the nation in the postwar period. The great terminals in Cleveland, Cincinnati, and elsewhere fell vacant. Only within the last few years has there been any indication that passenger traffic might revive, at least modestly. Amtrak service on three east-west lines across the state is holding its own at this writing, but the future is far from clear. Freight traffic is still heavy on the railroads, but many once-important lines are now considered expendable by some experts. Local industries served by these lines urge their retention. As with the debate over passenger service, this question is far from settled.

Ships from around the world visit Ohio ports. A Swedish vessel at Toledo. (9)

Huge machines dump coal into ship's holds at Toledo, while iron ore is unloaded at neighboring wharves (left). (10)

An Ohio Portrait

"Big Lucas" handles heavy cargo at the Port of Toledo. (11)

Waterborne transport is flourishing. The most dramatic development of the postwar period was the opening in 1959 of the St. Lawrence Seaway, which brought oceanborne commerce to Cleveland, Toledo, Conneaut, Ashtabula, and other Ohio ports. The Lakes trade continues to flourish as ever larger ore carriers bring record loads of iron ore south. Shipments of coal back north to ports on the upper lakes make Toledo the world's largest coal shipper. Some of the giant ore carriers are built in the American Shipbuilding yards at Lorain. On the Ohio River, barges pushed by "towboats" transport enormous quantities of bulk cargo at a price that cannot be matched by alternative forms of transport.

Ohio has profited handsomely from construction of the federal system of interstate highways. These, connected with "outerbelt" roads around major metropolitan areas, allow the pleasure and commercial traveler easy transit across the state. Of course it was the Ohio Turnpike, opened in 1955, that persuaded Ohioans of the necessity and convenience of modern highways. Under the competent management of the Ohio Turnpike Commission, this arterial link has carried so much traffic that revenues promise to pay off construction bonds faster than scheduled.

Facilities for air travel and for air freight are widespread in Ohio. Thanks to the dispersion of her major population centers, Ohio has major airports in every section of the state except the southeast. Cleveland Hopkins International Airport is the state's largest facility. Cincinnati's new port serves southwestern Ohio though actually located in Kentucky. Dayton, Columbus, Toledo, Akron-Canton, and Youngstown airports attract major carriers. Under another recent development program, every Ohio county now boasts an airport. Some of these facilities serve local indus-

tries by speeding communication with outside areas. Air travel and shipping loom large in Ohio's future. There is currently considerable debate about the need for new and expanded air facilities with perhaps the most interesting problem being whether or not to build a super-port in the greater Cleveland vicinity. Some planners urge that a completely new port be dredged out of Lake Erie off downtown Cleveland, but this vision is opposed by environmentalists who fear the potential for polluting the lake.

Ohio's industrial progress and her record in business activities generally are closely associated with the position of organized labor. In the recent era, Ohio has been a stronghold of organized labor. The craft unions of the A.F.L. and the industrial unions like the United Steel Workers, Teamsters, United Auto Workers, United Rubber Workers, and others swing a good deal of influence in state affairs. Organized labor is generally credited with defeating an attempt to add a "right to work" amendment to the state constitution in 1958. For all its economic strength, however, organized labor has not figured as large in state politics as its membership might suggest. Generally backing candidates of the Democratic party, labor has often found itself involved in the divisive infighting so common in Ohio Democratic politics in recent years. One of the most significant labor developments for the immediate future would appear to be the organizing of certain public employees, including teachers. The increased militancy of organized labor poses a whole new set of problems for legislators, courts, and the public.

Another marked trend in labor is the inclusion of blacks, women, and other historically excluded groups in the movement. Some portions of the labor movement in Ohio still resist opening membership to these groups, but there

The I-70 and I-77 interchange at Cambridge, billed as the world's largest. (12)

Carl Stokes and his wife during his tenure as Cleveland's mayor. (13)

seems little doubt that the barriers will ultimately fall.

On the political front, Ohio's post-World War II record is not distinguished by adherence to any one political group or creed. The sharing of power by Republicans and Democrats, both in national and in state politics, has been rather evenly balanced. Despite its preponderance of Democratic voter registrants and its character as an important industrial and urban state, Ohio had the largest Republican delegation in the United States Congress in the late 1960s and early 1970s. The old rural Republican bastions in the state had their influence minimized by reapportionment of the general assembly and redistricting of Congress in 1966 along the court-mandated one-man-one-vote principle. Nevertheless, much of the support lost by Republicans in rural areas was made up by support from the newly expanded suburban areas. Reapportionment reconstituted the Ohio General Assembly, which now has thirty-three members in the senate and ninety-nine members in the house of representatives. Redistricting changed United States Congressional Districts. As a result of the accelerated growth in certain other states reflected in the 1970 census, Ohio lost one of its congressional districts and now has twenty-three.

It has long been claimed by political pundits that Ohio is essentially conservative in its voting behavior and in its political makeup. Its general adherence to the Republican party and the politics of big business from the Civil War to the 1930s is a matter of record. In 'more recent decades, however, interpreting Ohio's attitude is more difficult. Apparently the state is still politically conservative for an industrial, heavily urbanized state. Many elected Democrats have been as conservative in economic and social outlook as candidates of the Republican party. Frank

Lausche of Cleveland, governor and senator from Ohio, is a case in point.

Lausche is also a good example of the importance of ethnic politics in Ohio, especially in that most ethnic city, Cleveland. Mayors of the Forest City like Lausche, Locher, and Perk have openly catered to ethnic groups. The Cleveland city council roster reads like a roll call of European countries. Complicating Cleveland's political picture in recent years has been the rise to power of blacks who are seeking there, and in several of Ohio's other cities, the political recognition that formerly escaped them. Springfield can boast that it was the first sizable city to have a black mayor, but the election of Carl Stokes as mayor of Cleveland in 1967 marked the first time in American history that a black person was chosen to head the administration of a major city. Since that time, several other Ohio cities have had blacks in top leadership positions. No Ohio city of much size has yet had a woman mayor, but it would appear that this too might happen in the near future as women become more assertive politically.

Mae Stewart, President of the City Commission of East Cleveland. (14)

With the election of John Gilligan as governor in 1970, Ohio chose a man pledged to the enactment of a state income tax. Since 1934 the sales tax has been, and still remains, Ohio's chief source of revenue. Additional sources of income were needed, however, and the graduated state income tax was the Gilligan administration's answer. This taxing source has yielded a significant amount of revenue, but as is usually the case, it has not accomplished all that its backers claimed it would. Still, efforts to repeal it have failed. Even with this new tax source, Ohio citizens remain among the least heavily taxed in the nation. The other side of that coin is that Ohio spends proportionately far less for state services than do many other states. A recently enacted state lottery is Ohio's latest attempt to provide modest additional revenue.

Developments in education have been noteworthy in the period since World War II. Ohio's public schools have traditionally been supported from local property taxes. The inequities of this approach became a matter of deep concern to certain legislators and professional school administrators. Within the past decade, amendments to the School Foundation Formula have sought to rectify some of the imbalance through the distribution of state funds to districts of greatest need. If the public schools are hard pressed to finance operations, the private school systems are experiencing even greater difficulties. Roman Catholics have had to close some schools or consolidate selected institutions in order to maintain the remainder. Along with certain Protestant-directed schools and other private schools they have sought various forms of state relief. Nearly every effort to direct public tax money to parochial schools has been ruled unconstitutional by the courts. However, an enormous burden would be placed on the public school systems in Cleveland, Cincinnati, and other major cities if parochial schools closed. Efforts to aid private schools continue.

Another pervasive educational problem of the post-war era concerns racial mixing in order to equalize the quality of educational services received. Ohio's large cities have many schools that are nearly 100 percent black or 100 percent white. Many suburban schools have no black students whatsoever. Spokesmen and spokeswomen for black communities, along with many educators, claim that few of the schools whose students are predominantly black provide educational services which are equal to those found in predominantly white schools. Some observers say the answer is busing; some claim that residential integration provides the only long term solution; others believe in leaving children in neighborhood schools while upgrading inadequate educational services. This issue remains to be reconciled.

An offshoot of the women's liberation movement of the 1960s and 1970s is the increased attention given to discriminatory practices against girls and women in education. On the student level, girls will have free access to courses, such as industrial arts, which were formerly reserved for boys. Girls also participate in all but a few varsity sports activities, and money alloted to girls' athletic and other activities must be proportionate to the amounts available for boys' activities. On the professional level, there is pressure to see that no qualified candidate for an administrative position is held back because she is female. Open, freely competitive opportunities for hiring and promotion are increasing.

Perhaps the chief new direction taken by Ohio's school systems is the move toward vocational education. Much of the early initiative in this direction came from political leaders who felt that vocational education was one answer to the problem of unemployment. Certain educators felt that it would be a constructive outlet for students whose orientation was practical rather than academic. Joint vocational school districts have been organized around the state, and attractive new facilities are found in every corner of Ohio. The verdict on the long-range results of this new emphasis is not yet in. Only time will tell whether or not the move has the merits ascribed to it by its backers.

Public higher education in Ohio has boomed in unprecedented fashion in the last two decades. The state college and university system has mushroomed. In 1946 there were six state universities in Ohio; by 1970 there were twelve. To the original group — Ohio, Miami, Ohio State, Kent State, Central State, and Bowling Green — were added three former municipal universities — Akron, Cincinnati, and Toledo — and Youngstown State, which was founded as a YMCA college; Cleveland State, developed from the nucleus of Fenn College; and Wright State, formerly a Miami University branch operation at Dayton. In addition, the Medical College of Ohio at Toledo was established by the state, and state money helped subsidize medical schools at Cincinnati and at the recently combined Case Western Reserve University. The Medical College of Northeastern Ohio, a medical school in Dayton, and a college of osteopathic medicine at Athens are recent additions to the state institutions of higher education. Many new community colleges and university branches have been created. They provide two years of education and encourage transfer to four year institutions.

This entire, complex system is supervised by the Ohio Board of Regents, a body of nine citizens appointed by the governor. The regents oversee the broad policies under which public higher education operates in Ohio.

Another important element in the life of Ohioans — organized religion — is hard to assess accurately since so much of its activity is inadequately reported. In keeping with the experience of other states, Ohio churches reported membership increases in the 1950s and then experienced a leveling off in the following decade. New church buildings appeared on the landscape. The denominations which flourished most in postwar America were those whose theology tended to be most dogmatic. So-called liberal churches did not increase their numbers in the same proportion as did their more conservative neighbors. This phenomenon was attributed in part to a search for security, a need for positive assurance in a rapidly changing world.

The Roman Catholic faith claims the largest number of communicants among Ohio's churches. In the Protestant tradition, the Methodist church has the largest membership. But old membership lines are blurred in many Protestant denominations by an ecumenical movement which merged formerly separate groups. The size and impact of black congregations increased also in this period. Much of the initiative for social change came from these congregations and their leaders. As ethnic neighborhoods changed in the larger cities, some Roman Catholic parishes formerly identified as the Italian parish, the Slovak parish, or the Irish parish found newcomers of different backgrounds moving into the parish. The major changes in Catholic practice, however, were the elimination of Latin in the service and the increased involvement of the laity.

Earlier Ohio pastors used radio to reach a wide audience; currently some Ohio pastors employ television. This is a very expensive business, however, and quite beyond the means of most

An Ohio Portrait

In the midst of a modern campus, Ohio University's
Cutler Hall (1816) is a link to the beginning of
public higher education in Ohio. (15)

congregations. Ohio's most fully developed television ministry emanates from the Cathedral of Tomorrow in Summit County. More than 350 stations in the United States and various foreign countries broadcast attractively programmed services from the cathedral.

The appeal of fundamentalist Protestantism in Ohio is apparent throughout the state; local tabernacles replete with their own bus fleets bring people by the thousands to services that feature "Bible preaching." Much support for these efforts comes from persons who migrated into Ohio from sections of the country where this approach to religion has traditionally been favored.

Judaism in Ohio has held its own in the postwar decades. The migration of Jews from old neighborhoods near the central city to the newer suburbs has caused a corresponding relocation of their houses of worship. The Orthodox, Conservative, and Reformed Jewish practices are all represented, although the Jews, in common with their gentile neighbors, have moved increasingly toward a broader humanistic base of belief and practice. A countermovement of sorts has appeared among some young Jews who have moved toward a more traditional outlook, possibly in the same effort to find roots and meaning that has motivated Christians to move toward more dogmatic beliefs and traditional practices. Approximately 165,000 Ohioans belong to Jewish congregations.

As one would expect in any complex society, Ohio has experienced its share of spectacular events during the past three decades. Some of them have been traumatic — wrecks, skydivers plunging to their deaths in Lake Erie, tornadoes, the collapse of the Silver Bridge into the Ohio River, the Sam Shepherd murder trial, tragic nursing home fires. But some by their very na-

ture reflect problems of the larger American society.

The prolonged struggle in Indochina, intense civil rights activity, and the "sexual revolution" contributed to an escalation of social tensions which reached a climax in Kent, Ohio. In May, 1970, four Kent State University students were killed and several wounded by gunfire from units of the Ohio National Guard which had been sent to maintain order on campus during antiwar demonstrations. It was the tragic climax of months of protest on American college campuses, a protest stemming largely from student disenchantment with the Johnson and Nixon administrations' involvement in the war in Indochina. Reaction to the shootings revealed how deep the split in American society had become. To many, especially young anti-establishment segments of society, Kent State represented the extreme to which a "repressive" society would go to quell dissent. Others, who feared student "radicals," felt that the authorities were justified in suppressing demonstrations, even by extraordinary measures. Most of Ohio's large public campuses and some private ones as well found it necessary to close operations briefly in the aftermath of the Kent State affair. Classes were suspended and on some campuses students were sent home for the remainder of the term.

During the sixties campus violence and unrest was paralleled in several of Ohio's major cities, where actual rioting or the imminence of violence created tensions and fear. Much of the urban crisis was related to the frustrations of black communities within the cities, who felt that government was unresponsive to their needs. Cleveland's Hough riot (1966) and the Glenville "shootout" (1968) were the most widely publicized of these outbreaks. In 1968 when civil rights leader Dr. Martin Luther King, Jr. was

271

Contemporary Ohio

Tear gas disperses students in May, 1970 on the
Kent State University campus. (16)

Ohio National Guardsmen on duty at the Hough
riots, Cleveland, 1966. (17)

assassinated in Memphis, Tennessee, anger and
frustration again built up in the inner cities of
Ohio's metropolitan areas. Cleveland's Mayor
Carl Stokes and his associates personally walked
the streets to keep tempers in check.

Cities have been explosive places throughout
American history, so it would be foolish to say
that the periods of trauma are over. However,
there are positive signs which give hope for improvement. Increased political participation by
minority representatives in both elected and appointed positions may improve communications
about the needs of inner city constituents. A
broadening of opportunity in various occupations, especially in public service positions and the
professions, improves the chances for many capable people to secure employment in keeping
with their talents. Visible achievement on nearly
all levels by accomplished black Americans provide models of success for the young to emulate.
Problems of great magnitude remain, but a growing pool of concerned people of all races bodes
well for efforts to make Ohio an optimum social
environment for all its people.

Another major concern of the postwar era
affecting Ohio and its people is control of the
environment. In the interest of luring and holding industry, some public officials have been willing to allow continuing pollution of air and water. A state Environmental Protection Agency,
charged with monitoring environmental regulations, lacks adequate personnel and funds to
cover all of its responsibilities. Many public officials and numerous private citizens have kept up
efforts to salvage Ohio's basic resources, especially its air and water. It was not a matter of pride
when Lake Erie was repeatedly cited as perhaps
the worst example of large-scale water pollution
in America. Erie, said the experts, was a "dying
lake," lacking oxygen, filled with poisons, and

Mr. & Mrs. John H. Bustamante of Cleveland. Mr.
Bustamante started Cleveland's First Bank and
Trust Company. (18)

An Ohio Portrait

The old Ford Trimotor still makes regular flights from Catawba to the Erie Islands. (19)

slowly filling with sediment. A once prosperous commercial fishing industry has been virtually wiped out by pollution. One of Erie's principal feeder streams, the chemically polluted Cuyahoga River, actually caught fire, much to the chagrin of Ohioans who resented seeing their state held up before the nation as a ludicrous example. Along the southern extremities of the state, the Ohio River was suffering from similar neglect, and its fish and natural life were largely eliminated.

A combination of official state action, federal participation, local concern, and private pressure has brought a potentially disastrous situation partially under control. A few species of fish have returned to waters now clean enough to support them. Veteran observers of Lake Erie claim that its waters are clearing since new sewage treatment plants and control of fertilizers and industrial wastes has been in effect. Numerous Ohio industrial plants have installed both air and water pollution control equipment. Cities like Steubenville, which ranked at the bottom of the clean air charts, appear to have some hope for improvement. Public consciousness of the continuing need for concern is stirred by local television stations with their air quality index charts, by conservation groups like the Sierra Club, and by a populace increasingly aware of the quality of life afforded them in their neighborhoods and their state.

Despite its problems, which are mostly local manifestations of national concerns, Ohio has much to offer its people. Though no longer as much of a national pace-setter as it was one hundred years ago, on the whole Ohio has matured and mellowed gracefully. Reflecting pride of accomplishment, Ohioans show a determination to recapture many of the sights and sensations of earlier days. A visit to Roscoe Village in Coshocton County, or to the Piqua Historical Area, or to German Village in Columbus will convince the skeptic of this truth. Canals have been restored and authentic replicas of canal boats ply their waters at several locations. The *Delta Queen*, last of the Ohio River paddlewheelers, got a special reprieve by Congress and is again taking sentimental journeys on the Ohio and Mississippi. The old Ford Trimotor which connects Catawba with the Erie Islands is favored by aircraft enthusiasts. Numerous restored mills again grind grains. Old glass and pottery patterns are resurrected for the pleasure of fanciers. A copper company in Bucyrus still makes copper ware in the traditional manner; and so it goes as Ohio looks to its past.

Any account of the Buckeye State should end on a forward-looking note, for that has been the characteristic direction of Ohio's energies. What could afford a better example of Ohio's concern for and involvement in the future than its role in space exploration? No state has been more fully associated with the development of flight and aircraft than has Ohio. Not only was Ohio the home of the Wright Brothers and other pioneers of manned flight, but it has been a focus of air research through the facilities of Wright-Patterson Field, the Guggenheim Airship Institute, and other centers. Cleveland has long hosted the National Air Races. A distinguished group of Ohio men and women have established air records and have earned world-wide acclaim for their feats.

This tradition in the air continues in the space age. Many Ohio companies construct equipment used in America's space vehicles. But it is people who make a program, and here too Ohio is well represented. Colonel John Glenn of New Concord was the first American to orbit the earth. Don Eisele and James Lovell are astronauts with Ohio backgrounds. And it is perhaps appropriate that the first human to step on the moon, Neil Armstrong, grew up in Wapakoneta in the rich farmlands of west central Ohio.

Visual pollution common to strip-city developments. (20)

Hope remains for a return of commercial fishing on Lake Erie as a dying lake is revived by pollution controls. (21)

A cruel dilemma: "smoke means prosperity," but it also creates health problems. A scene near Steubenville. (22)

A paper company plant poses pollution problems at Chillicothe. (23)

Epilog

This year, 1976, America celebrates the bicentennial of the American Revolution. Ohio is somewhat younger than the nation, but it was settled initially by the same generation of men and women who achieved independence from Great Britain and who formed a new nation. Some of their most productive ideas — the rectilinear survey and the policies for administering the public lands — were pioneered in Ohio. Ohio provided a new home and a new start for people of many traditions. No state can claim to be a better amalgam of these diverse peoples and traditions.

Foremost in both the agricultural and industrial life of America, well represented by both rural and urban interests, birthplace and/or residence of innovators and accomplished folk in every important area of life, national leader in the critical years between the Civil War and World War I, Ohio has a right to review her record with

The "good old days." Amish buggies at Berlin, Holmes County. (24)

satisfaction and pride. It has paid the price for policies that reflect some of the less wise decisions of earlier generations, and one would hope that these lessons have been well learned.

Everywhere in the buckeye state exists the juxtaposition of old and new, of past and future. Old river towns like Marietta and Gallipolis retain some sense of early times. Sections of Cincinnati still attest to its leadership in nearly every Ohio activity during the early years of statehood. But just outside Marietta and Gallipolis are enormous industrial plants complete with expensive new pollution control equipment, and Cincinnati's new Riverfront Stadium complex rests near the landings along the river once favored by pioneer travelers and traders. Columbus' historic German Village lies within sight of the new forty-one-story state office building. Oil refineries and huge industrial establishments lie on the outskirts of Lima and Findlay on lands adjacent to century-old farms. Huge ore carriers crowd Erie ports, where remnants of old pilings remind one of the little sailing vessels that formerly brought trade and commerce. Wilberforce College sits beside the newer buildings of Central State University, a silent commentary on the merging of two distinct educational traditions. And in Columbus, the Ohio American Revolution Bicentennial Advisory Commission, dedicated to enhancing Ohio's awareness of its past, occupies quarters in an ultra-modern building, product of a future-looking architecture. Perhaps nowhere is the juxtaposition of old and new more striking than in Wapakoneta. There the Aerospace Museum commemorating Ohio's role in space flight occupies land once part of a Shawnee capital. The very name of the town reminds Ohioans of how deep their cultural debts run, while the displays within the museum attest to Ohio's role in developing the future.

Restorations, like this schoolhouse at the Western Reserve Village at the Hale Homestead, Summit County, instruct the public about our heritage. (25)

A welcome home for astronaut Donn F. Eisele at Columbus West High School. (26)

The Air-Space Museum, Wapakoneta. (27)

(28)

PHOTO CREDITS

Key

ABJ *Akron Beacon Journal*
CHS Cincinnati Historical Society
CPD *Cleveland Plain Dealer*
CPL Cleveland Public Library
LCHS Licking County Historical Society
ODED Ohio Department of Economic and Community Development
ODNR Ohio Department of Natural Resources
ODT Ohio Department of Transportation
Ohio EPA Ohio Environmental Protection Agency
OGS Ohio Geological Survey
OHS Ohio Historical Society
OSU Ohio State University
PCHS Pickaway County Historical Society
Se.CHS Seneca County Historical Society
St.CHS Stark County Historical Society
Su.CHS Summit County Historical Society
WRHS Western Reserve Historical Society

I THE SETTING

Page
2 Black Hand Gorge; ODNR.
   Ohio River; Lefevre J. Cranstone sketches, Lilly Library, Indiana University, Bloomington, Indiana
2 Sixteen-gallon stoneware water cooler used at American House Hotel, Columbus. Impressed "Wm. Kelsey, American House, Columbus, Ohio," ca. 1845; OHS.
2 Pottery dog. Akron, Ohio area, ca. 1880; OHS.
2 Sheicks Hollow; ODNR.
   A map of the *Natural vegetation of Ohio at the time of the earliest land survey.* Prepared by Robert B. Gordon, chief geologist, 1870; OHS.
3 Buckeye leaves and fruit; OHS.
3 Lumberman; OHS.
4 (1, 2) OHS.
5 (3) OGS.
   (4) Tom Root, Plymouth, Ohio.
   (5) OGS.
   (6) OHS.
6 (7) ODNR.
7 (8) *Preliminary geological map of Ohio.* Prepared from the notes of the geological corps by J. S. Newberry, Chief geologist, 1870; OHS.
8 (9) OHS.
   (10) ODNR.
   (12) OHS.
9 (11) ODNR.
   (12) OHS.
10 (13) OHS.
   (14) Polished flint; ODNR.
12 (15) OHS.
   (16) ODNR.
13 (17, 18) OHS.
14 (19) OHS.
   (20) Miami Conservancy District.
   (21) OHS.
15 (22) ODNR.
16 (23) OHS.
   (24) S. Durward Hoag, Marietta, and OHS.

(25) OHS.
17 (26) Buckeye leaves and flowers; ODNR.

II FIRST ARRIVALS IN THE OHIO COUNTRY

Page
18 Decorated pottery vessel, Hopewell Culture; OHS.
18 Mica hawk's claw, Hopewell Culture; OHS.
18 J. Vincent half-stocked percussion rifle, ca. 1860; OHS.
18 Iron bullet mold for casting muzzle-loading rifle balls; OHS.
18 Double-edged sheath knife with six-inch blade and ivory handle, Sheffield, England, ca. 1860-1900; OHS.
18 Bullet bag and powder horn; OHS.
18 Box of 100 foil-lined, center-fire percussion caps; OHS.
18 Powder can, "Manufactured by Eureka Powder Works, New Durham, N.H."; OHS.
18 Fresh water pearls, Hopewell Culture; OHS.
18 Hawk effigy platform pipe, Hopewell Culture; OHS.
18 Wray stone figurine, Hopewell Culture; OHS.
18 Berlin sandstone tablet, Adena Culture; OHS.
19 Copper vulture effigy gorgets, Hopewell Culture; OHS.
19 "Mound at Marietta"; *Historical Collections of Ohio,* by Henry Howe, 1902, vol. 2; OHS.
20 (1) OHS.
21 (2, 3) *Historical Collections of Ohio,* by Henry Howe, 1902, vol. 2; OHS.
22 (4-7) OHS.
23 (8) OHS.
   (9) *History of the Indian Tribes of North America,* McKenney and Hall, 1842, vol. 1.; OHS.
   (10) Moravian National Archives, Bethlehem, Pennsylvania.
25 (11) Schoenbrunn; OHS.
26 (12) *History of the Indian Tribes of North America,* McKenney and Hall, 1842, vol. 1.; OHS.
28 (13) Engraved by R. W. Dodson from a portrait by L. W. Morgan.
   (14) From an engraving by B. West.
29 (15) Courtesy Smithsonian Institution.
   (16) From an engraving by B. West.
30 (17, 18) OHS.
31 (19) After McKenney and Hall's copy of the original in the Smithsonian.
33 (20) Crawford's sword; OHS.
   (21) Painting by Ed Lepper, 1906; SeCHS.
34 (22) *History of Ohio in Words of One Syllable,* Annie Cole Cady.
   (23) OHS.
35 (24) Adena pipe, Adena Culture; OHS.

III A STATE CARVED FROM THE WILDERNESS

Page
36 Arrow heads; OHS.
36 "British and American burying their dead after the Battle of Lake Erie";
36 William Henry Harrison on snuffbox cover, ca. 1840; OHS.
36 Connecticut Land Company; OHS.
36 Christopher Gist; one of the 18 original art renderings by Annette Salrin for the official Ohio Bicentennial calendar.
37 George Croghan medal; OHS.
37 Greene Ville Treaty peace medal; OHS.
37 Tecumseh, *The Pictorial Field Book of the War of 1812,* Benson J. Lossing, 1868; OHS.
38 (1) Virginia Military Survey, *Ohio Lands and Their History,* William E. Peters, 1930; OHS.
39 (2) One of the 18 original art renderings by Annette Salrin for the official Ohio Bicentennial Calendar.
   (3) Engraving by John Sartain in *Military Journal of Major Ebenezer Denny*

. . . , 1859; OHS.
   (4) OHS.
40 (5) *Map of the State of Ohio . . . ,* John F. Mansfield, 1806; OHS.
41 (6) Engraving by J. C. Buttre; OHS.
42 (7) *Harper's Magazine;* OHS.
   (8) OHS.
43 (9) Drawing by William Mark Young; OHS.
   (10) OHS.
44 (11) OHS.
   (12) *The New Popular Atlas of the World,* Mast, Crowell & Kirkpatrick, 1892; OHS.
45 (13) OHS.
46 (14) OHS.
   (15) Engraving by Samuel Sartain; OHS.
47 (16) OHS.
48 (17) Painting by R. T. Zogbaum; OHS.
   (18) Painting by Howard Chandler Christy, 1945; Ohio State House, Columbus.
   (19) OHS.
49 (20) From an old print; OHS.
   (21) Greene Ville Treaty Memorial Assn., 1935; OHS.
50 (22, 23) OHS.
51 (24) OHS.
52 (25-28) OHS.
53 (29) *History of the Indian Tribes of North America,* McKenney and Hall, 1842, vol. 1.; OHS.
   (30) Courtesy of Field Museum of Natural History, Chicago.
   (31) Portrait, 1814 in uniform of general by Rembrandt Peale. Grouseland House, Vincennes, Indiana. Owned by the Frances Vigo Chapter, Daughters of the American Revolution.
54 (32) Ohio State House, Columbus.
55 (33) OHS.
   (34) Ohio's first state seal; OHS.
56 (35) OHS.
   (36) Anthony Wayne Parkway Board; OHS.
57 (37) Anthony Wayne Parkway Board; OHS.

IV BUILDING A SOCIETY: THE MATERIAL SIDE

Page
58 Unidentified pioneer woman; OHS.
58 Flatbottom river boat. *A Journey in North America . . . ,* George H. V. Collot, 1826; OHS.
58 "Marietta at Harmar," Stereograph by J. D. Cadwallader; John Waldsmith Collection.
59 Canal boat at Piqua; OHS.
59 Portage County banknote; OHS.
59 Plow with iron share and wooden moldboard; OHS.
59 Cleveland steamboat landing, Stereograph view by H. D. Udall; John Waldsmith Collection.
59 Canal Bank of Cleveland bank note; OHS.
59 Cleveland Public Square, 1829; WRHS.
59 "Burning fallen trees in a girdled clearing." Engraved by W. J. Bennett, N.A. from the original painting by G. Harvey, ANA; OHS.
60 (1) OHS.
   (2) Grant Foreman, *The Last Trek of the Indians.* (Copyright 1946 by Carolyn Thomas Foreman; Copyright renewed 1974 by Mrs. C. Haines Lee) New York: Russell & Russell, 1972.
   (3) *Ladies Repository,* vol. XV (1855); OHS.
61 (4) OHS.
   (5) *The Growth of Industrial Art,* Benjamin Butterworth, 1892; OHS.
62 (6) OHS.
   (7) "Log Cabin in Ohio"; Lefevre J. Cranstone sketches, Lilly Library, Indiana University, Bloomington, Indiana.
   (8) *The Growth of Industrial Art,* Benjamin Butterworth, 1892; OHS.
   (9) OHS.
63 (10) "Farms and fences in Ohio"; Lefevre J. Cranston sketches, Lilly Library, Indiana University,

INDEX

Page numbers in italics
indicate illustrations